Theater of Fear and Horror:
The Grisly Spectacle of The Grand Guignol of Paris 1898 - 1962

Originally published as *Grand Guignol: Theatre of Fear and Terror*
from Amok Press (1988)

Includes bibliographical references.
ISBN 0-306-80806-4
Théâtre du Grand-Guignol—History. I. Gordon, Mel.
PN2636.P4G75   1997
792'.0944'36—dc21 97-17646
CIP

Theater of Fear and Horror:
The Grisly Spectacle of The Grand Guignol of Paris 1898 - 1962
© 2016 Mel Gordon

Translation of André de Lorde and Alfred Binet's *A Crime in a Madhouse* copyright ©1997 by André Gisiger and Mel Gordon. Translation of Leopold Marchard's *Orgy in the Lighthouse* ©2011 by Mel Gordon and Barry Richmond.
Original art by J.T. Steiny. All other art is from original Grand Guignol sources, which include program art, publicity stills, and posters. We have contacted copyright owners where known.

ISBN 978-1-62731-031-4

Feral House
1240 W. Sims Way Suite 124
Port Townsend, WA 98368

www.FeralHouse.com

Design by Sean Tejaratchi

THEATRE OF FEAR AND HORROR

THE GRISLY SPECTACLE OF THE
GRAND GUIGNOL OF PARIS
1897 ~ 1962

BY
MEL GORDON

FERAL HOUSE

*To Russell Blackwood,
the newest "bandit" of the Grand Guignol.*

Tragic pleasure consists in the imitation of horrifying and pitiful events which in itself, according to Aristotle, is delightful.

—Compendium of Tragicomic Poetry
by Giovanni Battista Guarini, 1599

The most sick, perverted, and pornographic drama on Broadway can never hope to match the thrillers staged at the Grand Guignol.

—RAGE *(a sensationalist New York magazine) March 1963*

TABLE of CONTENTS

ACKNOWLEDGMENTS
IX

FOREWORD TO THE **REVISED EDITION**
1

INTRODUCTION
5

THE GRAND GUIGNOL: A HISTORY
9

THE **INFLUENCE** OF THE **GRAND GUIGNOL**
43

STAGE TRICKS OF THE **GRAND GUIGNOL**
55

100 PLOTS FROM THE **REPERTOIRE**
OF THE **GRAND GUIGNOL**
65

COLOR PLATES AFTER PAGE 118

FEAR IN **LITERATURE: AN ESSAY**
by André de Lorde (1927)
141

I AM THE **MADDEST WOMAN** IN THE **WORLD**
by Paula Maxa (1938)
148

A **CRIME** IN THE **MADHOUSE**
by André de Lorde and Alfred Binet (1925)
156

ORGY IN THE **LIGHTHOUSE**
by Leopold Marchard (1956)
188

GRAND GUIGNOL
THEATRE DU GRAND GUIGNOL
ILS SONT ENTRES DANS LA NUIT
LE RENARD
GRENOUILLE

ACKNOWLEDGEMENTS

Like the Grand Guignol itself, this book—an expanded, third edition—is the product of many artistic talents.

Ken Swezey, Daniel Gerould, and Jeff Casper helped shepherd this unlikely project through its initial Amok Press publication in 1988. André Gisiger added much material for the second Da Capo Press edition in 1997.

And now Sean Tejaratchi has redesigned this new volume with still more Grand Guignol authority and theatricality. We have substituted the play *The System of Dr. Goudron and Prof. Plume* with the more provocative *Orgy in the Lighthouse* and included the "lost" autobiographical memoir by Maxa and a color selection of Grand Guignol posters.

Thanks to Feral House, *The Theatre of Fear and Horror* refuses to fade away or vanish from world culture.

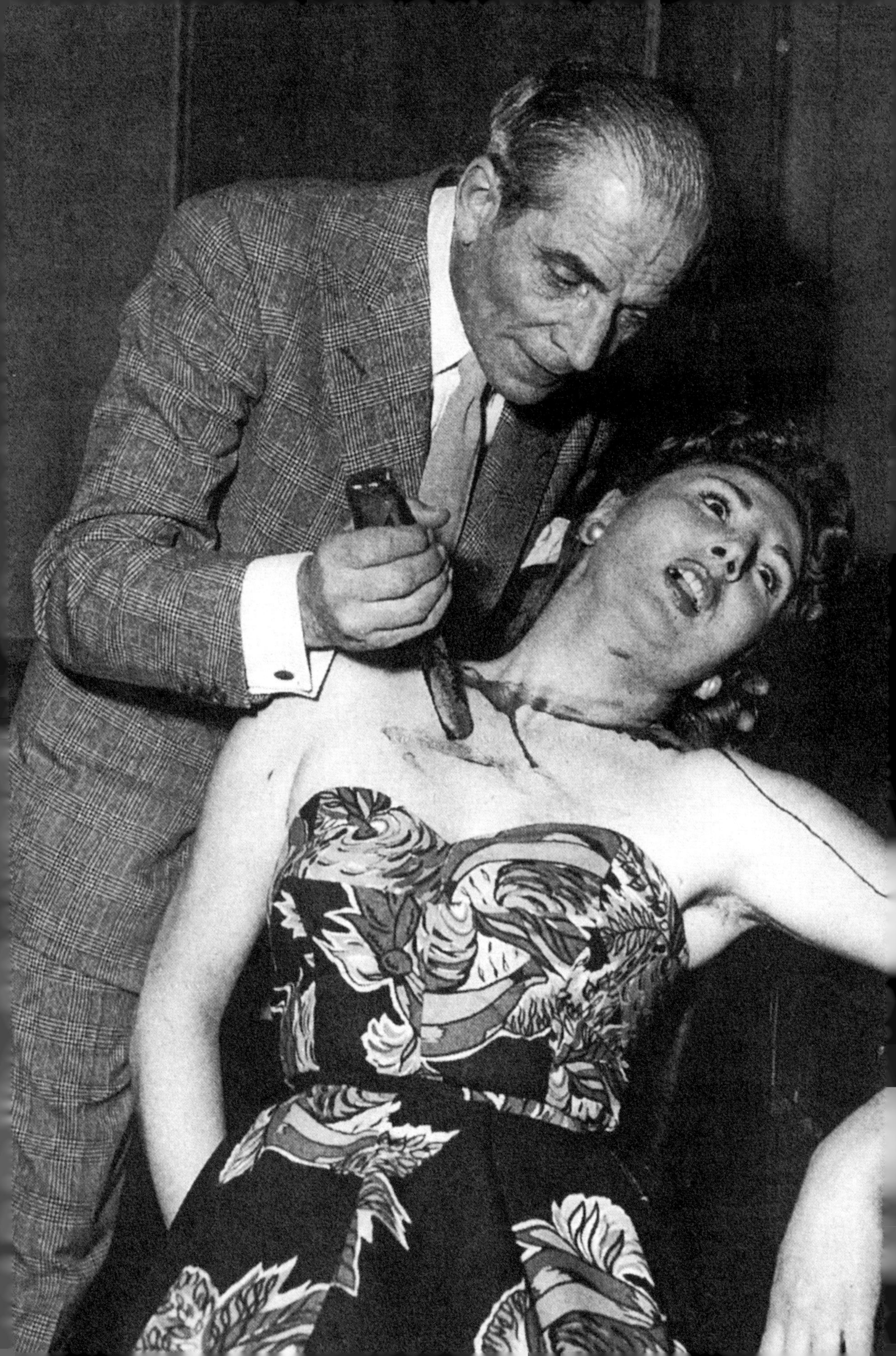

FOREWORD TO THE REVISED EDITION

A DRUNKEN and rampaging native militia discover an isolated lunatic asylum in a jungle clearing in Central Africa. They lock the doors and toss dozens of grenades through the windows. The mental patients begin to sing and dance hysterically, not knowing the charge and shrapnel from the grenades are meant to kill them. Two brothers, almost identically dressed, quietly sneak into the den of their upper-middle-class house and methodically gun down their parents, who themselves are transfixed by a television soap opera. Caught in a web of an absolute panic, three Black middle-aged sisters, fearing Satan's power unleashed in a hoodoo parish of Louisiana, flee to a small town in Texas, where they stop to gouge out the eyes of their possessed but acquiescent younger sister. A suicide cult, led by a castrated prophet, spends its last days on earth gleefully playing nickel slot machines in a Las Vegas casino, riding roller coasters, and searching for lost coins in an amusement park. Believing that his former wife has given him a deadly blood disease, a celebrity athlete cuts her throat in the middle of the night and repeatedly stabs an innocent

ABOVE: *LABORATORY OF HALLUCINATIONS*, 1922

FOYER OF THE GRAND GUIGNOL THEATRE, 1947.

admirer of hers. Although his blood is found everywhere at the crime scene, he is acquitted and lives out his days, playing golf and reconsidering his career options until he is caught again.

The Grand Guignol, the unimaginably gory theatre of terror and horror that addicted countless generations of Parisian theatre-goers and thrill-seeking tourists, never died. Its cruelties and perverse comedy seep into our daily lives. Unlike the Gothic melodramas of the nineteenth century, the Grand Guignol—from its inception in 1897 to its humiliating death in 1962—based its plots on bloody and murderous criminal exploits, which were taken from real life. The newspaper, the laboratory report, the prefect's roster—those were the sources of the Guignol's unpredictable and grisly productions. Audiences also sensed that this was a different kind of entertainment. When bones crunched and blood started to coagulate on the performer's matted hair, the aesthetic cessation of disbelief began. But this was quickly supported by the spectator's deepest understanding that the shocking stage display was a more truthful unveiling of the savage human soul than anything available on stage or in the cinema. Only life matched the horror of the Grand Guignol.

The folklore of the Theatre of the Grand Guignol is virtually endless. A few additional facts and surprises: during the last, confused years of WWI, horribly wounded French soldiers were trucked into

Paris for a day, where they were wined and dined in fine restaurants and in the evening brought to watch the Grand Guignol as a special treat. Internal French military files after the war reported that this worked as a great morale builder.

Alfred Binet, the French creator of the Binet Intelligence Test, was one of the most successful playwrights of the Grand Guignol and co-author of *A Crime in a Madhouse*. The American Psychological Society in the early twenties agonized over Binet's original examination, which asked such thought-provoking questions to young students as: "What is the first thing that you would do, if you came home after school and found your mother strangled and mutilated?" Nearly all of Binet's horrific essay tests were deleted in the American versions.

In the post-World War II era, all three owners and many of the directors of the Grand Guignol were women, including one of France's leading feminist intellectuals. Despite the Grand Guignol's disturbing reputation for graphic onstage mayhem against defenseless young waifs, it stood out as one of the few French institutions that gave full creative reign to female producers. But women-directed or not, the Grand Guignol quickly floundered commercially in its final incarnations.

Neither establishment theatre nor *outré* art, the Grand Guignol inhabited a marshy no-man's land of authentic, if historically expiring, popular entertainment in the fifties. The overall devotion among Parisian writers, society people, and artists to the Grand Guignol at the time is surprisingly

> *"All our nightmares of sadism and perversion were played out on that stage."*
> —Anaïs Nin.

difficult to assess. Many continued to attend its performances with fascinating regularity but without comment. Probably, like the assemblages of pornographic photographs sealed in wafer-thin wraps—Montmartre's backstreet specialty—the Grand Guignol was insufficiently primitive, ironic, or even esoteric enough to overtly influence their avant-garde sensibilities. The trip to 20bis Rue Chaptal apparently degenerated in that decade into an anthropological search for lost and curious theatre pleasures.

But the dying Grand Guignol had another legacy. Its bitter idealism, distrust of authority, and reckless sexual taunting was certainly passed on to a postwar generation of European artists—although in ways that are still too murky, too disguised and subterranean to be easily traced. Writing in her diary in the spring of 1958, Anaïs Nin typically bemoaned the Grand Guignol's current decline, yet she also revealed its deepest, truest, and most invisible impact on its knowing spectators:

"I surrendered myself to the Grand Guignol, to its venerable filth which used to cause such shivers of horror, which used to petrify us with terror. All our nightmares of sadism and perversion were played out on that stage."

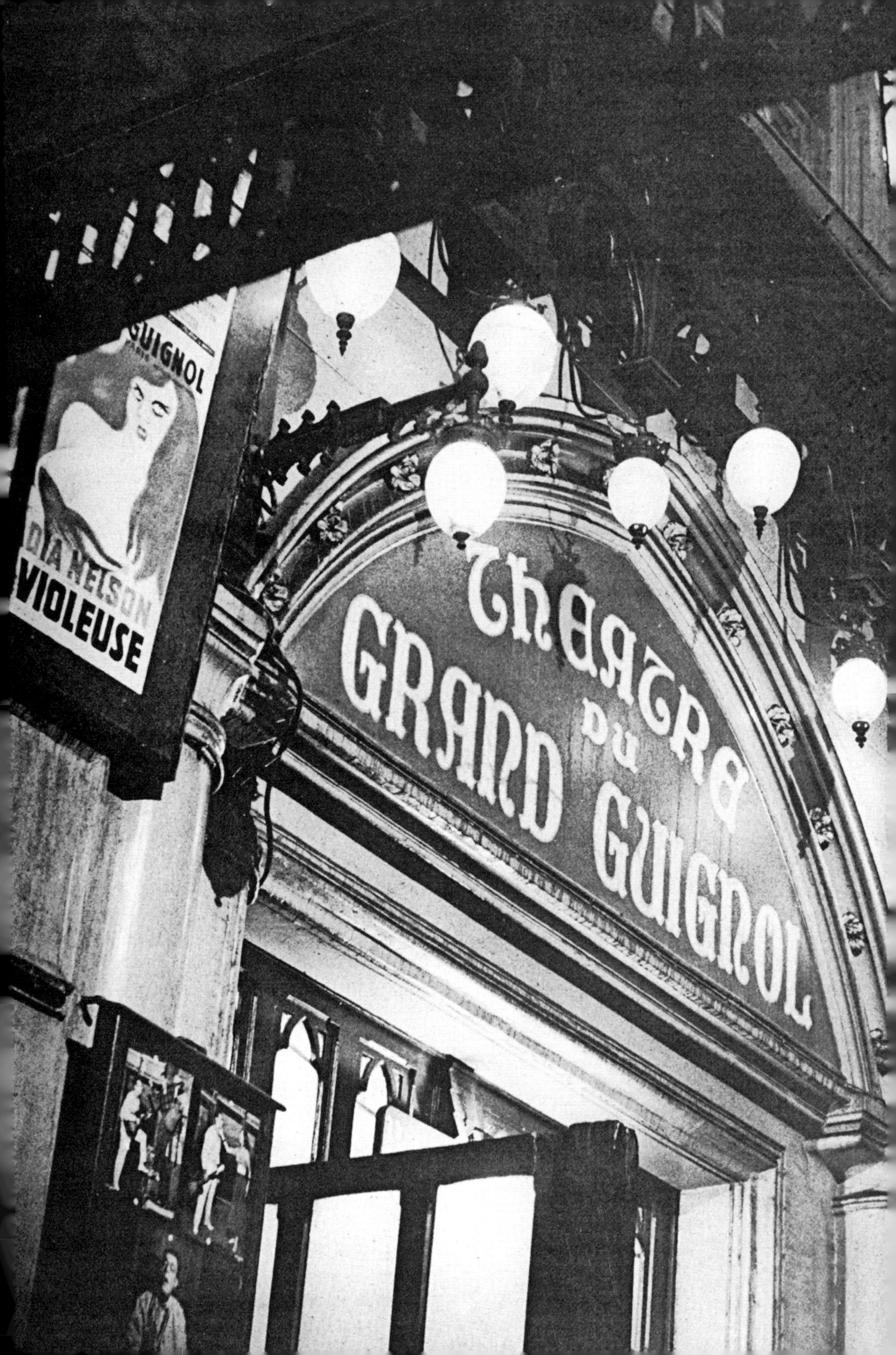
GUIGNOL
DIA NELSON
VIOLEUSE
THEATRE
DU
GRAND GUIGNOL

INTRODUCTION

≻⋅⋅⋅⋅⋅⋅⋅⋅⋅≺

THERE IS SOMETHING embarrassing about the Grand Guignol. Like a renegade sect or invented religion from another century, it still touches upon our secret longings and fears. A product of fin-de-siecle France, the Grand Guignol managed to transgress theatrical conventions and outrage its public as it explored the back alleys of unfettered desire, aesthetic impropriety, and nascent psychological trends in criminology and the study of abnormal behavior. Its supporters called the Grand Guignol play the most Aristotelian of twentieth-century dramatic forms since it was passionately devoted to the purgation of fear and pity.

Audiences came to the Theatre of the Grand Guignol to be frightened, to be shocked, while simultaneously delighting in their fears (or in those of the people around them). The more terrifying a performance was—that is, the more it tapped into its spectators' collective phobias—the greater its success.

If one had to single out one reason for the Grand Guignol's 65 years of prosperity and success from 1897 to 1962, a special genius for finding new audiences would have

ABOVE: *A KISS IN THE NIGHT*, 1922

TWO YOUNG GUIGNOLERS, 1950.

to be considered. In some decades, the Parisian Theatre of Fear and Terror was the darling of Paris' *epater les bourgeois* intelligentsia and their followers; in other times, its elite spectators consisted of an odd mix of cocaine-sniffing royal outcasts from a dozen lost Central European and Balkan Houses and thrill-seeking tourists. More often than not, seats were taken by regulars, a special class of spectator, the "Guignolers." But no matter when the actors performed or who watched, it played a topsy-turvy game with its audience's deepest instincts and underlying, repressed impulses for sex and savage retribution.

That studies of the Grand Guignol have been largely ignored in scholarly circles should come as no surprise. Here was a theatre genre predicated on the stimulation of

Laughter was the dark and hidden ingredient of the Grand Guignol.

the more raw and adolescent of human interactions and desires: incest and patricide; blood lust; sexual anxiety and conflict; morbid fascination with bodily mutilation and death; loathing of authority; fear of insanity; an overall disgust for the human condition and its imperfect institutions. For the vast majority of drama academicians, however, the Grand Guignol was little more than an unhealthy curiosity, unworthy of serious analysis or documentation. Despite its immense popularity and influence on other dramatic forms in the twenties and thirties,

THE LITTLE ROQUE BY ANDRÉ DE LORDE, 1923.

such as the Hollywood horror film and psychological thriller, no major theatre history text, even today, as much as mentions Paris' greatest twentieth-century stage attraction.

Part of the problem certainly lies with an intrinsic humor embedded in the Grand Guignol's plots and techniques. Journalists and critics made little distinction between the black and antinomian humor of violent fantasy, especially as it was played out in minute detail on the Grand Guignol stage, and the self-conscious, melodramatic enactments of camp parody. When tyrannical fathers are surgically mutilated, when innocent children are strangled in their beds, when mothers leave their infants to starve on their neighbors' doorsteps, when all the familiar taboos of social constraint and sex are challenged and then overturned in the most graphic manner imaginable, at first, laughter and derision seem to be the appropriate responses. But in a typical Grand Guignol evening, laughter was always followed by panic and, after that, by more laughter still. Laughter was the dark and hidden ingredient of the Grand Guignol. ⚜

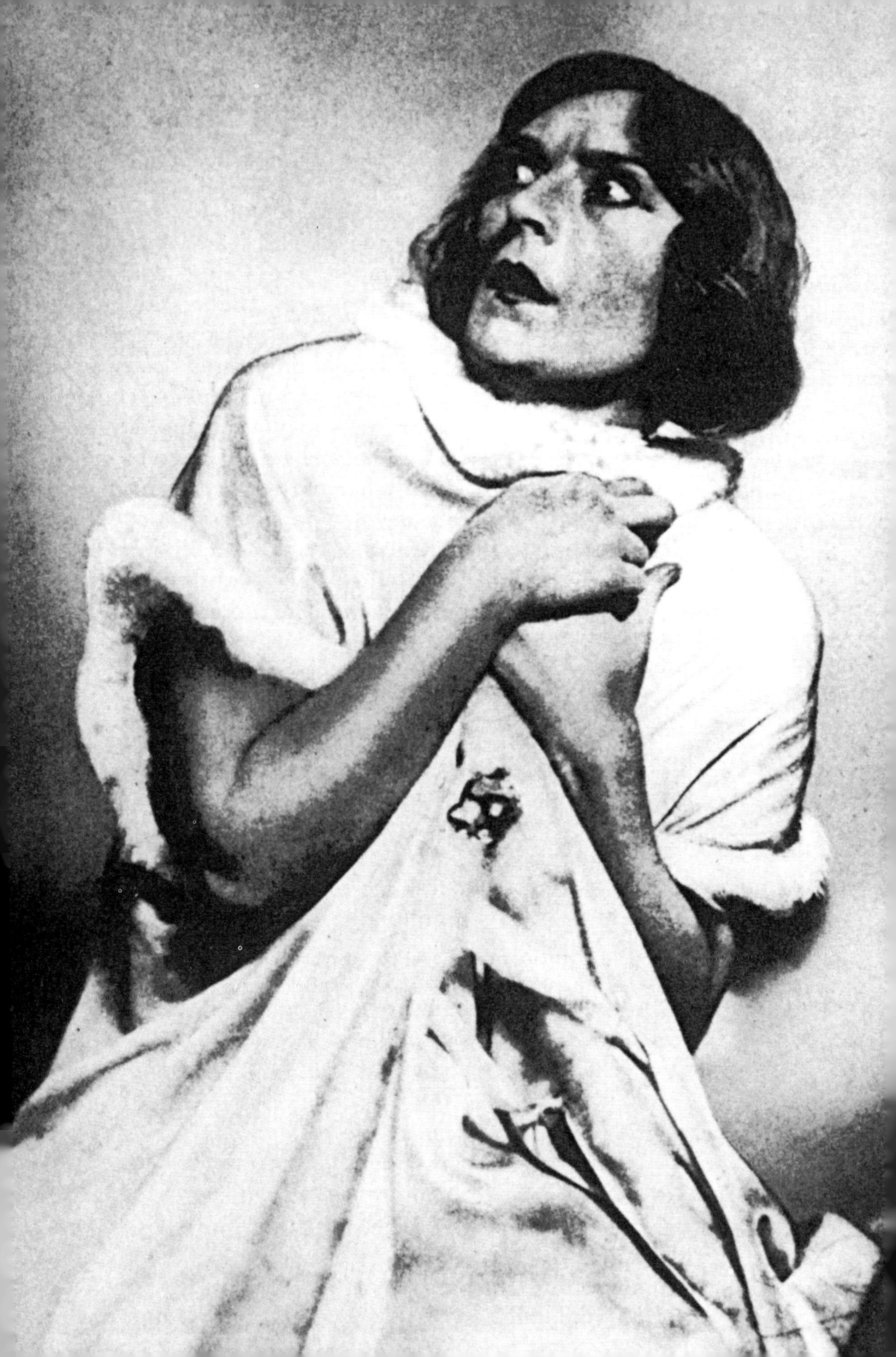

THE GRAND GUIGNOL: A HISTORY

I N A WAY, the Grand Guignol always existed. The impulse to shock, to display the extremes of human behavior, and then to demonstrate the divine punishments that follow for those individuals who violate society's taboos may have been the original social function of all performance. This attempt to force from theatre a seriousness—a playing with life and death—could take place within or outside the pale of official taste, which was later labeled "high" or "low" art. In the preliterate world, shamanistic enactments of self-mutilation brought fascinated tribespeople into new and altered states of awareness. Human, animal, and effigy sacrifices were the centerpieces of civilization's earliest ceremonies in Egypt and the New World.

OPPOSITE: SYBIL THORNDIKE IN H.F. MALTBY'S *THE PERSON UNKNOWN*, 1921.
ABOVE: *THE DEAD RAT, ROOM 6*, 1921.

Normally in Western cultures, horrific events on stage were permitted as long as they were obvious imitations. Yet Aeschylus so frightened his Greek audience during *The Eumenides* that "children died and pregnant women miscarried." Prompt books from the Middle Ages reveal an awful and bloody display of animal parts that realistically substituted for performers' severed limbs and organs. The early Elizabethan and Jacobean playwrights (Shakespeare excelling among them) feverishly constructed plots and dialogues that remain among the most unwholesome and disturbing in the world repertoire. (Artaud even included Shakespeare, Dekker, and Webster as charter playwrights in his Theatre of Cruelty.)

Pornographic dramatic entertainments were played out in the brothels of seventeenth and eighteenth-century Vienna and Paris while court poets dourly spelled out Neoclassical rules of writing and acting to playwrights and censoring boards. Around the Place de la Nation during the French Revolution's Reign of Terror, freshly-guillotined corpses were manipulated like oversized puppets in grotesque comedies. Throughout the eighteenth and nineteenth centuries, as the European theatre lost its royal patronage and audience as well as its artistic efficacy, other strange "blood-and-guts" performances were mounted in conjunction with the revival of occultism and Mesmerism. Once again, violence and sexuality reigned in these private rituals and "scientific" presentations, darkly conducted by shrewd director-prophets who reenacted milder but more sophisticated renditions of shamanistic trickery.

As the Industrial Revolution intensified during the first quarter of the nineteenth century, a thirst for new and lurid popular entertainment forms grew in Western Europe. Most of these traded on sensationalistic plots and the exploitation

> *Each play seemed to release a previously hidden psychic spring among the working-class people from Glasgow to Dresden, with its dramatic hub in industrial Paris.*

of their audiences' visceral curiosity over morbid criminal behavior and savage punishment. In a way, they acted as fantasy substitutes for the guillotine and its public celebrations. Guilbert de Pixérécourt, an unhappy graduate of the Counterrevolutionary and Republican armies, created an ironclad recipe for the newest subliterary genre called the melodrama. In his plays, everything began with the complete and unexpected victimization of poor and innocent people by a cruel and sexually corrupt oppressor, quickly followed by a superhuman struggle that always concluded with a swift—almost divine—punishment against the agents of human iniquity. By the 1810s, as many as seventy melodramatic productions a month opened on Paris' underclass thoroughfare, the Boulevard du Crime. Each play seemed to release a previously hidden psychic spring among the working-class people from Glasgow to Dresden, with its dramatic hub in industrial Paris.

But if the early melodrama gave crude organization to the feverish desires and imaginations of young proletarian Europeans, another popular artistic genre spoke more authoritatively still to the heart and head of those looking for grisly amusements. This was the *faits divers*, or the short news items printed in broadsheets or yellow journals. From the time of the French Revolution to the 1930s, specialized French newspapers and weeklys provided their readers with realistic and gory accounts of true-life crime stories and their frequently bizarre denouements. While the *fait divers* covered much of the same plot and character terrain of the gothic and cheap melodrama—abandoned infants, seduction and rape, public assassinations, forced prostitution, freaks of nature, suicides, sadistic abuse by the powerful, incest, drownings and suffocations, spiritualism, train wrecks, child abuse, mutilation, and other crimes of passion—they differed from de Pixérécourt's invention in three aspects. For one, the *faits divers*, as befitting their name, were short in length. Usually illustrated with garishly-colored drawings, they rarely needed to hold the reader's attention for more than a few minutes. Secondly, unlike the melodramas, which had to end happily, the *fait divers* normally concluded with a disturbing and vindictive note. Finally, the *fait divers*' plots were taken from life, not from the pens of fantasy-mad playwrights. In these ways, the *fait divers* prefigured exactly on the printed page what the Grand Guignol would be on the stage.

THE SCHOOL OF NATURALISM

The Theatre of the Grand Guignol was one of several offshoots from the Naturalist movement on the Parisian stage that began in the late 1880s. The *Théâtre Libre*, founded by a twenty-nine year-old gas company clerk, Andre Antoine, heeded Emile Zola's call that the theatre must become naturalist or nothing at all. Yet between Zola's manifesto for a "scientific" theatre, based on a methodical analysis of human behavior, heredity, and environment in 1873, and Antoine's stripped-down stage experiments, some fourteen years had elapsed. By 1887, naturalism and its accompanying radical philosophies no longer offended free-thinking Parisians.

> *More appalling still, many of the* **Théâtre Libre***'s short plays dealt with the mess and squalor of lowlife among Paris' underclasses.*

The *Théâtre Libre* (a wishful name, since it was paid for out of Antoine's dwindling resources) made its renown for other reasons. Actual used furniture, replete with nicks and stains, and objects from daily life, such as sides of beef and clucking chickens, were brought to the stage. Interestingly, some of these were hastily purchased from a derelict, second-hand furniture store when less dilapidated articles borrowed from Antoine's mother's apartment were stolen just before the *Théâtre Libre*'s opening night. Antoine also pioneered an innovative acting style that more or less ignored its audience. His spectators were startled to find the *Théâtre Libre* actors speaking to one another with their backs to the house as if the audience was secretly observing through an invisible wall. (A contemporary circus parody of Antoine showed a clown with two backs of a head instead of a face.) More appalling still, many of the Théâtre Libre's short plays dealt with the mess and squalor of lowlife among Paris' underclasses.

From the inauguration of the *Théâtre Libre*'s brave experiment in naturalist dramaturgy, Antoine demonstrated an artistic generosity and eclecticism uncharacteristic of the time. Since naturalistic dramas tend-

LE PETIT CRUCIFIÉ

ROMANCE
Créée par MARIUS RICHARD, à la Scala

Paroles de
RENÉ ESSE ✶ GASTON MAQUIS
Musique de

Petit format, 0 fr. 35

HENRI PASCAL, éditeur, 38, rue Tiquetonne, PARIS
Successeur d'Albert REPOS

Exécution publique et tous droits de traduction et de reproduction réservés. Propriété pour tous pays.

LA PHOTOGRAPHIE DANS LES PRISONS

ed to be diminutive in length, as many as five or six one-acts might comprise a single evening at Antoine's 373-seat theatre. But there were never enough talented naturalist playwrights to satisfy Antoine's needs. So besides naturalist plays, verse tragedies, adaptations from classic literature, comedies, even proto-Symbolist sketches appeared during the *Théâtre Libre*'s five-year heyday. And as the theatre's repertoire began to move toward the ethereal and ineffable mindscape of the burgeoning Symbolist movement, there was a corresponding pull toward extreme naturalism, or what would soon be called "sordid realism." These sensational and offensive plays, which often brought high-minded critics into civic and censorious action against them, fell into at least two separate camps: the dark, anti-clerical mystery fable and the grisly social documentary of modern Paris.

Typical of the handful of naturalist mystery plays was Auguste Linert's *A Christmas Story* (1890). Like a host of young French writers of his generation, Linert became fascinated with Edgar Allan Poe's hideous and irony-laced short stories, somewhat amplified in Baudelaire's colorful translations. In Linert's *A Christmas Story*, a familiar tale unfolded with a shocking conclusion: on Christmas eve, a peasant girl, in her last term of pregnancy, looks for a place

> *All the bourgeois concepts of love and loyalty followed a new and skewed logic.*

to give birth. Unable to find some kindly soul who will take her in, she murders her infant child and throws the remains to a farmer's pigs, while in the distance, neighboring peasants sing Christmas carols on their way to Midnight Mass.

No less disturbing were the *Théâtre Libre*'s documentary plays that recreated slices of life from Paris' underworld. Called *rosse*, or "crass," plays (from the street argot for a nasty or malicious person; literally "old horse"), these productions revealed a different, more primitive thought process, a universe of pure animal passion. Thievery, prostitution, alcohol addiction, sexual dependence and humiliation, jealousy, incest, child abuse, cheating, brutality to women, and vengeance were the most common and notorious themes. And if the characters lived in an atmosphere devoid of bourgeois mores and guilt, the plays themselves shattered the middle-class expectations of Antoine's spectators. All the bourgeois concepts of love and loyalty followed a new and skewed logic. Wrongdoers (that is, the criminals, sociopaths, and young hooligans: the *apaches*) were rarely punished or praised. Almost always, *apache* life with its anti-social, indigenous traditions and conventions continued unabated at the play's end.

In addition to their novel subject matter, the *rosse* productions created havoc with

FELICIEN ROPS, *LA BUVEUSE D'ABSINTHE*

the aesthetic and ironclad structural components of the well-made play. Here, none of the normative values of French society— good and evil, simple "right and wrong," the hierarchy of one class over another—existed. Nothing *had* to happen in a *rosse* play. Any conclusion was possible. Naturally, these amoral and unsettling naturalistic dramas proved to annoy the pundits of establishment mores even more than Antoine's tattered sofas and realistic acting. The Théâtre Libre was under immense pressure to rid itself of both the naturalist mystery play and social documentary. Only because the Théâtre Libre ran itself as a private enterprise limited to individual subscribers were local censors held at bay.

> **Rosse** *plays revealed a different, more primitive thought process, a universe of pure animal passion.*

OSCAR MÉTÉNIER

Formerly a secretary to the Police Commissioner of Paris and a writer for tabloid-like journals, Oscar Méténier was considered the master of the *rosse* play along with naturalist playwrights Georges Ancey and Jean Jullien. A co-founder of the Théâtre Libre in 1887, the twenty-eight year-old Méténier provided Antoine with many of his most controversial offerings. Having already scoured Paris' menacing red-light and working-class slum districts for over six years in a scientific search for naturalist material, Méténier brought an immediate and striking authenticity of character, atmosphere, and language into his writings and dramas. He also exhibited a genuine sympathy for his lowlife play figures, many of whom were based on real persons, and he found their instinctive and savage actions superior to the vain pretensions of Paris' bourgeois theatre-goers.

Méténier's *rosse* vignettes were brief, rarely longer than fifteen minutes, but lurid and effective. *In the Family*, the sensation of the Théâtre Libre's second evening, mounted on May 30th, 1887, glimpsed into the lives of the Parisian underclass. In an illicit shop for the purchase of stolen merchandise, a thoroughly alcoholic thug; his daughter, a streetwalker; and a son, who pimps for a living, meet for dinner. The son describes the public execution of his best friend by guillotine that day in crude, stinging detail. Preoccupied and untouched by the young man's story, the father and sister finish dinner and ready themselves for their nocturnal and illegal activities. *In the Family* was quickly labeled an affront to public morality and banned from production in public theatres. In 1889, *The Informer (La Casserole)*, Méténier's more full-length play, lasting some thirty minutes, again shocked and titillated the Théâtre Libre critics. Using real criminal types to play themselves in minor

NIGHTMARES BY ANDRÉ DE LORDE.

> *Méténier brought Antoine to a private viewing of the police execution of a criminal.*

parts and an actual circus strongman, the violent sketch unfolded in a cheap dance hall, recreated in naturalistic detail. There, in a bloody climax, a pimp grows enraged at a prostitute who has informed on his male lover and stabs her to death.

Méténier continued to work for the Théâtre Libre, once adapting Leo Tolstoy's *Power of Darkness* in a Parisian street argot that gained the approval of the Russian master himself. Another time, Méténier suggested that his untrained brother be cast for a part in a *rosse* play. But Antoine grew tired of the offensive and vulgar genre. In its unpredictability, it was predictable. To Antoine, the difference between a great *rosse* play and a hackneyed one seemed slight. And when Méténier brought Antoine to a private viewing of a criminal's execution, the director of the Théâtre Libre found much less enjoyment in the spectacle than the chronicler of *apache* life. Méténier and Antoine were moving in different directions.

Then, in 1893, six years after its beginnings, Antoine's Théâtre Libre disappeared from its Montmartre home. It had collapsed financially. Yet naturalism in the theatre had not spent its force. In just a few years, it would succeed wildly beyond anyone's prediction, except perhaps Zola's. The novelty of realistic sets and a more life-like style of acting invigorated the Parisian scene in the middle and late 1890s. The plots, though, would change, once again centering on the foibles and etiquette of middle class life. The shocking jargon of the streets that Méténier made stageworthy would now fuel the witty and slightly suggestive lyrics of the popular cabaret chansons.

> *He called it the Grand Guignol after the name of the popular Punch and Judy puppet character.*

Judy puppet character from Lyons, which had become a generic name for all puppet entertainments. It was to be a "Grand" (large) "Guignol" (puppet show) since the intended audiences were to be adults and the characters live performers. The mad behavior and violence that excite children in a normal guignol would be magnified for the pleasure of their parents. ("Grand Guignol" might have been borrowed from a contemporary satirical review of the same name.)

The actual space of the Theatre of the Grand Guignol had a curious and celebrated history. Erected as a Jansenist refuge and convent in 1786, it was gutted and sacked five years later during the Reign of Terror. In the early nineteenth century, a blacksmith with an artistic bent refurbished the chapel's remains as his workshop, leaving untouched the wooden angels hanging from the paneled ceilings in the foyer, and the pseudo-gothic designs cut into the thick oak doors. Throughout the 1870s, the conservative, fire-and-brimstone Dominican priest, Father Didon, used the back-alley Montmartre church as a pulpit to attack the purveyors of extramarital sex. Then in 1880, Georges Rochegrosse, a leading academic painter and designer, purchased the old baroque chapel for use as his studio.

THE FOUNDING OF THE GRAND GUIGNOL

In the spring of 1897, Méténier, who had now tried his hand at other literary pursuits, including the writing of vaudevilles, returned to his patented *rosse* genre. He opened the Theatre of the Grand Guignol at 20 rue Chaptal, not far from the original Théâtre Libre. In fact, his 285-seat theatre (variously given as 280, 272, 265 and 230 seats) seemed like a grisly extension of the Théâtre Libre. It was said that he called it the Grand Guignol after the name of "Guignol," the popular Punch and

GRAND GUIGNOL
THEATRE
DU
GRAND GUIGNOL
GRAND GUIGNOL
GRAND GUIGNOL

Finally, Maurice Magnier, a fanatical publisher with a shaky financial past, leased it in 1896, with the hope that he could ride the trend, inspired by Antoine, for intimate performances given in Montmartre chamber theatres. Calling his venture the Theatre-Salon, Magnier planned to mount a series of miniature dramas and one-act plays. But little went right. The forbidding, twenty-by-twenty foot stage seemed too small even for a cabaret theatre. One critic joked that it was so cramped inside that a front-row spectator could shake hands with the actors as he stretched his feet into the prompter's box. Literally, any audience member who arose from his pew-like seat during a performance unintentionally became a part of the show. Magnier failed again.

Oscar Méténier had different ideas about the old chapel. Like the blacksmith-artist before him, he retained the stiff and heavy architectural artifacts from the *ancien regime* period. He especially adored the wicked-looking cherubs with their crooked smiles that were carved into the beams of the vaulted ceilings, and the shallow church-like seats in the balcony. The anxious and cursed atmosphere of a huge confessional booth, mocked and wrongly used, appealed to his sense of the gothic. (Decades later, "Guignolers" would swear that they heard the actual whispers and chants of nuns during frenzied and agonizing segments of the horror plays.) Also, the claustrophobic confinement of the house could greatly improve the acoustics and, therefore, the nastiness of the *rosse* plays.

With a good deal of fanfare, Méténier

> **PROGRAM**
> *Evening of April 13th, 1897*
> • • •
>
> **GOSSIP FROM MADEMOISELLE GUIGNOL**
> *a curtain-raiser, by Hughes Delorme*
>
> **LITTLE BUGGER**
> *a rosse play in two scenes about marriage in the underworld, by Oscar Méténier*
>
> **GUN SHOT**
> *a comedy, by Georges Courteline*
>
> **WITHOUT A DOWRY**
> *a rosse play, by Jean Lorrain*
>
> **MONSIEUR BADIN**
> *another comedy, by Courteline*
>
> **THEIR FRIAR**
> *another rosse play, by Lorrain*
>
> **MADEMOISELLE FIFI**
> *A "shocker," about a prostitute who stabs a German officer, adapted by Méténier from Guy de Maupassant's story.*

inaugurated his Theatre of the Grand Guignol on April 13th, 1897. Dressed in black, as always, and accompanied by two body guards, as always, Méténier triumphantly walked down the orchestra aisle, shouting and accepting greetings in his bullfrog voice. The first program consisted of seven plays: a curtain raiser, two *rosse* plays by Méténier, two comedies by Georges Courteline, and two dramas by Jean Lorrain. The evening was unusual enough to be considered a success, even in a jaded Paris.

Méténier wanted the repertoire of the Grand Guignol to be different from the disbanded Théâtre Libre and the Théâtre-Salon. Short comedies would alternate with *rosse* plays. Each would intensify the other, like "hot and cold showers." After the first season, a typical bill of Méténier's Grand Guignol would consist of 1) a slapstick curtain raiser, 2) a light drama, 3) a comedy, 4) the horror play, and 5) a farce. Much like a vaudeville format, these plays could be replaced or repeated at will from week to week. *Mademoiselle Fifi* played continuously on one bill or another for seven months. The determining factor was the play's immediate and overall structural effectiveness on its audience. Méténier's formula of "hot and cold showers" was unwittingly responsible for saving the Continental one-act play from extinction.

MAX MAUREY

To accommodate the Grand Guignol repertoire, Méténier further divided his *rosse* plays into two categories: 1) Plays of Popular Manners, virtually actionless dramas of Parisian lowlife that indirectly ridiculed bourgeois morality and propriety, such as *In the Family* and *Little Bugger*; and 2) Newspaper Items (the *faits divers*), dramatizations of bizarre and aberrant events taken from police blotters and published in a few sentences in the daily paper, such as *Mademoiselle Fifi*. In both cases, Méténier seemed torn between wanting to shock his audiences, with or without spurts of stage blood, and proselytizing about the savage nobility of his *apaches*.

Essentially, for Méténier and his colleagues, the Theatre of the Grand Guignol, like the Théâtre Libre, was a literary and social venture. As a product of the Parisian avant-garde, it had to be ever-changing and evolving. Méténier felt that he could not sustain the novelty. And, in 1898, after four seasons, he sold his interest to Max Maurey, long considered the "true" father of Grand Guignol. After 1898, Méténier disappeared into history.

Max Maurey was a mystery. Not a man of the theatre, at least not known to the Montmartre crowd, Maurey was determined to make the Grand Guignol a financial success. He had little desire to attempt theatrical experimentation for its own sake; that was stuff for poets and painters. Maurey sought

> *Spectators fainted on the average of two per night.*

sure-fire formulas of terror and fear. And if Méténier focused on extreme naturalistic "slice of life" sketches, Maurey's interest pointed toward something different: what one critic referred to as the "slice of death" drama. Maurey's Grand Guignol was to be "pure theatre." That is, a place where every social taboo was cracked and shattered. This formula would attract the French public that slaked its blood lust and fascination with the morbid by devouring pulp novels and unlikely tabloid exposés. This clientele, in other times, flocked to country freak shows and wax museums that featured chambers of horror and sensational crime. Now, watching live realistic and gory enactments of mutilation, rape, torture, and murder, each spectator could play out his fantasies of victimization and retribution. Audiences could truly be purged of pity and fear.

Maurey did not abandon all of Méténier's techniques and dramatic methods. The "hot and cold shower" format (now called "laughter and tears"), if anything, became

A satisfied customer.

GRAND GUIGNOL CARTOON BY CHARLES ADDAMS

PRE-SHOW MEDICAL EXAMINATIONS OF GRAND GUIGNOL SPECTATORS IN THE FRENCH MAGAZINE *RIRE*.

Maurey sought sure-fire formulas of terror and fear.

more standardized. Longer, more fully developed comedies and horror plays alternated in constant tandem. Generally, two light comedies (or farces) and two horror plays filled out an evening. The socially ironic bite of Méténier's *rosse* plays were now much more likely to be found in the comedies than in the thrillers. Horror was immediate and physically shocking, even sickening, usually coming in the last minutes of a horror sketch. Psychological suspense replaced social and cultural sophistication.

Renowned for his perfectionism, Maurey had a habit of extensively rewriting scripts and toying constantly with the stage effects. Seated in the house with the trademark cigarette in his mouth, Maurey obsessively made each actor work and re-work scenes, frequently giving them exact line-readings. The fourteen permanent performers often maintained that they, under Maurey's direction, not the audience, suffered the most at the Grand Guignol. Séverin Mars, a leading performer and popular mime, became so frustrated with Maurey's drills that he almost threw the director's table at Maurey. Another time when Maurey shouted to the pianist that he was sick of his pedestrian playing, the pianist retorted, "I'm sick of your play." The rehearsal atmosphere of barely restrained hostility and frustration

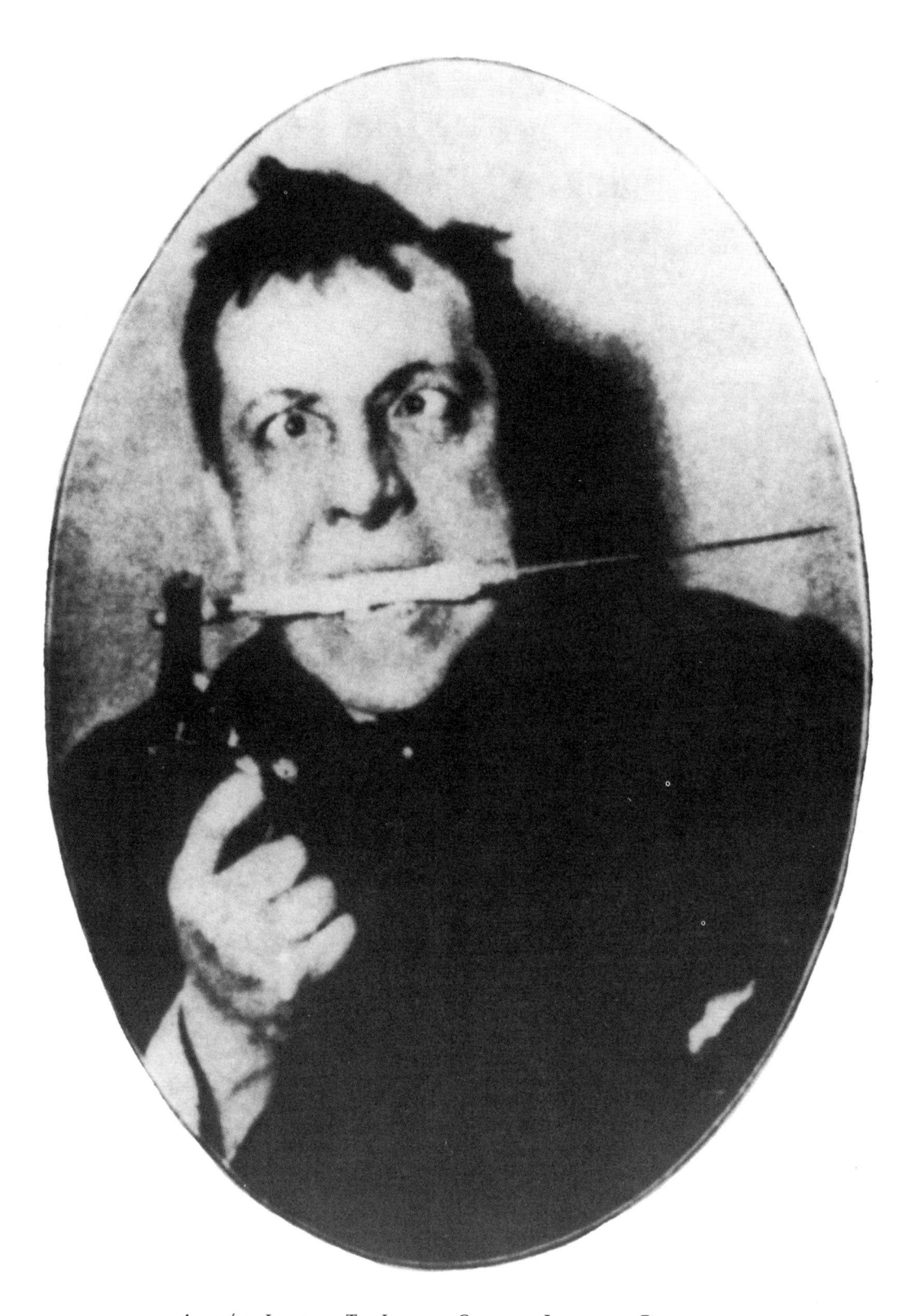

ANDRÉ DE LORDE IN *THE INVISIBLE ONE* BY DE LORDE AND BINET, 1912.

> **PROGRAM**
> *from 1913-14 Repertoire*
> • • •
> **THE SEDUCTRESS**
> *a farce about a woman who believes all men are trying to seduce her, by Robert Dieudonne*
>
> **THE THANATOGRAPH**
> *a horror play by Andre Vernieres*
>
> **THE TRIANGLE**
> *a sex farce by Alfred Sutro, adapted by Regis Gignoux and Charles Barbaud*
>
> **THE WHITE CELL**
> *a horror play in two acts about the execution of a Russian revolutionary, by Leo Marches and Gaston-Ch. Richard*
>
> **M. LAMBERT, SELLER OF PAINTINGS**
> *a comedy in two acts, by Max Maurey*

probably improved the evenings' work. And in exactitude and precision, Maurey was often favorably compared to Antoine.

Maurey also had a special gift for public relations. One of the most famous incidents in the Grand Guignol history is recounted in a cartoon from a 1904 issue of the *Journal*. Attempting to revive his wife, who has just fainted from the shock of a Grand Guignol production, a customer shouts for a doctor. In the theatre's foyer, Maurey replies that unfortunately the doctor too has collapsed. Although most readers passed the story off as the ultimate Grand Guignol joke, many "Guignolers" assert an event like it actually happened at the turn of the century. Another cartoon from the same period shows an old doctor, under orders from the Police Commissioner, checking the hearts of potential Grand Guignol customers before they were allowed to enter the "House of Horror."

ANDRÉ DE LORDE

If anyone was responsible for the Grand Guignol's ascension from a local Parisian sensation to international success, it was the playwright and essayist André de Lorde, known in his lifetime as "the Prince of Terror." The son of a physician, from an early age de Lorde developed a fascination for all things frightening and morbid. Outside his father's office, the young de Lorde would listen to the sobs and screams of the patients, imagining in detail the horrifying torments they suffered. Once, to rid his son of his dread and preoccupation with death, the elderly Dr. de Lorde took André to the apartment of a recently deceased man where, as a doctor, he was required to verify his departure. The young de Lorde waited

> *If anyone was responsible for the Grand Guignol's international success, it was André de Lorde, the 'Prince of Terror'.*

outside the bedroom, watching the women in mourning passing in and out of the room, as they placed funeral candles by the side of the dead man's body. The future master of horror knew what he envisioned in his mind's eye was even more terrifying than the sight of an actual corpse. The young de Lorde chose to remain outside. On another occasion, de Lorde's father forced the boy to keep vigil over his dead grandmother's body on the evening before the burial. The doctor wished to convince his son, once and for all, not to be afraid of death or pain. But just the opposite happened. De Lorde became obsessed with death—especially of the horrific and painful variety. All his life, de Lorde was haunted by it.

According to his therapist and dramatic collaborator, Dr. Alfred Binet, the director of the Psychological-Physiological Laboratory of the Sorbonne, de Lorde was a poor patient, always rushing off with new plans for a play, instead of dealing with his own dark and complicated psyche. Binet often compared de Lorde to his idol, Edgar Allan Poe (always referred to by the French as Edgar Poe). Both suffered from depression and were unusually sensitive to their adolescent fears and emotions. Like many poets and writers, de Lorde possessed "the soul of a child," but in de Lorde's case, the child remained traumatized by dread.

Between 1901 and 1926, de Lorde wrote over one hundred plays of fear and horror, often in collaboration with doctors and novelists. Besides the Grand Guignol, de Lorde's plays were mounted at the Théâtre Antoine (which continued in the naturalist tradition of the Théâtre Libre), the Odeon, the Théâtre Sarah Bernhardt, the Gymnase, the Vaudeville, and the Ambigu. Trained as a lawyer, de Lorde worked as a secretary to the Minister of Finance and later received an appointment as a chief librarian at the Bibliothèque de l'Arsenal. More than any previous writer for the Grand Guignol, de Lorde was a literary man, giving interviews to newspapers and magazines, publishing volumes of his horror plays, even writing manifestoes and explanations of his work.

In one preface to a collection of plays, de Lorde stated that men who flee fear through the day, flock to it after sundown

OPPOSITE AND ABOVE: *NIGHTMARES*, 1909

> *De Lorde wanted to write a play so terrifying and unbearable, the entire audience would flee from the theatre.*

at the Grand Guignol. The horror play was an essential feature of modern life as the gladiator contests, *autos-da-fé*, and guillotine beheadings had been in other times. And identifying with his American predecessor, de Lorde wanted to create one of Poe's dreams: to write a play so terrifying and unbearable that several minutes after the curtain rises, the entire audience would flee from the theatre en masse.

An avid reader and student of the newest trends in psychology and criminal behavior, de Lorde was the first dramatist to set plays in operating rooms and insane asylums. As a playwright, he mastered the two principles vital to effective terror: creating plots where the suspense continues to grow until the gruesome finale unfolds; and, the very opposite trick, preparing the audience for an inevitable conclusion they have already guessed. Either way, the anticipation of horror was the key—otherwise the terrifying and sickening conclusions would merely draw simple surprise or even laughter.

The collaboration of Maurey and de Lorde turned the Grand Guignol into an elite social entertainment despite the bloody climaxes and horrific violence. Just

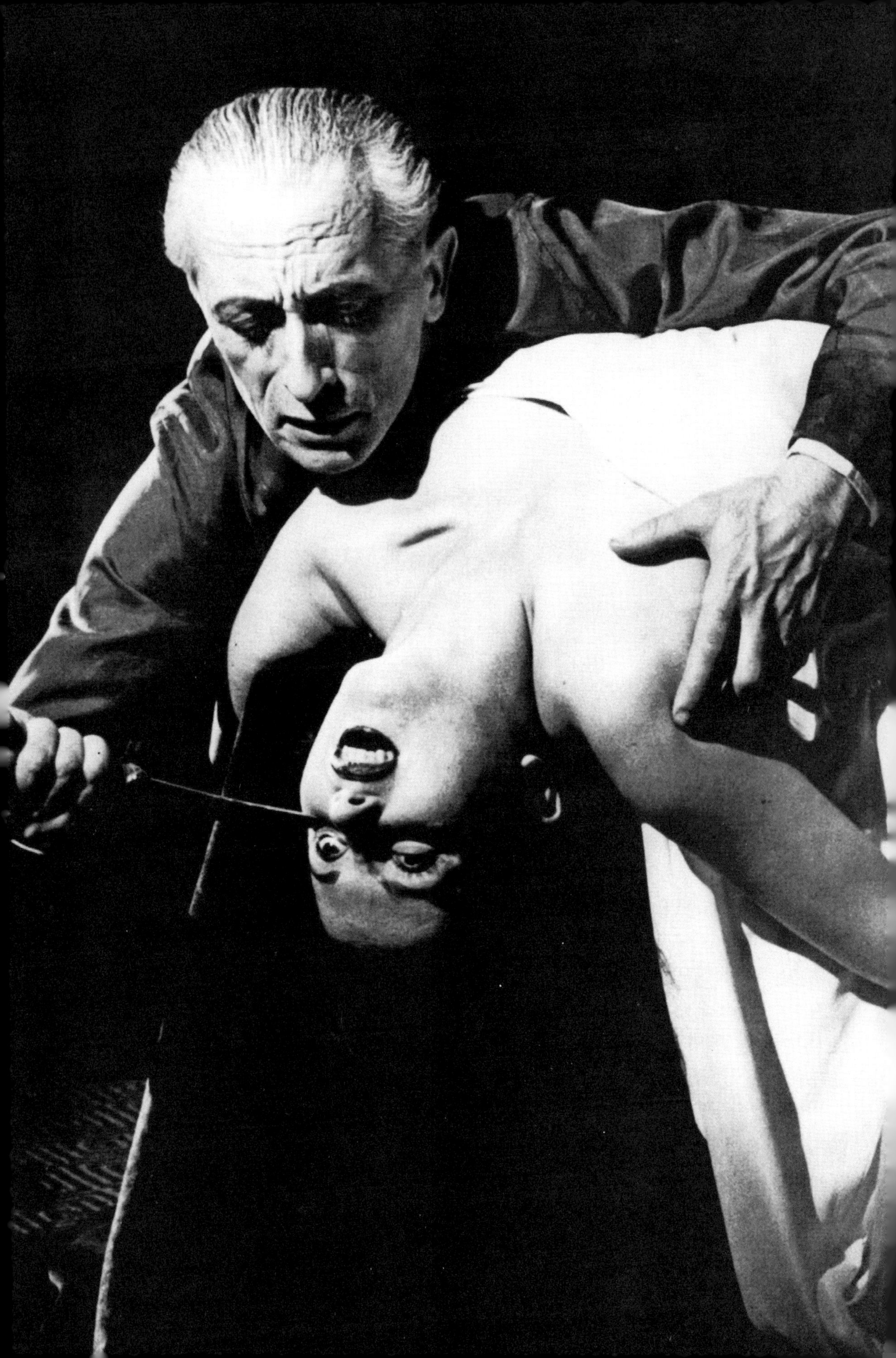

OPPOSITE: *THE BLOODY EMBRACE*, 1945. ABOVE: CHARLES ADDAMS ILLUSTRATES THE GRAND GUIGNOL, 1950

> *At the very height of the scenic action and the character's emotional displays, hidden trick properties had to be executed perfectly.*

as Méténier had used the Grand Guignol to perfect his own brand of sordid "slice of life" sketches to educate Parisian audiences how the underclass lived and thought, de Lorde had invented a new dramatic genre devoted to "slices of death." It spoke to mankind's universal dread. And society women, in particular, were drawn to it. The presence of attending doctors at the theatre was no longer a publicity stunt. Spectators fainted on the average of two per night. Interestingly, it was mainly male playgoers who swooned, probably because, unlike their female escorts, the men failed to cover their eyes during the horrifying moments.

Even the bloodless, *rosse*-type plays produced shocks in the audience. F. Berkeley Smith, the famous British travel critic, reported on one such reaction in the winter of 1902. After a Grand Guignol performance of the relatively mild *An Affair of Morals*, the spectators, having already laughed heartily at the previous play, a sex farce, became rigid when two prostitute characters marched the dead judge's body out of a restaurant singing the "Fireman's Anthem."

As the curtain fell, the audience seemed in a stupor. A woman beside me sat staring at the floor, crying. Men coughed and remained silent. Not until the pianist in the foyer struck up a lively polka did they leave their seats for a little cognac and a breath of air.
—How Paris Amuses Itself *(NY and London, 1903)*

Under Maurey's direction and continual publicity, the Grand Guignol was newly recognized as a unique French entertainment. Parisian guidebooks in every

> *Horror was to be immediate and physically shocking, even sickening.*

language recommended it. After the Eiffel Tower—but equally with the *maisons de tolerance* (the legalized brothels), Maxim's, and the Louvre—the Theatre of the Grand Guignol had become the best known tourist attraction in Paris by 1910.

CAMILLE CHOISY

In 1915 Maurey retired. Camille Choisy, a small well-groomed man with extravagant taste—he wore a ring on each finger—took over in a partnership with the Rumanian-born Charles Zibell. Choisy, a true *homme du théâtre*, was himself a character actor in second-rate theatres and a sympathetic personality. In writing about the new regime, however, Antoine, now an important arbiter of theatrical taste, felt that the Grand Guignol had used up its novelty. The First World War, then settling into the unheroic posture of trench warfare, had introduced a new realism and horror in life. But, for Choisy, the technology of death helped enlarge his hideous vocabulary of torture and death: poison gas, explosive devices, electrical cables, surgical instruments and drills replaced the old pistol, dagger, and primitive sword.

Actually, the Grand Guignol reached its artistic apogee after the First World War.

PROGRAM
from 1923 Season

•••

A THIRD ACT
a sex farce about two playwrights and a cuckolding wife, by Serge Veber

ON THE SLAB
a horror play about an apache who hallucinates that a corpse has come alive, by André de Lorde and Georges Montignac

THE SYSTEM OF DR. PLUME AND PROF. GOUDRON
a horror play about a lunatic asylum that has been taken over by its inmates, by de Lorde

SAUCE FOR THE GOOSE
a comedy about an embittered man who, before he can tell his lover that he is marrying someone else, learns that she too is engaged to another, by Robert Diendonne

> **PROGRAM**
> *Premiere, February 8th, 1929*
> • • •
> ONE NIGHT OF EDGAR POE
> *a horror play, by André de Lorde*
>
> HARMONY
> *a comedy in three scenes,
> by Henri Duvernois*
>
> DESTINATION UNKNOWN
> *a horror play in two acts and four
> scenes, by Bernard Zimmer*
>
> THE MOROCCAN BREAKFAST
> *a comedy, by Jules Romains*

In the early and middle thirties, the Grand Guignol lost its novelty and appeal.

Its familiar array of acting techniques that once showed off a heightened realism—within gruesome circumstances—now transformed itself into a particular and discernible style of performance. Instead of the single-minded, Antoine-like naturalism in the creation of character and action, a more colorful and complicated behavior was expected from the players under Choisy. According to a 1923 press release, the Grand Guignol actors present "the realities of life—with its ardours, its violences, its enchantments, and also its beauties."

More than ever, Grand Guignol performers were expected to inhabit real characters with a full range of powerful and animalistic impulses—as they secretly manipulated the catches on fleshy prosthetic creations, intricate spring contraptions, and a host of blood-filled devices. Naturally, it was at the very height of the scenic action and the characters' emotional displays that the hidden trick properties had to be executed perfectly. When a beaker of fuming vitriol was unexpectedly thrown into the face of a character by his lover, a look of horror had to register on the actor's face at the same moment his skin transmogrified into a smoking, bubbling, and cracked mass of ooze. The smallest manual slip or false note in the acting could thoroughly ruin a twenty-minute scenario. Each Grand Guignol actor had to possess a double skill in stage concentration and sleight-of-hand trickery. And the French audiences of the teens and twenties became excited since they had a new yardstick by which to judge Choisy's productions.

MAXA

The most celebrated performer during the Grand Guignol's heyday was Maxa, known in the newspapers as "the High Priestess of the Temple of Horror." A glamorous actress with an instinctive understanding of the macabre, Maxa was said to have played all of her roles as if she "were carrying a torch." During her relatively brief career, she was murdered more than 10,000 times and in some 60 ways. A few examples: devoured by a ravenous puma, cut into 93 pieces and glued back together, smashed by a roller-compressor, burnt alive, cut open by a traveling salesman who wanted her intestines; she was also raped over 3,000 times under a dozen circumstances. Camillo Antona-Traversi, Choisy's secretary and an early historian of the Grand Guignol, calculated that on the stage, Maxa cried "Help!" 983 times, "Murderer!" 1,263 times, and "Rape!" 1,804 and one-half times. In her memoirs, Maxa wrote about the value of timing; a line or gesture said too fast, or slow, could easily ruin the tension built up over ten or fifteen minutes and destroy the evening.

Choisy encouraged the work of new playwrights by not rewriting each and every scene—at least not until after opening night. Maurey rarely extended that courtesy to dramatists and often had problems retaining their services after one or two experiences with his style of Grand Guignol. Yet even with the difficulties they created for their playwrights and adapters, both directors ultimately preserved and encouraged the writing of one-act plays, an art that quickly faded after Symbolism's collapse before World War One. Choisy also inten-

> *Maxa cried "Help!" 983 times, "Murderer!" 1,263 times, and "Rape!" 1,804 and one-half times.*

sified the Grand Guignol atmosphere by going to extra lengths for verisimilitude in set design. The scenic environments for Choisy's productions often consisted of modern ships, blimps, submarines, railroad cars, factories, and mines. Consequently, the naturalistic settings grew considerably in fantastic and expensive detail.

Of course, the public's actual reaction to the Grand Guignol shockers ran the gamut from outright revulsion to ironic detachment and playful amusement. For premieres, audiences often attended in evening dresses and tuxedos, bringing their own champagne and glasses. Resident millionaires from every continent, and royalty and their families came regularly. Among the best-known "Guignolers" in the Choisy-era were the King of Greece, Princess Wilhelmina of Holland, the Sultan of Morocco's sons and daughters, and the wife of the deposed King Alfonso XIII, who invariably arrived on All Saint's Eve. When King Carol of Rumania was forced into exile with his red-haired mistress, Magda Lupescu, they pub-

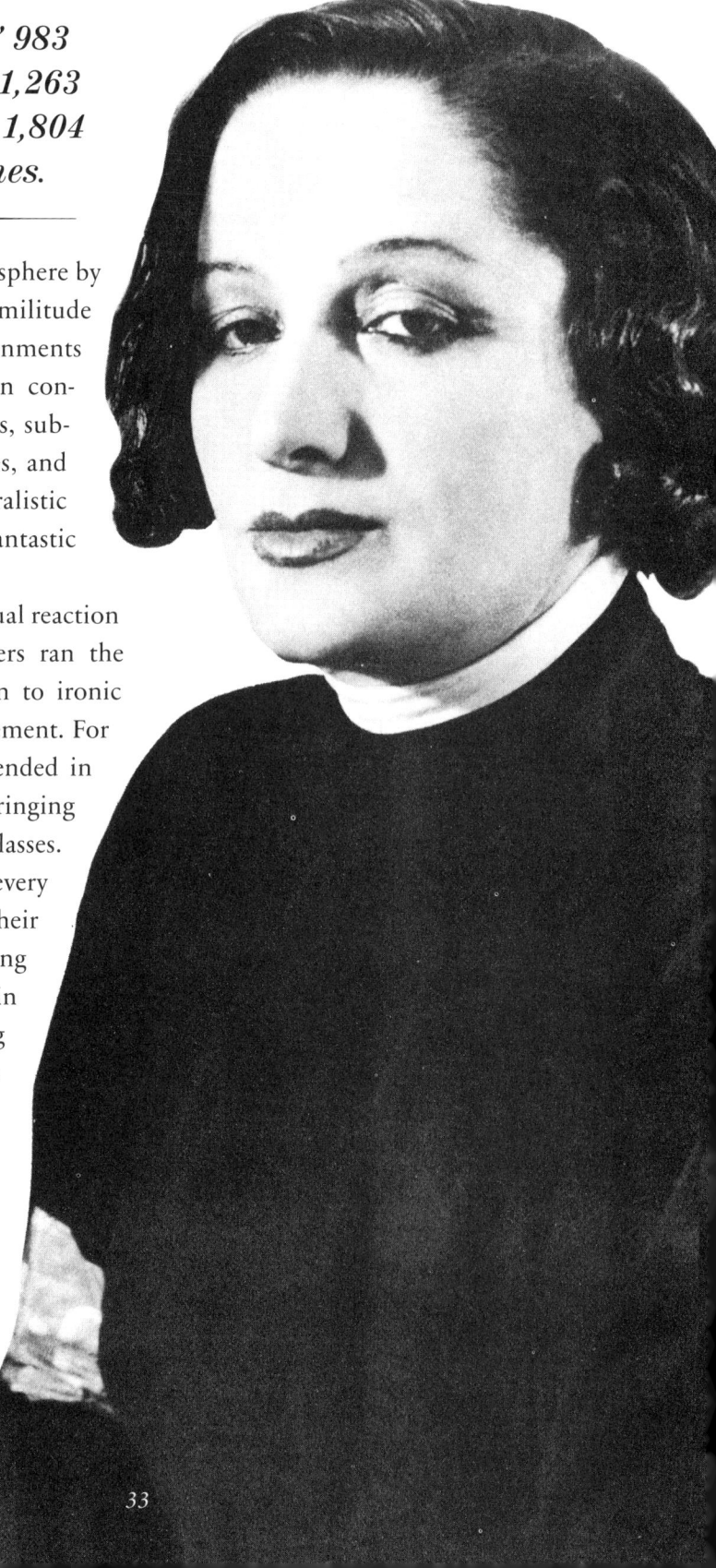

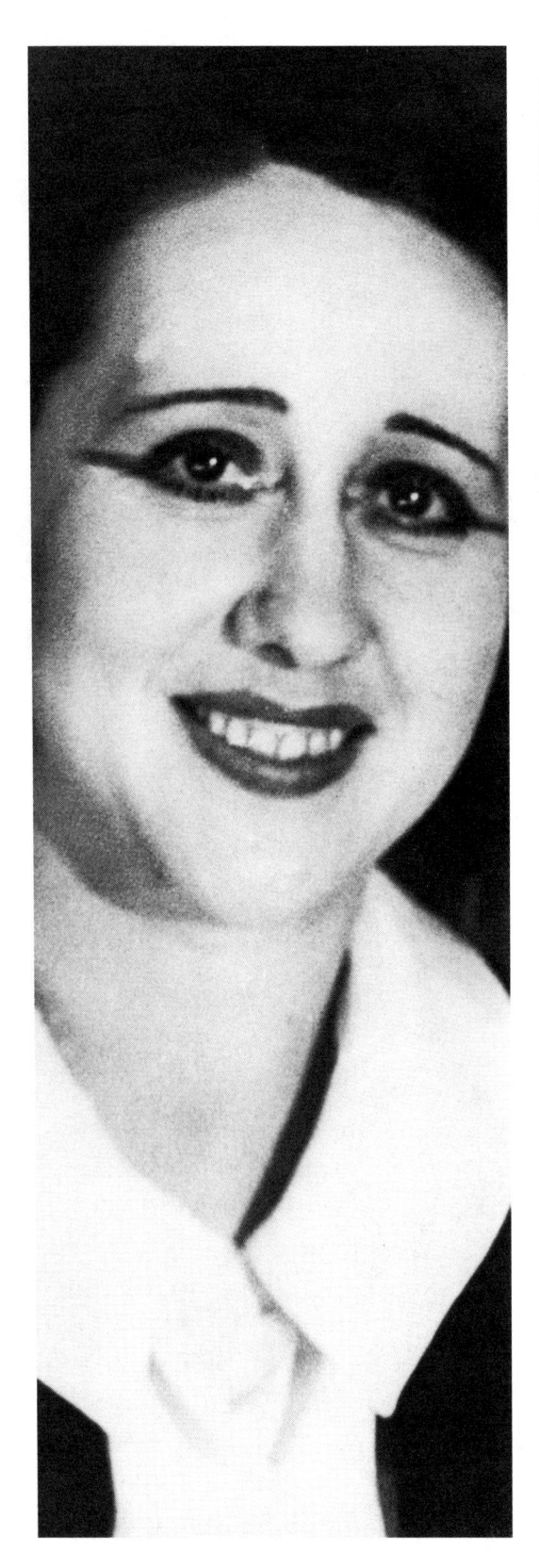

GRAND GUIGNOL   THEATRE OF FEAR AND HORROR

> **PROGRAM**
> *from the 1932 Season*
>
> • • •
>
> THE NEED FOR YOUTHFULENSS
> *a comedy, by Edmond Gilbert*
> (Jack Jouvin)
>
> ZANZIBAR
> *a horror play, by J. de Heeckeren*
>
> SEXUALITY
> *a horror play, in three scenes,*
> *by S. Ramel (J. Jouvin)*
>
> NEITHER DANDIA
> NOR BOUBOUROCHE
> *a comedy, by E. Gilbert*
> (J. Jouvin)

licly appeared at the Grand Guignol in Paris. And, after the tables turned in Rumanian politics, the King's pretender Prince Nichols fled to France and, like his father, was taken in by the murderous antics of the Grand Guignol. Still lesser types made up the bulk of the audiences. One such devoted patron was the Vietnamese political refugee Ho Chi Minh, then a noodle and pastry cook at a Chinese restaurant.

The involvement of some playgoers was so strong that they sometimes shouted "Assassin!" at the various "villains," just as their forbears did in the 1830s Boulevard du Crime melodramas. "Guignolers" liked to repeat the number of times that the house physician was called to treat temporarily sickened spectators. At one performance, six people passed out when an actress, whose eyeball was just gouged out, re-entered the stage, revealing a gooey, blood-encrusted hole in her skull. Backstage, the actors themselves calculated their success according to the evening's faintings.

During one de Lorde horror play that ended with a realistic blood transfusion, a record was set: fifteen playgoers had lost consciousness. Between sketches, the cobble-stoned alley outside the theatre was frequented by hyperventilating couples and vomiting individuals.

JACK JOUVIN

Charles Zibell, having lost most of his fortune during the war and in the inflation that followed, sold his share of the Grand Guignol to the playwright, director, and producer Jack Jouvin in 1926. Jouvin's uneasy collaboration with Choisy only lasted three years. Choisy departed in 1928 and, within a year, opened the rival *Théâtre du Rire et de L'Epouvante* ("Theatre of Laughter and Fright") at the Varietés Theatre under the direction of Jacques Albert.

Maxa, too, fired by Jouvin (supposedly because of her personal success in drawing an independent following of "Guignolers"), started her own terror-and-comedy type playhouse in the Montmartre, "The Theatre of Vice and Virtue." Yet, despite a superior repertoire and style of acting, neither Choisy or Maxa's theatres lasted more than a few seasons. The copyrighted name of "Grand Guignol" proved to be an attraction of its own.

In 1930, Jouvin announced a new Grand Guignol repertoire. He played down the de Lorde tradition of physical violence and flesh-searing torture, retaining only three of the Prince's masterpieces altogether. Jouvin's modern horror plays mixed psychological and sexual menace within the traditional crime and laboratory formats. Mental cruelty, homosexuality, hysteria, unexpected betrayal, and suspense fueled the plots. Most of the silly sex farces were eliminated. Even the "hot shower" comedies became less bawdy and physical. Jouvin created unifying themes for the programs, such as staging an evening of comedies and hor-

LABORATORY OF HALLUCINATIONS, 1947

> **Resident millionaires and royalty from every continent attended regularly.**

ror plays all authored by the same writer. Under the pseudonyms of Edmond Gilbert and S. Ramel, Jouvin wrote many of these dramas himself. It was all to no avail.

In the early and middle thirties, the Grand Guignol lost its novelty and appeal—except to American tourists and French university students out for a hoot. The theatre's balcony proved to be an ideal and daring place to engage in necking sessions and more pronounced sex play. In addition, Hollywood sound films, like *Dracula* and *Frankenstein*, borrowing the very techniques of terror and laughter from the Grand Guignol, became fierce competition. Only the ubiquitous glistening-red stage blood that still splattered and flowed in pailfuls caught the spectators' attention differently.

EVA BERKSON

In 1937, the dynamic British-born actress Eva Berkson bought out Jouvin and invigorated the old vehicle. Even Maxa returned briefly to once again be stabbed, burnt, scalded, shot, and torn to bits. During an episode of prolonged screaming, however, Maxa seemed to have permanently damaged her vocal cords; her audio range was forever reduced to normal speaking level. Intermixing some of the oldest farces with up-to-date horror plays, Berkson seemed to have found the perfect formula. She even mounted a horror play in 1939 that dealt with Nazi atrocities in Poland. The Grand Guignol flourished until the German invasion in 1940. With other British nationals, Berkson fled to England and waited out the war there, joining a women's auxiliary to the R.A.F.

During the Nazi occupation of Paris, the Grand Guignol found a familiar spectator, the non-French-speaking spectator. Most of the repertoire reverted to Choisy's old bills and the theatre became very popular with the enemy troops. Hermann Goering in particular enjoyed the productions; but, for the Gestapo and the SS elite, the Grand Guignol—with its gratuitous violence and lewd pornographic interludes—was a penultimate example of *Entartete Kunst* ("Degenerate Art"). Nazi censors vainly attempted to ban the popular French decadent entertainment. Only when German victory was assured, it was declared, could the Grand Guignol be liquidated and excised from the culture of New Europe.

One year after the Allied liberation of Paris in 1944, Berkson returned with her husband, Alexander Dundas, to piece together her beloved Grand Guignol. Initially, among the newly patriotic French theatre-goers, there was some resentment against the Théâtre of Horror and Terror, although these ill-feelings paled when compared with their real hatred toward the "legitimate" theatres, revue-houses, and cabarets that regularly entertained Nazi troops. Choisy, who kept the Grand Guignol running profitably during the Nazi occupation, fortunately died before the Committee of Liberation got around to trying him for wartime collaboration.

As a returning Englishwoman and

EVA BERKSON AND HER HUSBAND, ALEXANDER DUNDAS, 1946

> **PROGRAM**
> from the Season of 1953-1954
> ...
> THE PROSTITUTE AND THE ANGEL
> *a horror play in eight scenes, by Frederic Dard*
>
> AGLAEE
> *a comedy, by André Ransan*
>
> THE CHAUFFEUR
> *a classic comedy about country bumpkins who do not know how to drive an automobile stuck in a backyard, by Max Maurey*

a wife of an R.A.F. pilot, Berkson did not need to exonerate her wartime activities. Besides, the current occupiers of Europe, the Americans, took to the Grand Guignol themselves. When General George Patton, on leave from his German headquarters, visited it one evening, a French newspaper headlined "'Old Blood and Guts' at the Grand Guignol." The next day, excited audiences queued up for tickets, thinking that a new play had just opened.

The postwar years were difficult for Berkson. The Second World War, unlike the First, left the Grand Guignol's potential viewers hungry for hideous events—but real ones, not those imagined by Montmartre playwrights. Hundreds of sensational books and magazines describing the Nazi tortures and massacres were pinned up on the posts of the book kiosks along the Seine. Documentary footage of the Nazi death camps and medical experiments on humans that was shown in neighborhood movie houses became impossible competition. Audiences guffawed or laughed at de Lorde's pseudo-atrocities at the Grand Guignol. In 1947, Berkson confessed, "I've

> *Documentary footage of Nazi death camps shown in neighborhood movie houses became impossible competition.*

come to the conclusion that the only way to frighten a French audience since the war is to cut up a woman on stage—a live woman, of course—and throw them the pieces!" She tried several new formulas, including full-length dramatizations of foreign novels. These, although superb and terrifyingly produced, only worked for a time. The ageless former actress retired in 1951.

THE LAST YEARS OF THE GRAND GUIGNOL

Between 1951 and 1954, Charles Nonon, company manager, took over temporarily under the ownership of Max Maurey's sons, Denis and Michel. Nonon also attempted various formulas, now including full-length satires and even music revues. Again, the performances were good, but the Grand Guignol began to lose its special identity.

From 1954 to 1958, the crime writer and feminist journalist Raymonde Machard took over and improved the reputation of the Grand Guignol dramatically. For one, she used better and younger writers. Yet, the

> **PROGRAM**
> *from the Evening of the 1962 Season*
>
> • • •
>
> PARODY OF DEATH
> *a horror play in two acts, from Peter Randa's novel, adapted by Maurice Renay*
>
> EYES WITHOUT A FACE
> *a horror play in two acts, from Jean Redon's novel, adapted by Renay*
>
> TWO WOMEN IN POWER
> *a comedy in two acts, by J. Marevu*

By 1959, a camp quality had overtaken the Grand Guignol performances.

acting finally suffered, becoming sloppy and occasionally dangerous. One actress almost hanged herself in a leather contraption; another was badly burnt during an incineration scene. Still one more had a nervous breakdown on stage.

Some critics believed that this had to do with a "New Realism" in the acting, but a few of the events were pure hocus-pocus: like the publicity stunt where a Grand Guignol actress, playing a character who was kidnapped in *No Orchids for Miss Blandish*, disappeared herself and was declared held for ransom before opening night. Yet a number of the Grand Guignol's "problems" in the fifties could not be faked. The playwright of *The Machine to Kill Life* actually did die on opening night. And the technical adviser for a 1956 play about a Le Mans race car wreck, *The Death of Ralenti*, was one of 71 who died that year in a Le Mans disaster.

By 1959, when Fred Pasquale replaced Machard, a camp quality had overtaken the Grand Guignol performances. The audiences consisted of 50% tourists and many of the French fans were cheering on the stage madmen. In 1961, Nonon once again assumed the directorship. Despite horrific effects—like the tips of a woman's nipples being snipped off with a hedge shears followed by a gouging of her eyes (they were scooped out with a soup spoon and jackknife)—the Grand Guignol itself was dying. Nonon lamented that "We could never equal Buchenwald. Before the war, everyone felt that what was happening on stage was impossible. Now we know that these things, and worse, are possible in reality."

In November 1962, the Théâtre of the Grand Guignol closed its doors. The naughty joke, which once attracted the attentions of Paris' elite, now had gone stale and soft. It also became financially hopeless. Small-scale pornographic versions of the Grand Guignol in other theatres and nightclubs had already captured the bulk of German and British tourists wandering through Pigalle. The playhouse on Rue Chapel temporarily reopened as Théâtre 347, featuring a repertoire of science fantasy plays. But, in March 1963, with much fanfare, the portico and front entrance of the Grand Guignol were totally destroyed—comically, somewhat in the manner that a harmless but aging vampire is dispatched in bad films. A squad of bereted laborers, hoisting picks and shovels, grinned, then struck with their primitive implements at the weak and ancient facade. Second-string journalists and newsreel cameramen, ironically about to be forcibly retired themselves, captured the final *coup de grâce*. The Grand Guignol as a French institution died in 1963, but, only, as the "Guignolers" then claimed, to be replaced by something else. Interestingly, Nonon and several of the Grand Guignol performers went into the restaurant trade.

SUMMER SEASON

DIRECT FROM PARIS!

THE FAMOUS PLAYS OF THE

GRAND GUIGNOL

Thrills - Chills - Horrors - Never Seen in America!

FIRST SERIES
- "A DEAD RAT IN CABINET 6"
- "ON THE SLAB"
- "THE STRANGE CASE OF THE INSANE VIRGIN"
- "THE SYSTEM OF Dr. GOUDRON AND PROFESSOR PLUME"

2nd Series... to be announced...

THE PLAYGOER
Repertory Theatre

THE INFLUENCE OF THE GRAND GUIGNOL

THE GRAND GUIGNOL has long been considered a unique French entertainment. Although it attracted a large international audience to its Montmartre lair and appeared prominently in foreign-language guidebooks of the City of Light between 1905 and 1940, the Théâtre of the Grand Guignol itself was a poor export. Under Maurey's direction, the Parisian performers played successfully across France in summer months but in the spring of 1908, their first tour to London ended in a financial disaster. The political rivalry between the two leading colonial powers was at its height, and British critics savaged the Gaullic shockers as "mild amusement." A similar fate befell the tour in Berlin and Rome.

In the early twenties, Choisy's troupe traveled to Rio de Janeiro, Montreal, and New York. These ventures too often ended with short seasons and poor notices. Foreign play reviewers, who seemed to like neither the terror dramas nor the sex farces, had a greater sway and affect on the tastes of the local audiences than their equally critical Parisian counterparts.

ABOVE: *ON THE SLAB*, 1923

THEATRE

Only in French-speaking Montreal did Choisy find sold-out houses and an enthusiastic following. The theatre critic of the *Montreal Herald* (October 9th, 1923) summed up the fervent reception of his fellow Quebequoise:

> The work of the Grand Guignol is like nothing else in the world of theatre. It is devoted to the visualization of a pitiless analysis and dissection of the elemental human emotions, but it mainly concerns itself with the psychology of fear, terror, horror, and the reaction of the human conscience and the human need to influence both real and imaginary, working in and through certain suggestive atmospheric environments and upon the retina of imagination. It absorbs the attention of the beholder utterly.

Just one week later at New York's Frolic Theatre, a diminutive playhouse over the New Amsterdam Theatre, the same French-speaking troupe and its repertoire were met with a different reaction. Critics of all the major newspapers found problems with the Grand Guignol's acting, *mise en scéne*, and writing. The Selwyns, who produced the ten-week season in Manhattan, may have oversold the theatrical novelty, calling it an "even greater event than the coming of the Moscow Art Theatre" which played to frenzied American spectators the previous year. Typically, *The New York Tribune* (October 16, 1923) characterized the evening as "respectable, and not particularly flesh-creeping."

BRITISH GRAND GUIGNOL PROGRAM
Premiere, September 1st, 1920

•••

HOW TO BE HAPPY
a morality play, by Pierre Verber

G.H.Q. LOVE
a drama by Sewell Collins, adapted from Pierre Rehm's play

THE HAND OF DEATH
a horror play, by André de Lorde and Alfred Binet

OH, HELL!
a "revuette", by Reginald Arkell and Russell Thorndike

Promotional artwork for Grand Guignol at London's Little Theatre.

> *The Grand Guignol experience seemed to be limited to the physical confines of the French-speaking world.*

For a week's program, Alla Nazimova, the Stanislavsky-trained Hollywood starlet, joined the Grand Guignol. Having been banned from the Keith Vaudeville Circuit in a contract dispute over her suggestive sketch, *The Unknown*, the Russian femme fatale's notoriety should have brought in crowds of curiosity seekers and fans but, largely because of critical pressures, did not. The Selwyns' grandiose project closed somewhat ignominiously after five difficult the Grand Guignol sketches successful in and of themselves. Often the horrific effects became muted or were edited out completely.

In 1913 at the Princess Théâtre in New York, the celebrated American actor and director Holbrook Blinn introduced Grand Guignol plays into his second season of the Princess Players. Adapted to emphasize their mysterious and occult features, rather than the traditional gruesome or shock value, even horror plays like *Hari-Kari*, *Room Number Six*, and *The Kiss in the Dark* appeared vapid and greatly resembled the accompanying American mystery dramas given by the Princess Players. Then, four years after the Selwyn fiasco, George Renavent established the American Grand Guignol, Inc. at the Grove Street Théâtre in Greenwich Village in December 1927. This and other efforts, during the next five years, at the Temple Theatre, the Palace, and the Chanin Auditorium rarely lasted a complete season. The last venture, in the best Grand Guignol style, advertised the presence of a doctor and nurse—and mortician, if necessary—at every performance. Still, in the twenties and thirties, an avid American spectator seeking the true Grand Guignol would have to cross the Atlantic. (Other American Grand Guignol imitations surfaced briefly in Pittsburgh, New York, and San Francisco in the post-World War II era.)

weeks. The Grand Guignol experience, despite the multi-lingual and cosmopolitan nature of its audiences in Paris, seemed to be limited to the physical confines of the French-speaking world.

A few Grand Guignol playwrights, like de Lorde and Sarténe, savored a growing international popularity as their dramas were translated (or adapted) into a dozen European languages, as well as Japanese and Hebrew. Most of these foreign-language versions, however, were mounted in evenings of assorted short plays in an effort to preserve the art of the one-act play. Rarely were

Outside of Paris, only two Grand Guignol theatres attained a noted degree of success. The first, located at Rome's Teatro Metastasio, began under Alfredo Sainati's directorship as the result of the Parisian Grand Guignol tour in 1908. Although challenged by a rival group, "The Grand Guignol International" in 1910 and 1911, the original Roman Grand Guignol prospered, staging both Italian versions of the Grand Guignol classics and indigenous shockers. Among the many talented writers that Sainati managed to attract to his energetic ensemble was Luigi Chiarelli, the doyen of the Italian School of the Grotesque. Here the Italians diverged from their French colleagues with a heavy theatrical emphasis on social and metaphysical problems. Grotesque comedy blended effortlessly with grisly attacks on the social order. The Italian Grand Guignol theatre performed uninterrupted from 1923 to 1928.

JOSE LEVY

In 1920, Jose Levy opened a Grand Guignol theatre at London's Little Theatre, a small playhouse tucked away from the central Strand district. Obsessed with producing a theatre of terror north of the Channel long before World War One intervened, Levy finally managed to engage the services of one of England's great acting families: the Thorndike-Cassons. Sybil Thorndike, soon to create the part of George Bernard Shaw's Saint Joan, acted with a truth of character and feeling that few British actresses had exhibited since Sarah Siddons performed Lady Macbeth in 1782.

Like Maxa, Sybil Thorndike suffered every torment and humiliation that the British Grand Guignol could invent, being crushed by a collapsible ceiling; murdered and stuffed into a trunk; blinded and strangled; terrified as her husband was tossed to a ravenous band of wolfdogs; and encased in a block of plaster. Thorndike sought realistic images to feed her supernatural acting needs. She discovered that spiders rested their bodies and psyches while their simple musculature remained rigid. In a Georgian diary, she found a reference to a man who became helpless after falling into a wagon filled with thorns; "every nerve almost strained to a violent degree." These were her inspirations for Grand Guignol acting. Russell Thorndike, Sybil's brother, compared performing at Levy's theatre to a powerful kind of religious confession. He claimed that it even cured him of an unending and hideous stream of nightmares that plagued him for years, all of which returned unfortunately when the British Grand Guignol folded in 1923.

Both adaptations of traditional Grand Guignol classics and newly written horror plays and comedies formed the core of Levy's Grand Guignol. As devoted as the British actors were, the public censors

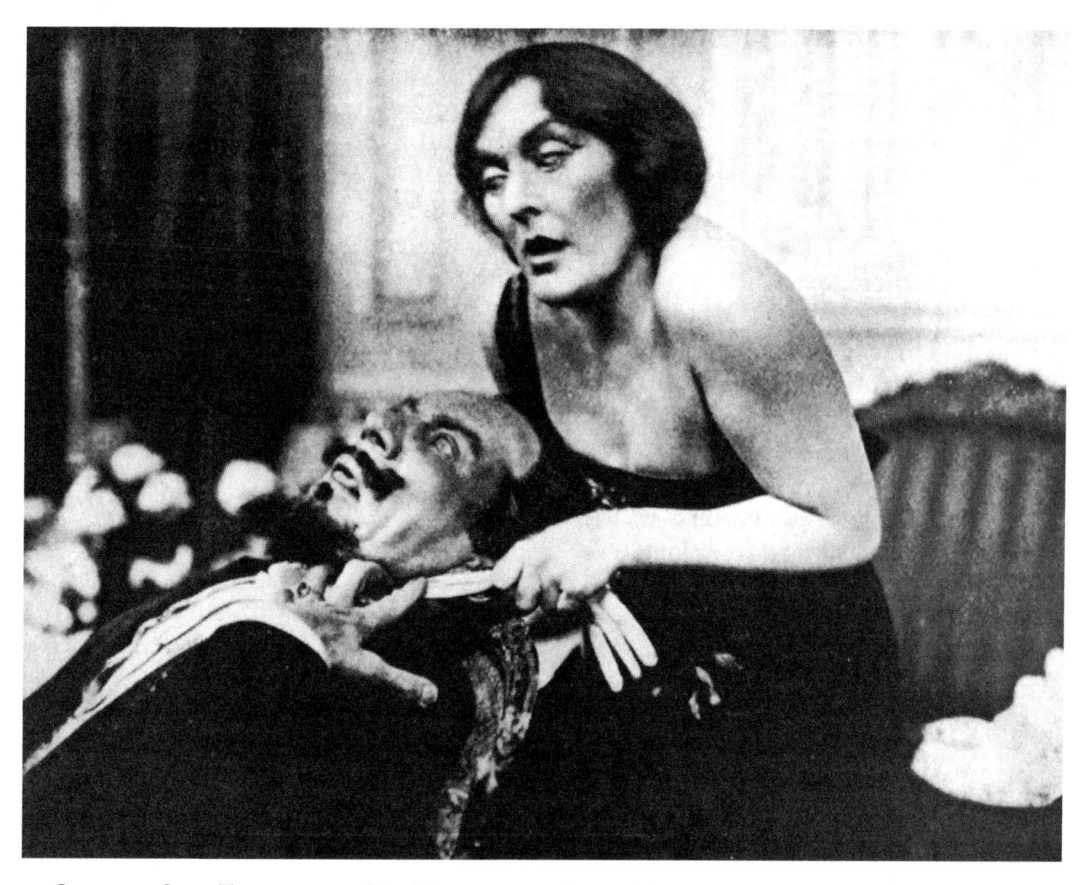

OPPOSITE: SYBIL THORNDIKE IN *THE MEDIUM*, 1920. ABOVE: THORNDIKE IN *PRIVATE ROOM NO. 6*, 1920.

felt even more strongly about the theatre. While most newspaper critics praised the work of the Little Theatre, others attacked its unwholesome qualities such as setting a sketch in a lavatory. Actually, the play *G.H.Q Love* took place in a cloak room outside the clearly-marked W.C.s for men and women. No matter. Other institutions quickly followed suit. The Society for the Prevention of Cruelty to Animals complained about the backstage torturing of wolfhounds to achieve the sound effects for *The Kill*. In fact, it was the actors' lungs that suffered since the howling yelps were produced by blowing furiously into glass pipes. Posters of the Grand Guignol

Sybil Thorndike sought realistic images to feed her supernatural acting needs.

were banned from London's underground trains, owing to their "immoral" nature. In the end, the success of Levy's Grand Guignol brought about its downfall. Sybil Thorndike, her husband Lewis Casson, Russell Thorndike, and several other performers, by 1923, were too well known for the arcane venture and finally were lured into more legitimate avenues of theatre.

MOTION PICTURES

The Grand Guignol's most significant influence on world culture can be found in the popular sub-genres of the Hollywood film. While the scary phantasmagoric style and primitive psychological thriller existed from the very beginnings of the European motion picture industry, the Grand Guignol had a major impact on their look and development by the end of World War One. De Lorde himself scripted eleven silent movies in France between 1911 and 1914, including a cinematic short of *The System of Dr. Plume and Prof. Goudron*. In fact, the hideous ironies of plot and character, unexpected brutalities, and overall mad feeling of the German Expressionist film had less to do with Expressionism from the German stage than the influence of the Grand Guignol.

Robert Oswald, the indefatigable Berlin film director, formally introduced Grand Guignol plots in his two film anthologies, *Unearthly Stories* (1919) and *Five Unearthly Stories* (1933). *The Cabinet of Dr. Caligari* (1920), the keynote German Expressionist film, actually was rejected by Expressionist writers in a series of bitter manifestoes as an alien example of Expressionist style and philosophy. Hypnotic spells; the ultimate superiority of wicked, insane authority over bourgeois power; gratuitous violence; the frailty of love were the characteristic features of the Grand Guignol, not German Expressionism. Only the frame of a dreamer's nightmare over

> *Lon Chaney, John Barrymore, Bela Lugosi, Peter Lorre, Boris Karloff, and Charles Laughton all personified the acting styles that Choisy and his troupe perfected in the twenties.*

the core of the *Caligari* plot, tacked on late in the production, along with the decor and acting style exhibited theatrical Expressionism's attributes.

In Hollywood, the "old dark house" mysteries of the silent era, like Paul Leni's *The Cat and Canary* (1927) and horror spectacles like *Phantom of the Opera* (1925), owed much more to the Grand Guignol than Expressionism. In 1928, Robert Florey directed the first acknowledged Hollywood-Grand Guignol film, *The Film Coffin*, which was criticized as "queer" and "impressionistic," terms that accurately defined the real Grand Guignol. Both in the silent and sound eras, Todd Browning created the films that borrowed most heavily from the Théâtre of the Grand Guignol. Especially in *The Unholy Three* (1925), *The Unknown* (1927), *Freaks* (1932), and *The Devil Doll* (1936), Browning established a particular, unhealthy atmosphere that closely resembled pure grand-guignolesque. Lon Chaney, John Barrymore, Bela Lugosi, Peter Lorre, Boris Karloff, and Charles Laughton all personified the acting styles that Choisy and his troupe perfected in

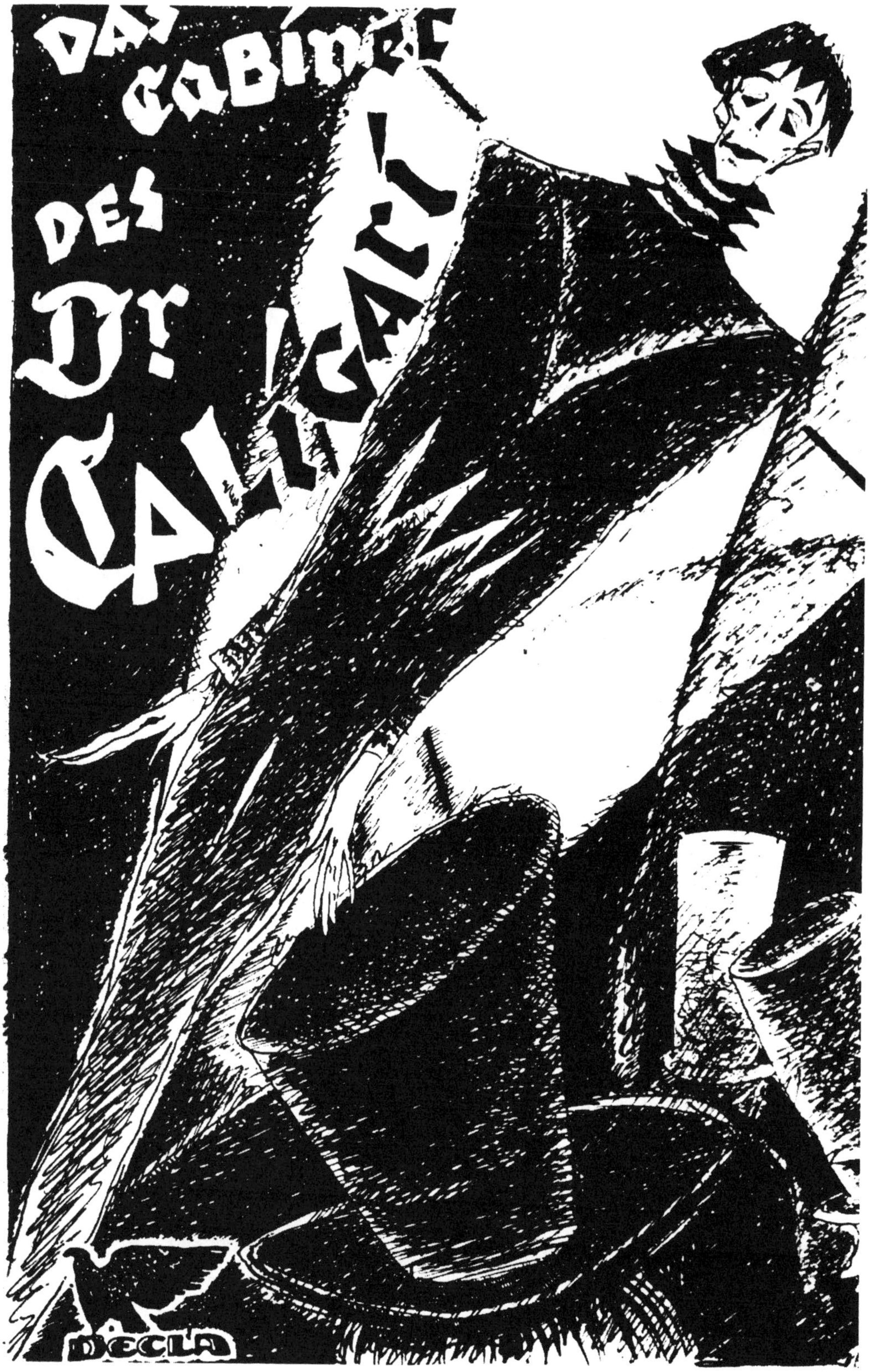
DAS CABINET
DES
Dr.
CALIGARI
DECLA

SILENT HORROR FILM *THE CABINET OF DR. CALIGARI*, 1920.

the twenties. Finally, in 1935, Karl Freund, the celebrated ex-patriot German cameraman, as a kind of recognition, directed a Peter Lorre vehicle, *Mad Love*, that utilized a Grand Guignol setting for his remake of "The Hands of Orlac" story.

After *Mad Love*, however, the Grand Guignol as a cultural icon disappeared from Hollywood. And with it went all its stepchildren. By the end of the thirties, vampires, zombie-masters, lunatics, werewolves, insane scientists and their vengeful creations became the subjects of silly parodies and low-grade shockers. Sadistic Gestapo officers and puffy-faced Southern sheriffs now satisfied Hollywood's thirst for perverse and monstrous archetypes. Curiously, American radio picked up the

> *The overall mad feeling of the German Expressionist film had less to do with Expressionism from the German stage than the influence of the Grand Guignol.*

dramatic outcasts. By 1939, the Grand Guignol and its plots showed up repeatedly on Arch Oboler's phenomenonally successful horror series *Lights Out!* as well as in its many broadcast imitations like *The Haunting Hour*, *The Weird Dr. Strange*, *The Creaking Door*, and *Inner Sanctum* (which mixed low-comedy and terror like the original Grand Guignol).

The Influence of the Grand Guignol

ARTWORK FOR HERSCHELL GORDON LEWIS' 1963 *BLOOD FEAST*, CONSIDERED THE FIRST GORE FILM.

American directors in the mid-70's developed their own Grand-Guignol-like sub-genre.

Occasional anthology films emphasizing horror and the occult appeared in Great Britain and France in the immediate postwar years, but not until the Technicolor and three-dimensional splash of Vincent Price and Christopher Lee monster movies in the fifties and early sixties did the horrific find its way back into the commercial cinema. Unhealthy black comedies that revealed the gothic undertrappings of contemporary life, like Alfred Hitchcock's *Psycho* (1960) and Richard Aldrich's *What Ever Happened to Baby Jane?* (1962) surfaced in the same period and led Hollywood back into the filmic grand-guignolesque. The height (or low point) of the kids-slashed-by-an-insane-avenger format was reached in the mid-seventies when young independent American directors developed their own Grand Guignol-like sub-genre. (Herschell Gordon Lewis originated the sickening "we can see your organs" film with the 1963 *Blood Feast*.) In France, the Grand Guignol settings appeared in two major films, *The Seduction of a Vampire* (1967) and *Grand Guignol* (1986). More than anything else, the later movie attempted to find an accomodation of psychological terror from the traditional *film noir* genre with an historical appreciation of the Grand Guignol's waning days. ⚜

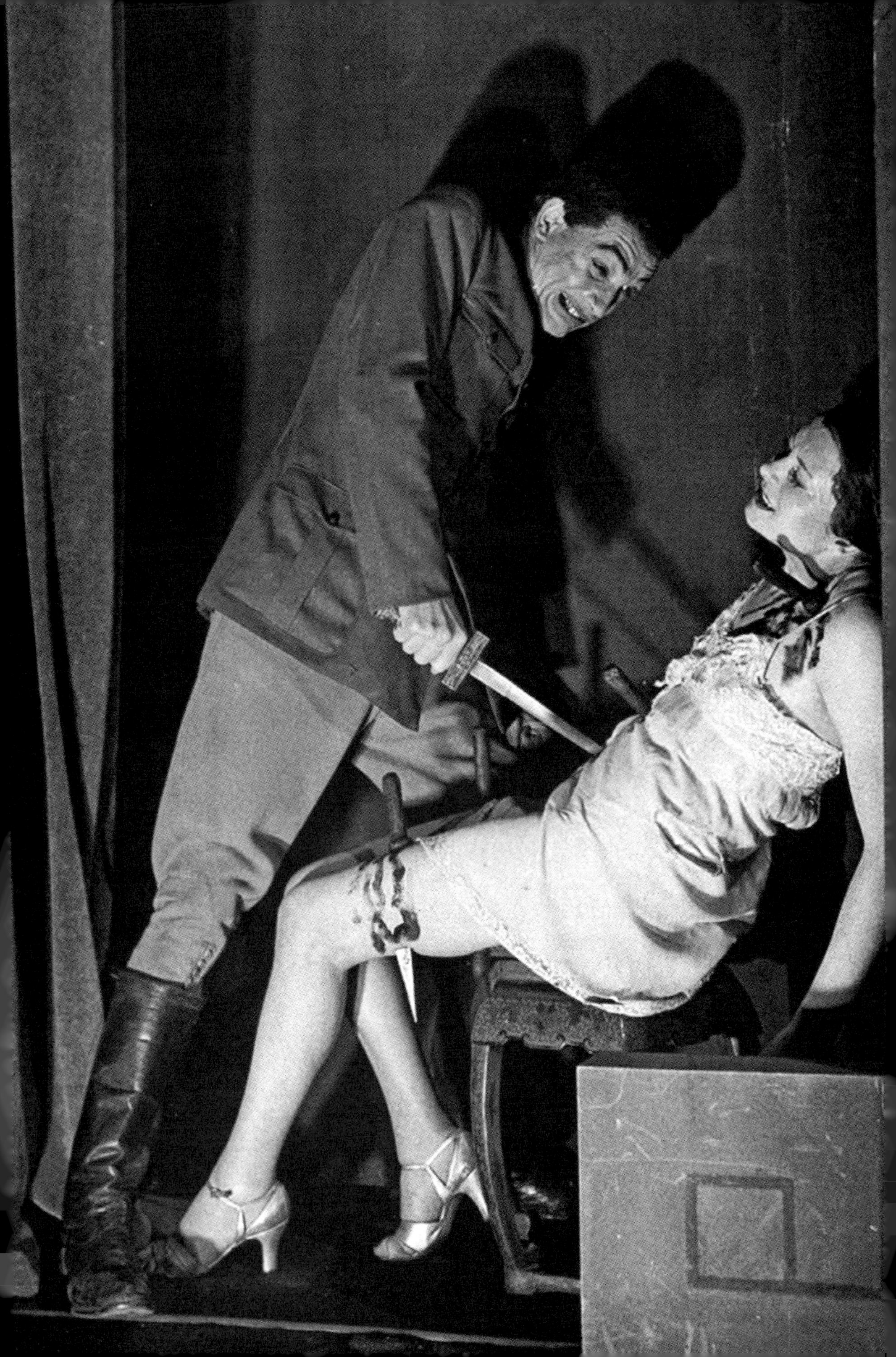

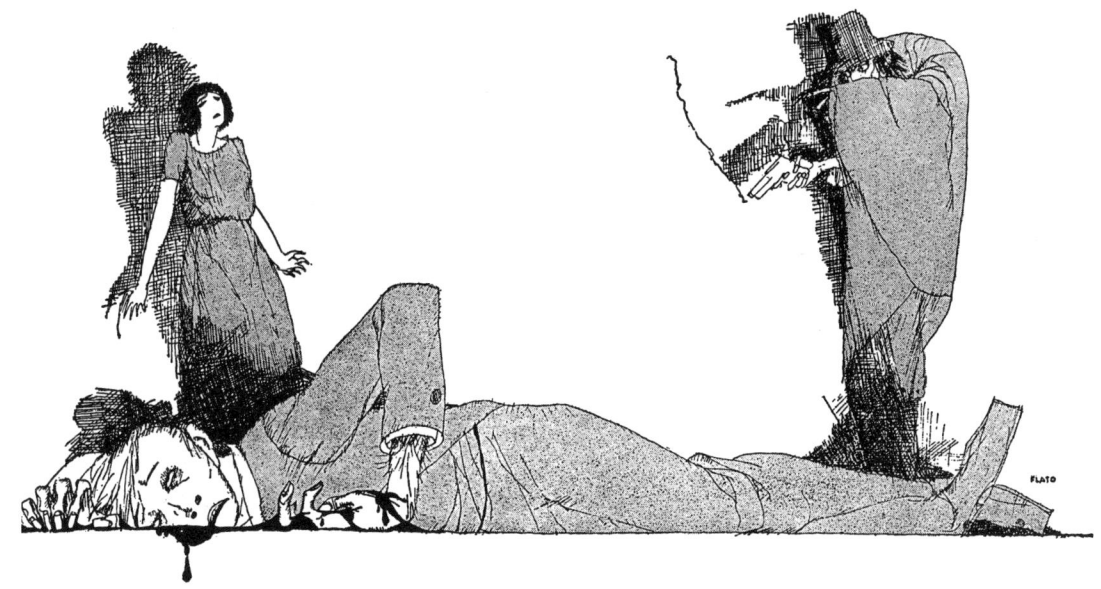

STAGE TRICKS OF THE GRAND GUIGNOL

UNTIL 1939, most of the scenic techniques, including the bloody stage tricks, of the Grand Guignol were a tightly guarded secret. A number of them were even patented. The secrecy probably had more to do with concealing their simplicity of design than a desire to prevent other theatres from using them. The Grand Guignol audiences wanted to believe in the reality of the gory stage actions, and, therefore, by their shocked reactions unconsciously assisted in the life-like presentations of grisly murders, torture, corporal mutilation, and bleeding wounds.

Following Antoine's naturalistic formula for exact, realistic detail, many of the Grand Guignol's frightening techniques were little more than well-crafted stage trickery. The manager of the Grand Guignol, Paul Ratineau, known as the "Third Bandit of Horror" (after de Lorde and Choisy), invented ingenious devices to create the sound of a harsh rain storm or a creaking door. He discovered the further away the sound source was from the audience, the more effective (or chilling) it was. Choisy spent whole days just orchestrating the sound design and lighting effects of a production. At the Grand Guignol, scenic atmosphere was as important as the

OPPOSITE AND ABOVE: *Night of Terror*, 1946.

> ## STAGING FOR THE "RIBBON OF FLESH" TORTURE
>
> from The Garden of Torture by Pierre Chaine (1922)
>
> • • •
>
> Before Ti-Bah's second entrance, prepare the following backstage: On Ti-Bah's back, at the level of her shoulder blades, affix a thin strip of adhesive plaster colored red on the bottom and flesh-color on top.
>
> When Han says: "I said it," Li-Chang grabs Ti-Bah, forces her to her knees and, facing the audience, tears off her shirt. As soon as Han gives the knife to Ti-Mao, Li-Chang, with one knee to the ground next to Ti-Bah, holds her wrists with one hand and with the other grabs her by the hair and pulls her head down. Ti-Mao uses this moment to simulate making two slits in her back. In reality, he bloodies her back with fake blood contained in a small tube or vial, which he then hides.
>
> As soon as Ti-Mao has finished this preparation, Li-Chang pushes down on the back of Ti-Bah's neck, forcing her forehead to the ground, exposing her back to the audience. At the same time, Ti-Mao seizes the top end of the plaster and tears it very slowly down her back so everyone sees the bloody scrap peel off of Ti-Bah's shoulders.

acting and plot in an evening. From the time the curtain arose, a special sensation of strangeness and mystery had to envelop the audience. In part, this was caused by a shadowing effect in the overhead lights and an imperceptible, hazy illumination of red and green colors in the corners of the proscenium. According to Maxa, the partially darkened stage decor produced an unconscious shock in the spectator: Something was about to happen, something hidden was about to appear from the shadows.

The Grand Guignol adhered to Dracula's biblical dictum: "Blood is the life!" Their single most celebrated secret involved patented blood recipes. Although varieties of stage blood have existed at least since the time of the classical Roman theatre, the Grand Guignol made something of a fetish of them. A dark, sticky stage blood

Daggers with retractable blades spurted blood when the blood-filled handles were squeezed.

signified old wounds; a lighter, dripping fluid showed new ones. The standard formula consisted mostly of a heated mixture of carmine and glycerin. Combined daily in a cauldron, the crimson liquid flowed like blood but also coagulated after a few minutes to form scabs. In quiet moments, spectators could sometimes hear the property woman whisper backstage, "Edmond, hurry! Warm up the blood." But because of the extensive cleaning bills in later years, even the use of the famous blood compounds followed a rule-of-thumb direc-

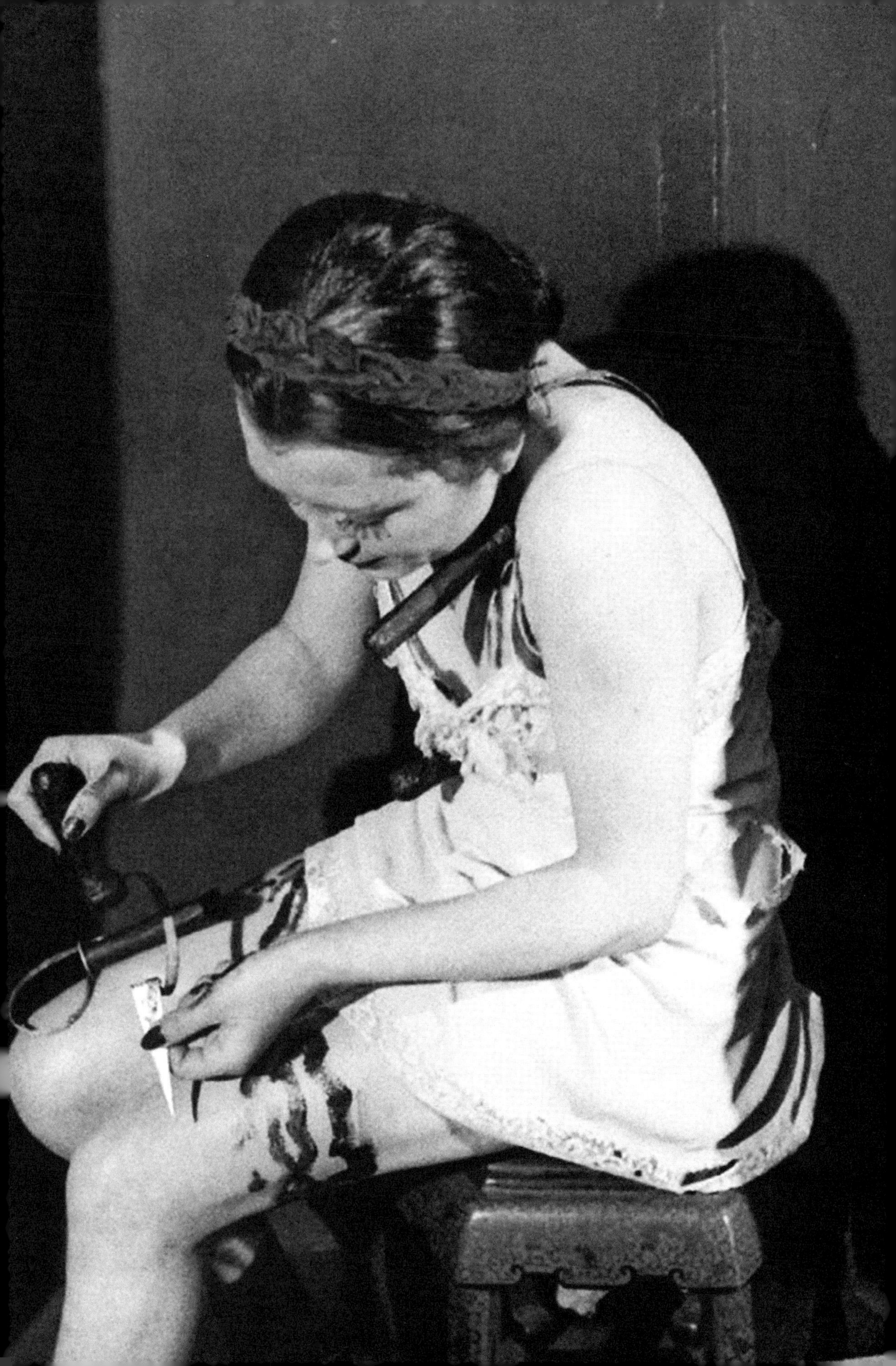

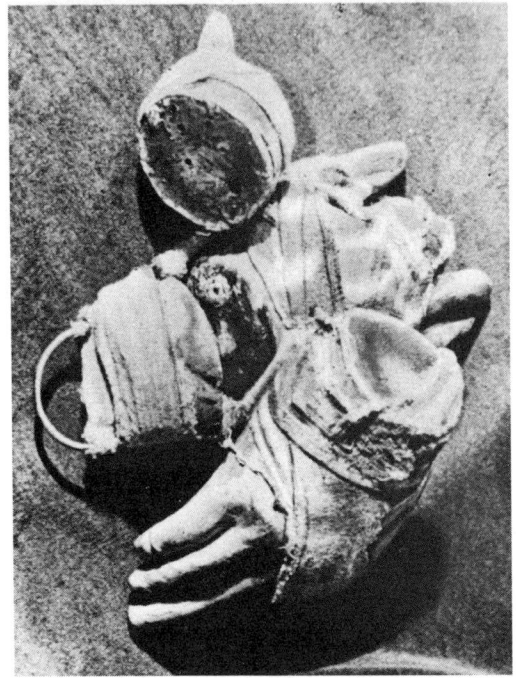

The partially darkened stage decor produced an unconscious shock in the spectator: Something was about to happen, something hidden was about to appear from the shadows.

tion: Large body wounds were limited to women (smaller costumes to clean) and head wounds for men (less hair to clean).

The most famous tricks of the Grand Guignol involved the realistic execution of violent actions and instantaneous sleight of hand transformation. Daggers with retractable blades spurted blood when the blood-filled handles were squeezed. Dying victims could reveal throat and facial wounds by tracing their blood-soaked fingers over the imagined area. Sword or knife-wielding murderers could seemingly penetrate their victims' limbs by using a stage weapon with an empty curved clasp between the handle and blade. Out of nowhere, lunatics could suddenly foam at the mouth simply by chewing on a hidden bit

GRAND GUIGNOL THEATRE OF FEAR AND HORROR

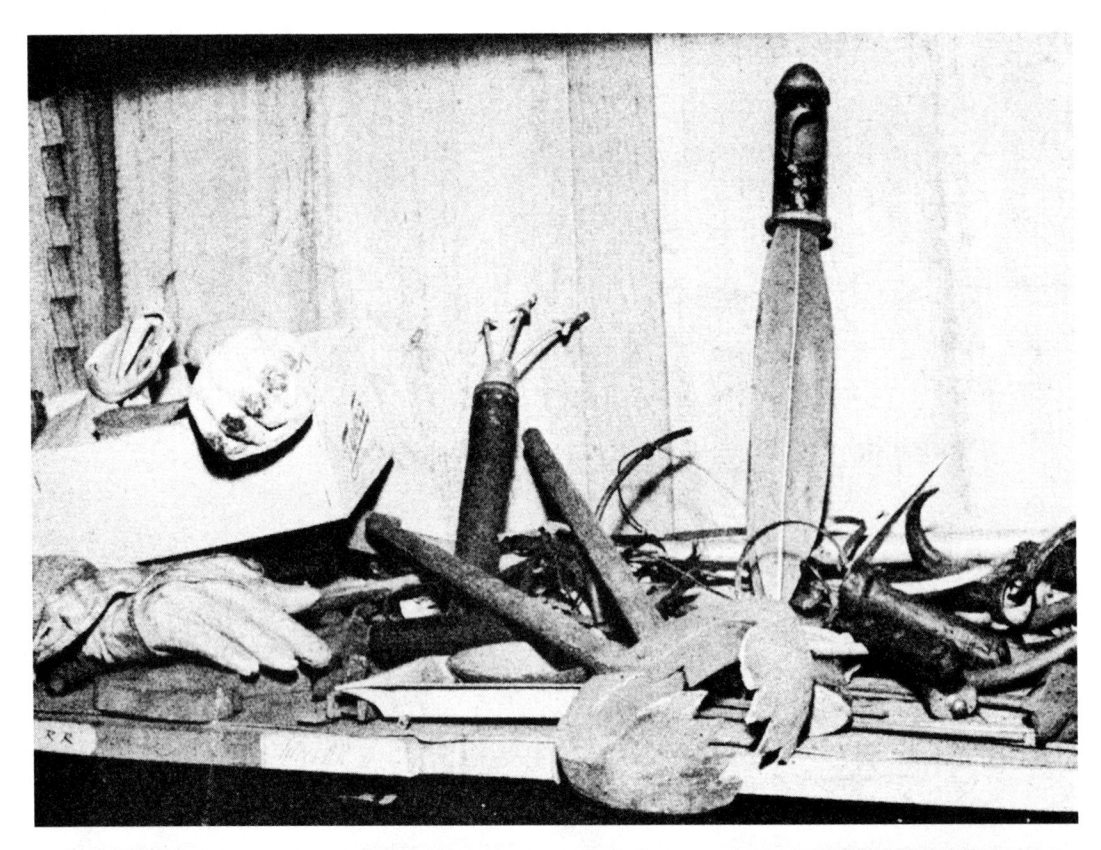

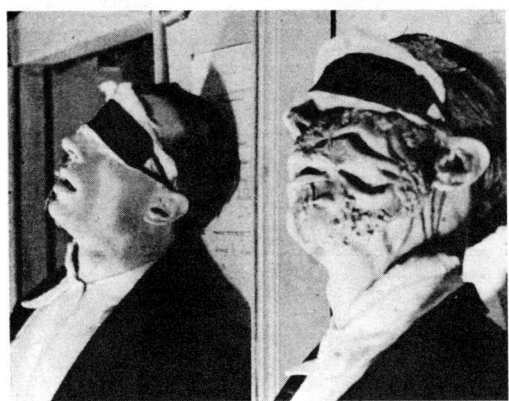

of soap. Mirrors, facial masks, concealed rubber pieces for wounds and burns, fake heads and limbs, all the paraphernalia of magicians, when expertly used—during moments of darkness or out of the spectators' view—created an atmosphere of sickening and eerie realism. Nonon frequently purchased different animal eyeballs from taxidermists—not only for visual realism, when characters eyes were gouged out, but for the organs' ability to bounce when they hit the stage floor. ⚜

OPPOSITE: AMERICAN G.I. FAINTS
AND IS REVIVED, 1953

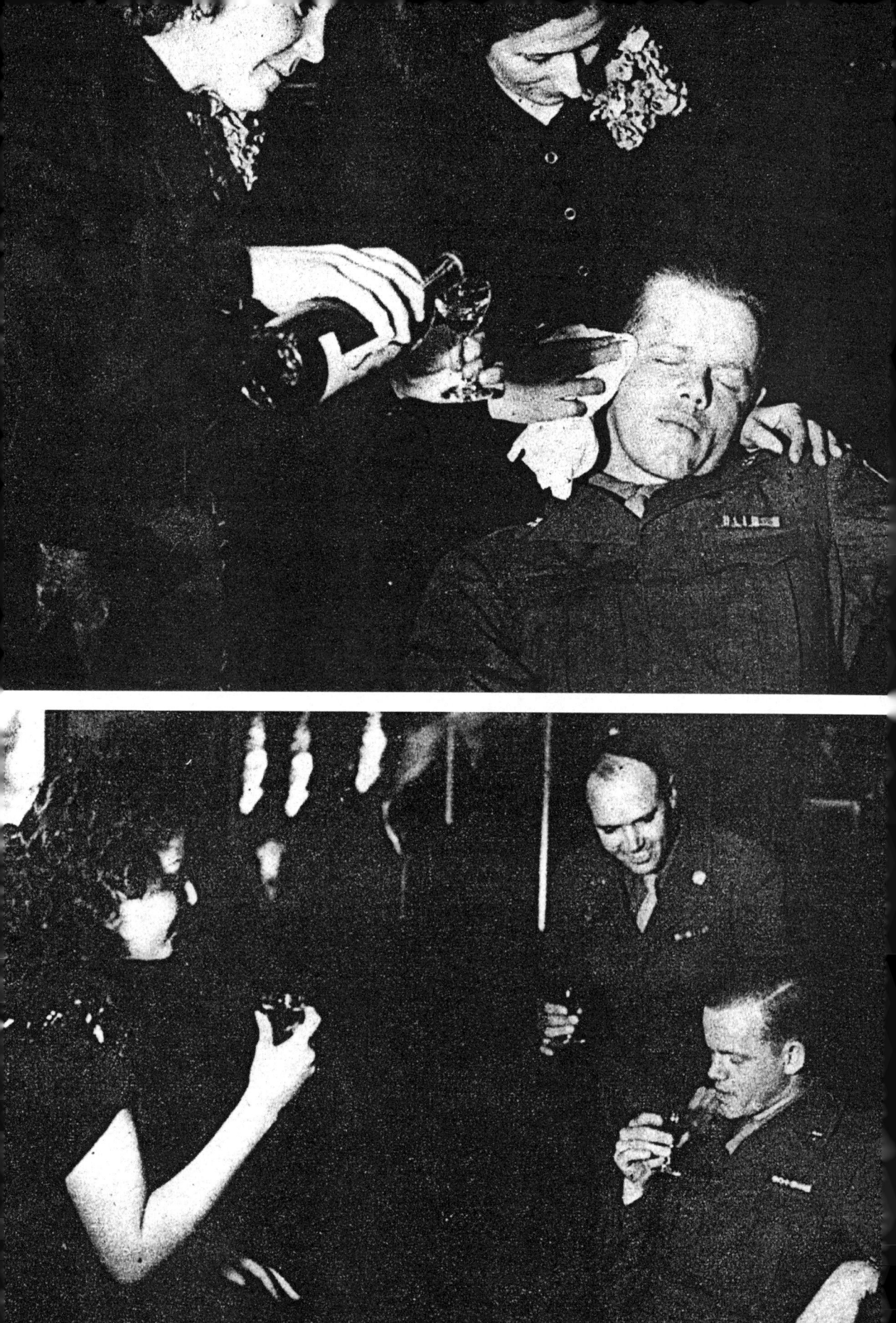

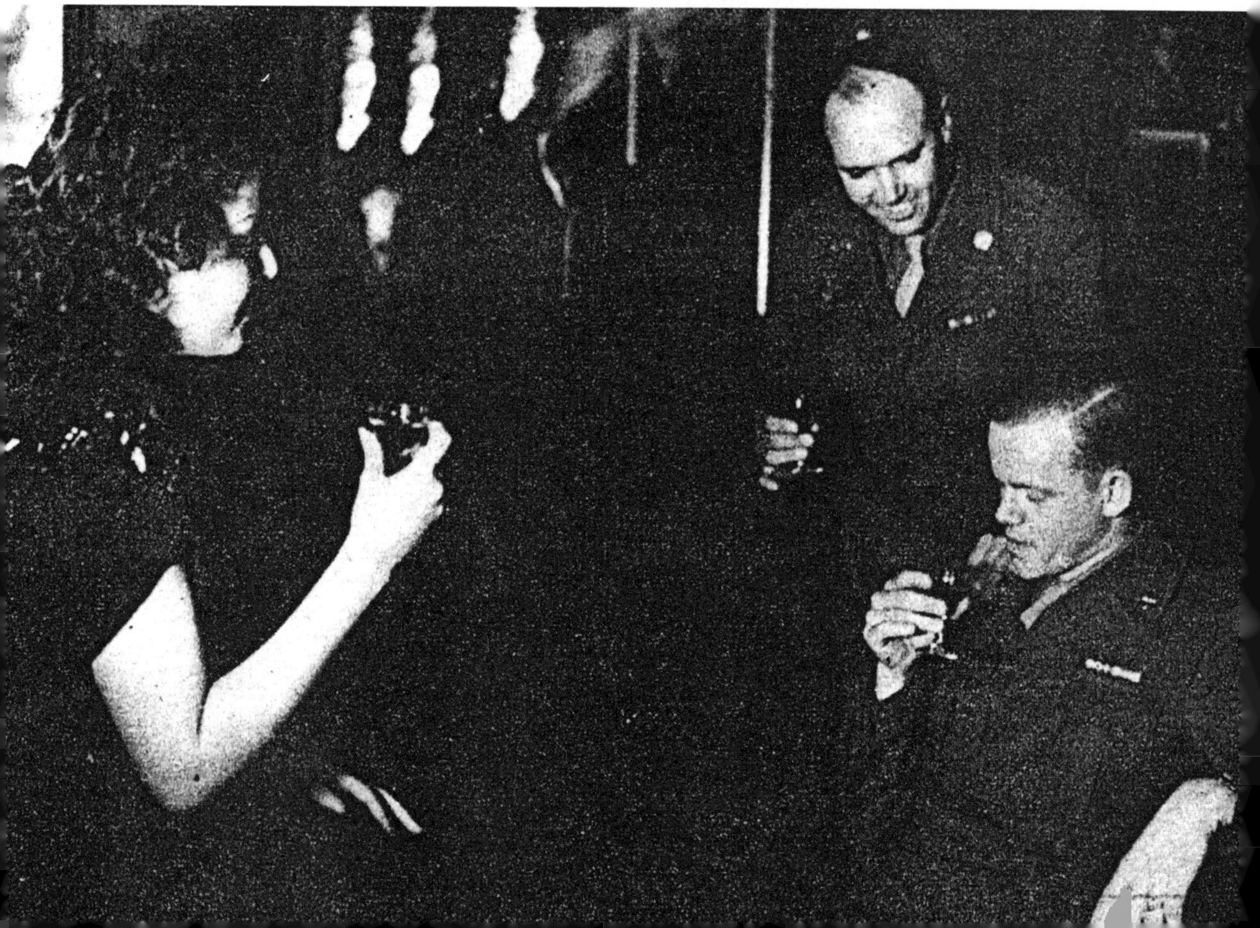

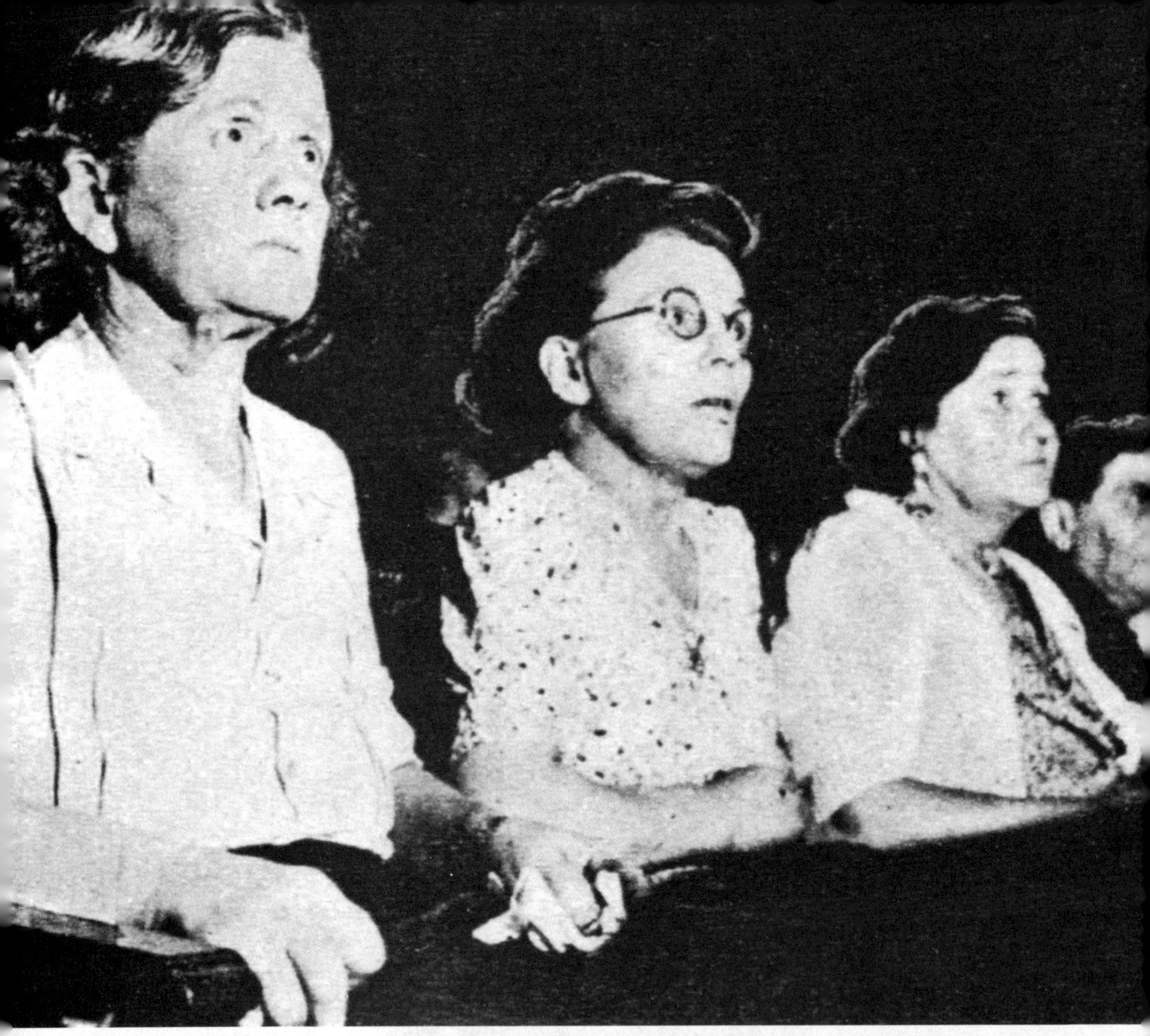

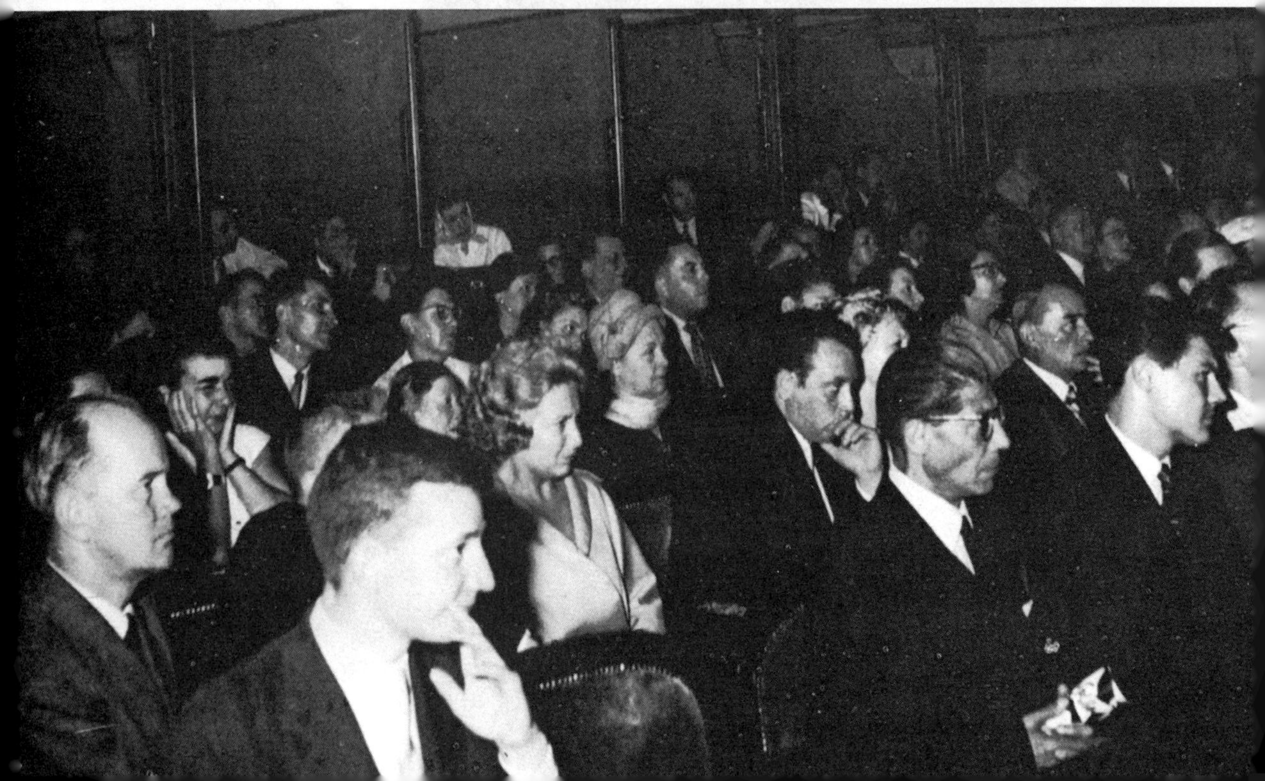

CONCLUSION

A QUESTION ALWAYS ARISES WITH the Grand Guignol: Why study it? Other than treating it as some gross-out joke of theatre history. Although the Grand Guignol seemed to have greatly influenced other theatres and genres, what could make it a worthwhile theatre of its own? The answer is one that becomes more and more important in contemporary and popular art: Censorship and gratuitous violence and sex in art.

In the United States, millions of otherwise liberal, "right-thinking," adults oppose government censorship in the arts, especially motion pictures, unless gratuitous violence is involved. On that issue, they frequently take an inflexible stand: violence on stage or screen can lead children or others into anti-social, physical activity. Gestapo agents in Paris believed much the same thing. During the heyday of the Grand Guignol, in the 1920s and 1930s, there was probably less violent crime on the street or by the state in Paris than in any major European capital. The reverse situation was true in Nazi Germany, where theatre and film censorship achieved its glory. Does that imply then that the Grand Guignol relieved its Parisian public of violent impulses, that it "purged" them of fear

ABOVE: *ANGUISH*, 1923

ABOVE: MAXA WITH CAMILLE CHOISY
IN *THE CLAIRVOYANT*, 1936

and pity? Probably not. Only that the relationship between violence in art and its affects on human behavior is rooted firmly in individual cultures. The connections between what people see and what they do is not clearly manifested, except to compulsive censors of art. Each particular culture informs its children differently. Sometimes, barbaric stage activity only produces health-giving chills and laughter. Such was the case of the Grand Guignol. ⚜

Selected Bibliography
...

"Le bazar de la terror," *Voilà* (Paris), October 20th, 1939.

Camillo Antona-Traversi, *L'Histoire du Grand Guignol* (Paris, 1933).

Comoedia Illustré (Paris): July 1913; January 1914; September 1920; July 1922; May 1st, 1924; and 15 June 1924.

Frantisek Deak, "The Grand Guignol," *The Drama Review* (NY), March 1974.

Daniel Gerould, "Oscar Méténier and *Comedie Rosse*," *The Drama Review* (NY), Spring 1984.

Grand Guignol Annual Review (London, 1921).

"Grand Guignol" Files of the Bibliothèque de l'Arsenal, Paris.

Mary Homrighous, *The Grand Guignol* (unpublished dissertation, Northwestern University, 1963).

Paris Plaisirs (Paris) #102 December 1930.

Francois Rivière and Gabrielle Wittkop, *Grand Guignol* (Paris, 1979).

P.E. Schneider, "Fading Horrors of the Grand Guignol," *The New York Times Magazine*, March 17th, 1957.

F. Berkeley Smith, *How Paris Amuses Itself* (NY and London, 1903).

Le Théâtre (Paris) 1969, Number 2. Grand Guignol Issue, edited by Arrabal.

100 PLOTS FROM THE REPERTOIRE OF THE GRAND GUIGNOL

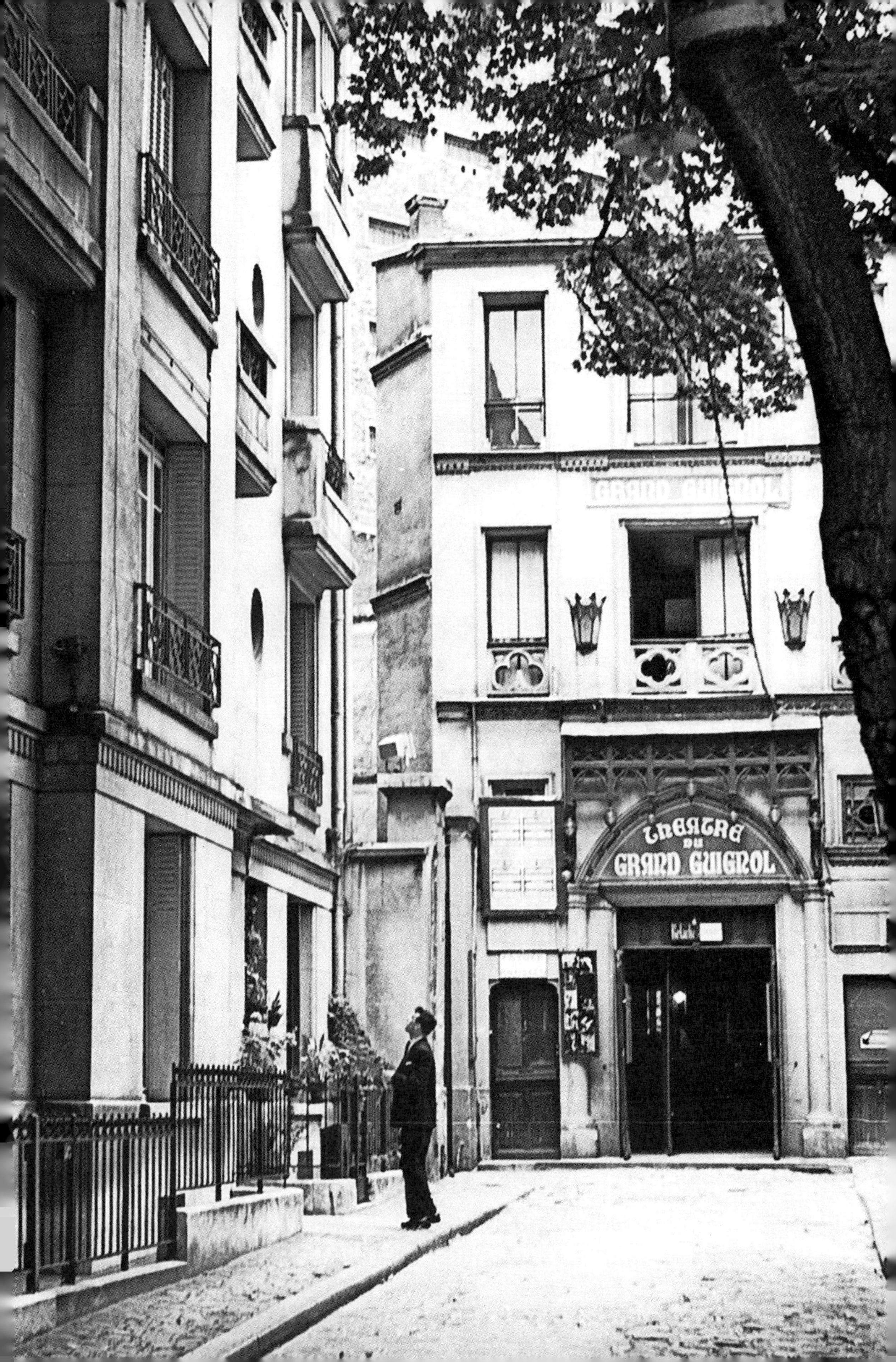
GRAND GUIGNOL
THEATRE DU GRAND GUIGNOL

ALTHOUGH somere French historians have claimed that there were between 4,000 and 7,000 scripts written for the Théâtre of the Grand Guignol of Paris and its short-lived competitors between 1897 and 1962, those figures are not only extraordinarily overstated but arithmetically impossible if they are referring to produced performances. The majority were, most likely, "accepted" into the repertoire but not staged. The number of produced plays is much closer to 1,200 different dramas and sketches, of which one-third were frequently restaged over several seasons. Some eighty or ninety appeared in print, either individually in contemporary journals and limited edition volumes or in play collections.

What follows are synopses of 100 of the most popular, or frequently performed, plays of the Grand Guignol—about one-tenth of the entire 65-year repertoire. My source material includes the published scripts, accounts of spectators and journalists, descriptions in programs and press releases, and various literary analyses, including M. E. Homrighous's *The Grand Guignol*. (It should be noted that descriptions in the programs and playbills were occasionally inaccurate.)

A typical evening of the Grand Guignol normally fell into the simple alternating dramatic divisions of three comedies (and farces) and three horror plays (or psychological dramas). The patented whiplash effect of laughter and tears was known as "hot and cold showers." For this listing, I have divided the plots into three categories: Horror Plays, Comedies and Farces, and Dramatic Plays. Within each section, I have attempted to characterize the overriding themes, or emotional play.

The Horror themes have been separated into the following subsections: Helplessness, Infanticide, Insanity, Mutilation, Mysterious Death, Suffering of the Innocent, Suicide, Surgery, and Vengeance. The categories of the Comedies and Farces are Bourgeois Morality, Cuckoldry, Sex Farce, and Suffering of the Innocent. Dramatic plots are divided into "Crass" Manners, Guilt, and Injustice.

In addition, six subsidiary themes are noted: Exoticism, Hypnosis, Imprisonment, Parisian Lowlife, Play-Transforming-Into-Terror, and Prostitution.

Certainly, the plots of many Grand Guignol plays—especially those written by André de Lorde—contain more than one theme, for instance: Helplessness, Insanity, Surgery, and Vengeance. Yet the horror (or humor) felt by the audience was normally predicated on a single overriding fear or emotion. While the overlapping and related themes make some plays difficult to affix to any one definitive group, I have attempted to place them in the category that best reveals their subliminal efficacy as a theatrical vehicle rather than a literary product. Included in the synopses are the authors' names and the date of the first performance of the play. Unless noted, the plays and sketches take place in one scene or act.

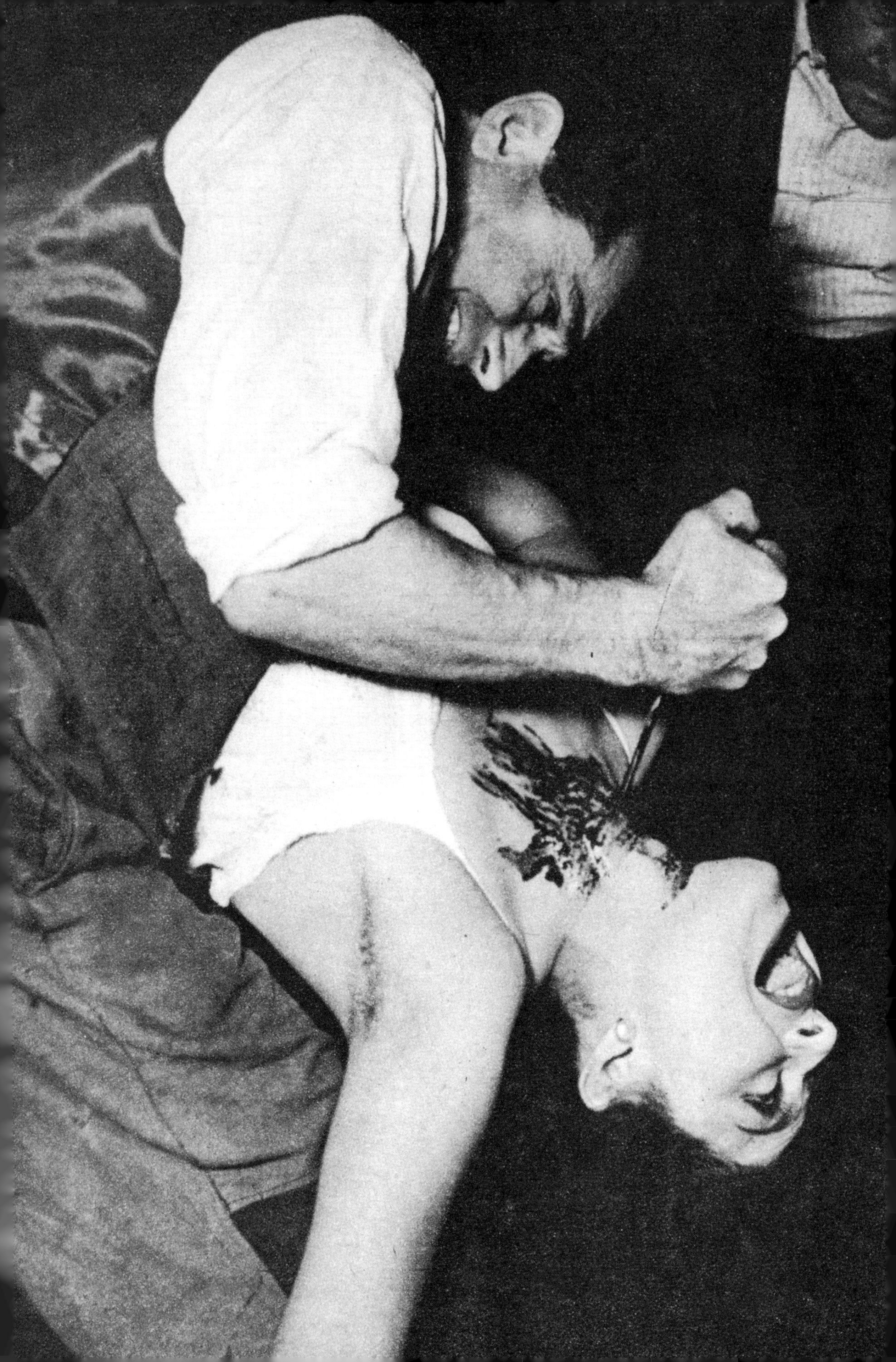

HORROR PLAYS

HELPLESSNESS

AT THE TELEPHONE
André de Lorde
and Charles Foley, 1902

A two-act play, which was one of the best-known dramas of the Grand Guignol, with the additional themes of Imprisonment and the Suffering of the Innocent. It was first presented at the Theatre Antoine.

André Marex, a prosperous Parisian businessman, has rented a backwoods country home for his wife, six-year old son, and his two elderly servants, Nanette and Blaise. Its unwholesome rustic quality and isolation are a great irritation for Marex. Only the newly installed telephone allows him to communicate with the outside world. In order to arrive in Paris the next day, Marex is forced to leave for a distant neighbor's house in the midst of a storm. To calm Martha, his wife, he shows her where his pistol is located. After Marex departs, a tramp visits the house and clandestinely pockets the pistol. Blaise, the old man servant, is notified that his ancient mother is ill. Martha persuades him to go immediately to her sick bed.

Later after dinner at his friends' home, Marex receives several telephone calls from Martha. She is frightened by the noises outside the country house. Each time, Marex attempts to allay her fears. Finally, when Martha calls, Marex realizes that intruders are breaking into the house. He listens in helpless agitation as members of his family are strangled.

OPPOSITE: *ABANDONED*, 1953

At the Telephone: 1. André Marex says good-bye to his family at their isolated vacation home.

2. After dinner at the Rivoire's, Marex takes his brandy and dessert.

3. Marex's wife calls to tell him that she has been hearing noises around the house. Marex assures her that they are imaginary. Later, Marex receives a second telephone call from his wife. While talking to her, Marex hears the sounds of her being brutalized and his son being murdered by tramps.

Workshop for the Blind, 1911

THE LAND OF FRIGHT
André de Lorde and Eugene Morel, 1907

A horror play in three acts with the additional themes of Exoticism and Imprisonment. Based on an actual incident in 1902, this play was first performed at the Theatre Antoine.

In an underground penal colony in Martinique, French prisoners hear rumblings above the earth. They soon realize that a huge volcano has erupted. Trapped below the ground and abandoned, the prisoners panic. One claims that they are in the safest place. Another predicts that the fumes from the lava will soon consume their supply of oxygen. Slowly the sulphurous clouds suffocate the prisoners.

THE WORKSHOP FOR THE BLIND OR SEVEN BLIND MEN
Lucien Descaves, 1911

A horror play with the additional theme of Imprisonment.

A group of seven blind men toil in a public workhouse making brushes. Each expresses his individual feeling about his daily condition: one is grateful to have a roof over his head; another feels that they are being exploited; still another preaches rebellion and revenge against their benefactors. When the blind men threaten the foreman with their knives, he locks them in the room and runs for the police. Outside their room the winter winds howl and the stove makes a roaring sound. Now in their solitude and separation from the outside world except for the strange noises by the window, the blind men are thrown, little by little, into a state of panic. The wind and sounds of the water pump make the blind men suddenly imagine that their building is on fire. They try to break down the door. A fight ensues and they attack each other with the knives. One throws himself out of the window.

IN THE FACE OF DEATH
Alfred Savoir
and Léopold Marchand, 1920

A three-act horror play with the additional themes of Cuckoldry, Guilt, Imprisonment, Mysterious Death, and Vengeance.

In an outpost of a small colonial settlement in French Equatorial Africa, Christian, a French hunter, hears three gunshots. His African servant, Gildas, has been ordered by Dr. Plassant to kill all dogs, including his own, to curtail an outbreak of rabies. Eve, the doctor's wife, runs through the jungle to be with her lover, Christian. She complains they are so isolated from civilization that no one can be cured in time to prevent a maddening death by the highly-contagious rabies. They declare their love for one another. Dr. Plassant appears at Christian's door and Eve hides in another room of the cabin. The elderly physician discusses his sexual and family problems with Christian. Both Plassants have inadvertently mentioned to Christian that they have decided to keep one small dog in their house. The doctor departs. Christian attempts to bring the lascivious Eve home to her husband but as night falls she seduces him in his cabin. Silently, Dr. Plassant enters Christian's bedroom. Finding his wife asleep in Christian's arms, Dr. Plassant prepares two syringes and injects each lover. He locks the doors and windows of the cabin. When the couple awakens, the doctor tells them that while they slept he injected one of them with a dose of the African disease.

The lovers are locked in the room with a sharp knife for protection. Each of them believes that the other is contaminated from the injection. In their hysteria, accusations fly, and Eve finally runs madly toward Christian, who stabs her in a moment of self-preservation.

After his wife dies, Dr. Plassant enters. He accuses Christian of murder. The serum he injected in both of them was a harmless solution. Christian has killed a harmless woman. To prove his case, Dr. Plassant kisses his wife before Gildas—shouting from the outside—can warn him. Eve, in fact, contracted rabies from her dog. Now her husband has the disease. The doctor runs out. Christian discovers that he has cut his hand on the knife during his struggle with Eve. He, too, will die from the epidemic.

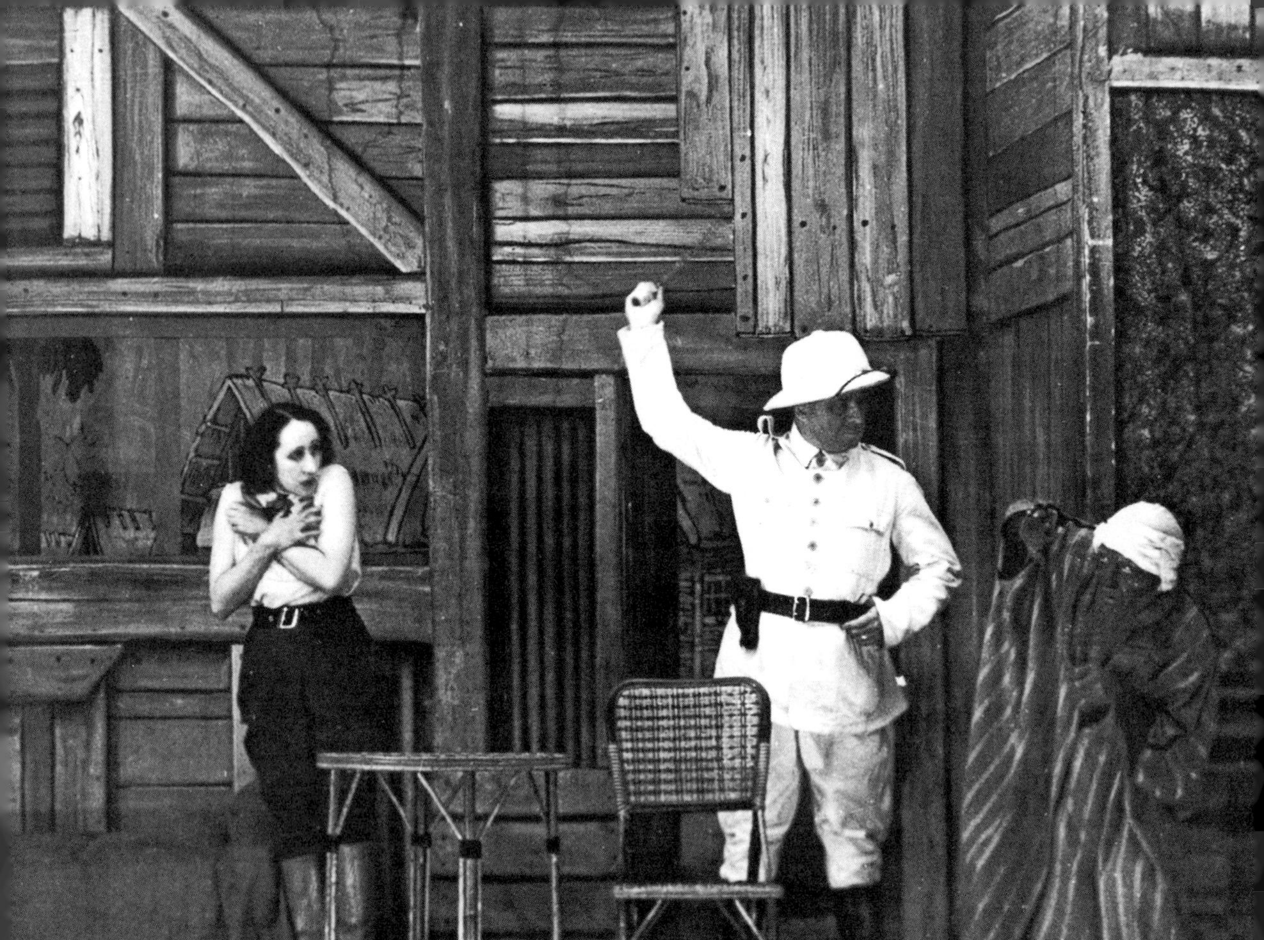
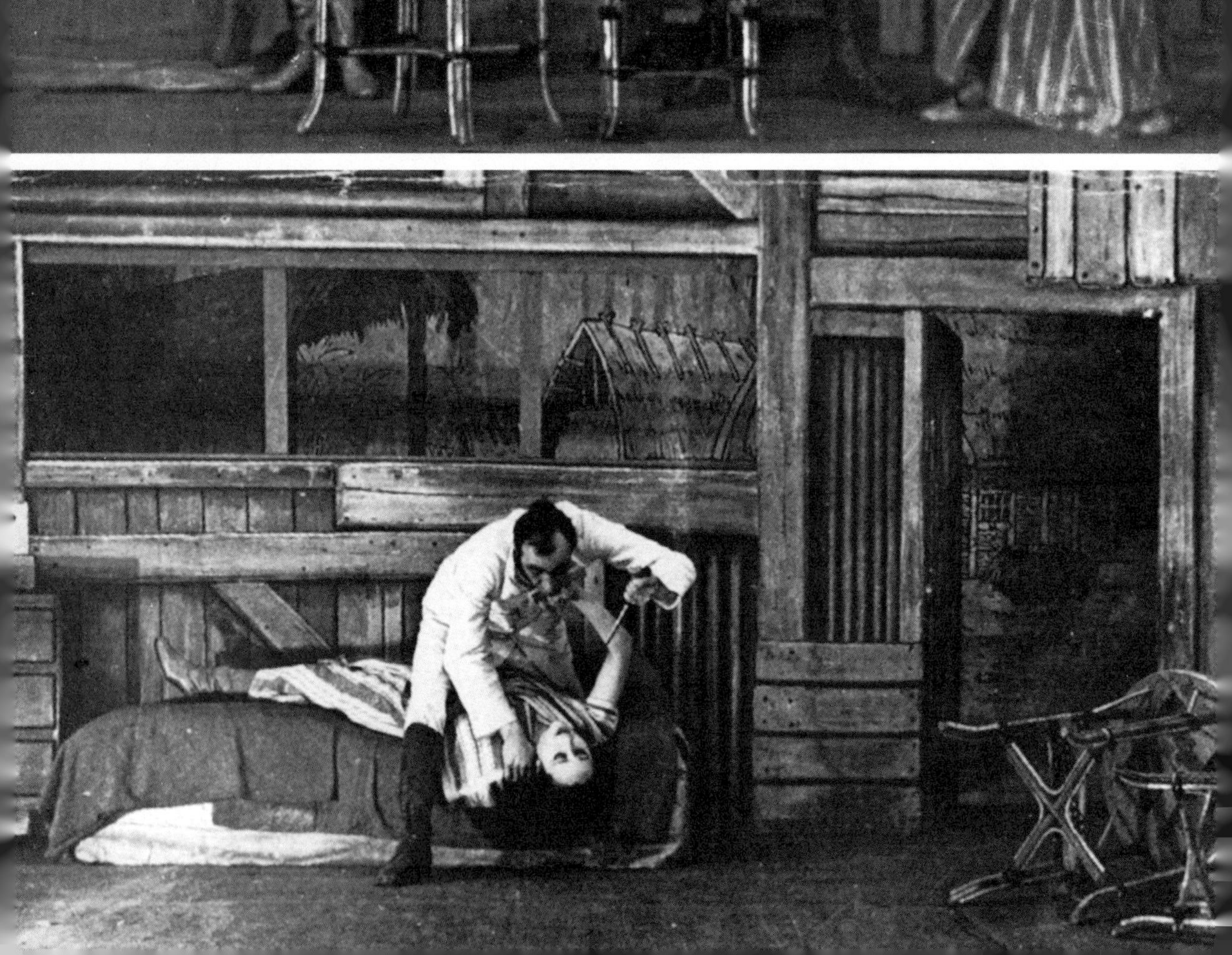

THE GRIP OF DEATH, OR THE HANDS OF HARDOUIN

Jean Sartène, 1922

One of the most frequently produced horror plays—it played some 1,000 times by 1933 and was translated into most European languages as well as Japanese. The play contains the additional themes of Cuckoldry and Vengeance.

The Hardouins are a family of successful wine-growers in Burgundy. Now 80 years old, speechless, totally paralyzed, and confined to a wheelchair, the patriarch Jean-Marie was once a vigorous worker with amazingly strong hands. His son, Hippolyte, a man of 50, has married Rose, a woman of 24, against Jean-Marie's will. With her young lover, Etienne, Rose plans to take over the Hardouins' property. Jean-Marie witnesses Rose's treachery, which she flaunts before him, but is powerless to tell his son about it. While Hippolyte is away, one of his workmen almost falls to his death on the rotten stairs to the two-story-deep cellar. The son returns and starts down the same stairs for a bottle of wine. The father, speechless from paralysis, looks on but cannot warn him. At first, Rose says nothing and Hippolyte starts down to a certain death. Just as he falls down the stairwell, Rose screams and kneels beside the old paralyzed man. Suddenly Jean-Marie regains control of his muscles and strangles her with his celebrated hands.

OPPOSITE: *Black Magic*, 1935
ABOVE: *The Grip of Death*, 1922

THE BLIND SHIP

Max Maurey, 1927

A horror play that closely resembles Maurice Maeterlinck's 1890 Symbolist masterpiece, The Blind. *It contains the additional themes of Imprisonment and Insanity.*

The entire crew of a freighter, sailing in the vast ocean, is struck blind in a flash epidemic. When a steamer is heard in the distance, the sightless sailors desperately flash SOS signals. The steamer ignores them and the ship continues out into the endless and empty waters.

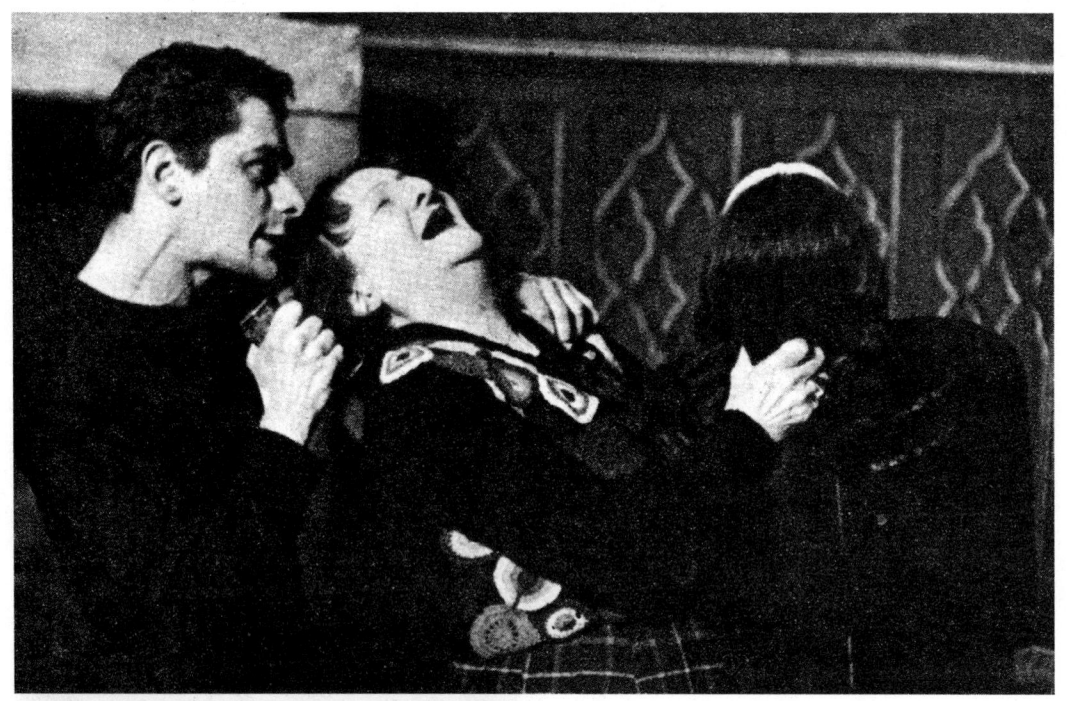

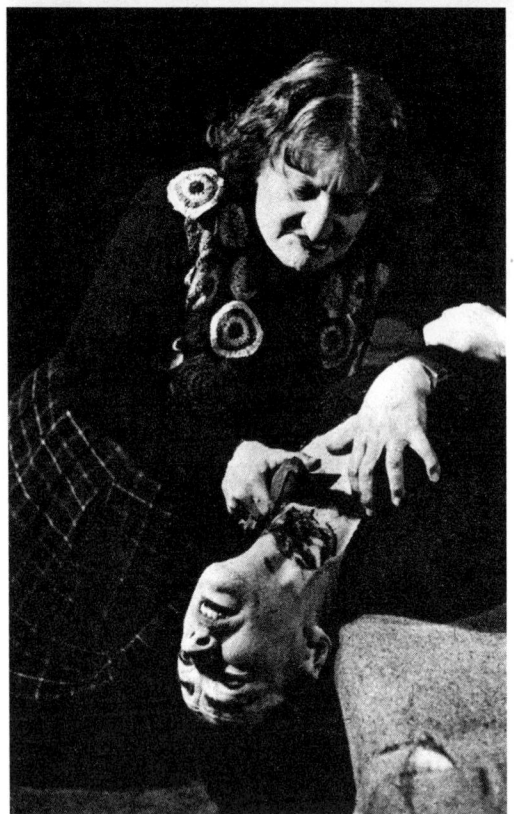

NO ORCHIDS FOR MISS BLANDISH

MARCEL DUHAMEL, 1950

This was a full-length, two-hour production adapted from the British mystery novel by René Raymond. Also with the additional themes of Exoticism, Imprisonment, Suffering of the Innocent, and Vengeance.

The psychotic American gangster, Slim Grisson, kidnaps the blonde Miss Blandish and holds her hostage. During her incarceration, where she is tied down in her bra and panties, she is sexually threatened by the drooling Grisson. Old Ma Grisson, the boss of the gang, beats Miss Blandish with a rubber hose so that she will silently submit to her son's pleasure. Both Grissons are finally killed in a police shoot-out.

THIS PAGE: *NO ORCHIDS FOR MISS BLANDISH*, 1950
OPPOSITE: *THE FINAL TORTURE*, 1956

INFANTICIDE

THE FINAL TORTURE

ANDRÉ DE LORDE AND EUGENE MOREL, 1904

A celebrated horror play with the additional themes of Exoticism, Guilt, Helplessness, Imprisonment, Insanity, and Mutilation.

During the 1900 Boxer Rebellion in China, the French consulate outside Peking has been surrounded for thirty-two days. Appeals to France have brought no response. Several Frenchmen in the isolated building have attempted to escape but without success. One heroic marine, Bornin, returns to the consulate with his hands cut off as evidence that the Chinese will show no mercy. Showing his bloody stumps, Bornin describes the atrocities that the other captured Europeans have suffered, then dies. The head consul D'Hemelin, realizing what will happen to his daughter, Denise, when the Chinese overrun the consulate, asks his subordinate, Georges Gravier, to kill her. In love with the daughter, Gravier refuses, forcing D'Hemelin to shoot his own daughter to prevent her torture. At this tragic moment, the Allied army arrives. A bugle sounds, the consulate is saved. D'Hemelin becomes insane.

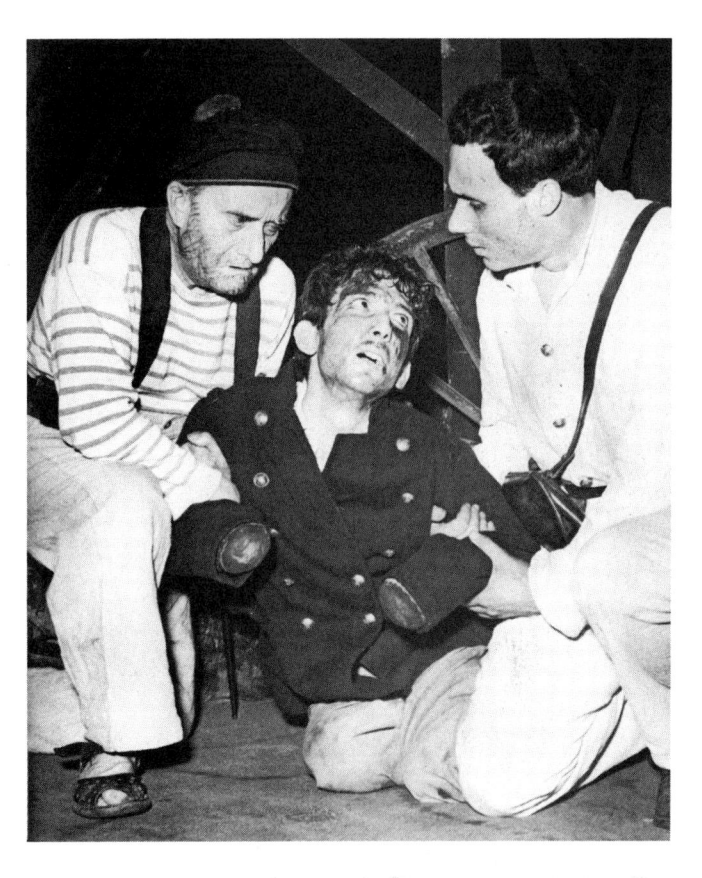

THE OBSESSION
André de Lorde and Alfred Binet, 1905

A two-act horror play with the additional theme of Insanity.

Jean is cursed with the obsession to kill his young son, Pierre. A Parisian psychologist explains that he is the victim of a progressive and incurable hereditary disease. Within a short period of time, Jean will be totally insane and unable to curb his murderous impulse. The psychologist advises that Jean commit himself to a mental asylum immediately. Jean, however, refuses to do so and returns home.

He confesses to his wife that he, not his daughter, accidently hit Pierre the other day. She thinks little of it and sends him into Pierre's room to apologize and bid the boy goodnight. In the room Jean strangles his son.

THE KEEPERS OF THE LIGHTHOUSE
Paul Autier and Paul Cloquemin, 1918

One of the most popular horror plays with the additional themes of Guilt, Insanity, and Imprisonment.

A father and son are the keepers of a lighthouse off the coast of Brittany. It is winter and they are completely shut off from the world for two months. A terrible storm is raging. Waves are beating against the lighthouse. The son tells a story of how one lighthouse keeper died at the beginning of his duty and his partner was forced to stay with the corpse for the whole two months. A few days earlier, the son confesses, he was bitten by a dog which may have had rabies. Suddenly, the son is seized with hydrophobia and insanity. He realizes that he is doomed to die in a most painful fashion. He begs his father to kill him. The thirst and madness worsen. Then the young man, foaming at the mouth, attacks his father and the father is torn between saving his son and signalling a chartless ship, which will soon dash against the rocks. He strangles his son and just manages to switch on the beacon of light, which saves the lives of the sailors on the boat.

SABOTAGE
Charles Hellem, W. Valcros, Pol d'Estoc, 1910

A horror play with the additional themes of Guilt and Surgery.

Called to the house of a sick child in a working-class district, Dr. Margy quickly realizes that only immediate surgery can save the girl's life. Using a neighbor as a nurse, Margy performs a make-shift emergency operation. Everything looks successful, except suddenly the electric lights go out. After a long search for a candle and matches, the child's mother, Angele, finally lights the candle's wick. Now Margy informs her of the bad news: her little girl expired during the dark lull. A door opens. Returning from a union demonstration against the local power station, the child's father enters the room triumphantly. While his fellow workers sing the "Internationale" outside the family's house, the father explains that it was his idea to cut the electricity in the district as a way of showing the bosses the workers' strength. Angele grabs him by the throat and calls her husband a murderer.

RAPID 13

Jean Sartène, 1921

A horror play with the additional themes of Guilt and Helplessness.

An embittered switchman of the railroad company decides to wreck one of the newest trains, the Rapid 13, when it passes his station by not pulling the proper lever. In the control room with his daughter, the switchman is reminded at the last minute that his granddaughter is on the oncoming Rapid 13. He suffers a paralyzing heart attack and cannot grip the necessary switch. Responding to his gestures and nods, the railman's daughter throws a switch, but it is the wrong one. As the two hold each other in desperation, the Rapid 13 hurls into still another train, undoubtedly killing the switchman's granddaughter, his daughter's daughter.

THE DEAD CHILD

André de Lorde, 1918

A three-act horror play with the additional themes of Cuckoldry, Insanity, Mutilation, and Vengeance.

A celebrated sculptor, Le Hirec returns home from abroad. He discovers that his wife has left him for another man. She has also abandoned their ill baby, who has since died.

Le Hirec, insane from grief, takes the boy's bones, nails, and hair from his grave and fashions a wax mannequin of his son.

Sometime later, Le Hirec's wife returns to him in remorse. Her initial happiness turns to disgust when Le Hirec shows her his effigy-child. She attempts to escape when he forces her to hold the wax model. Le Hirec has locked the doors. She runs upstairs to the child's room. Le Hirec follows her inside and strangles her, reappearing to murmur that she will never leave him again.

Following page: *The Clairvoyant*, 1936

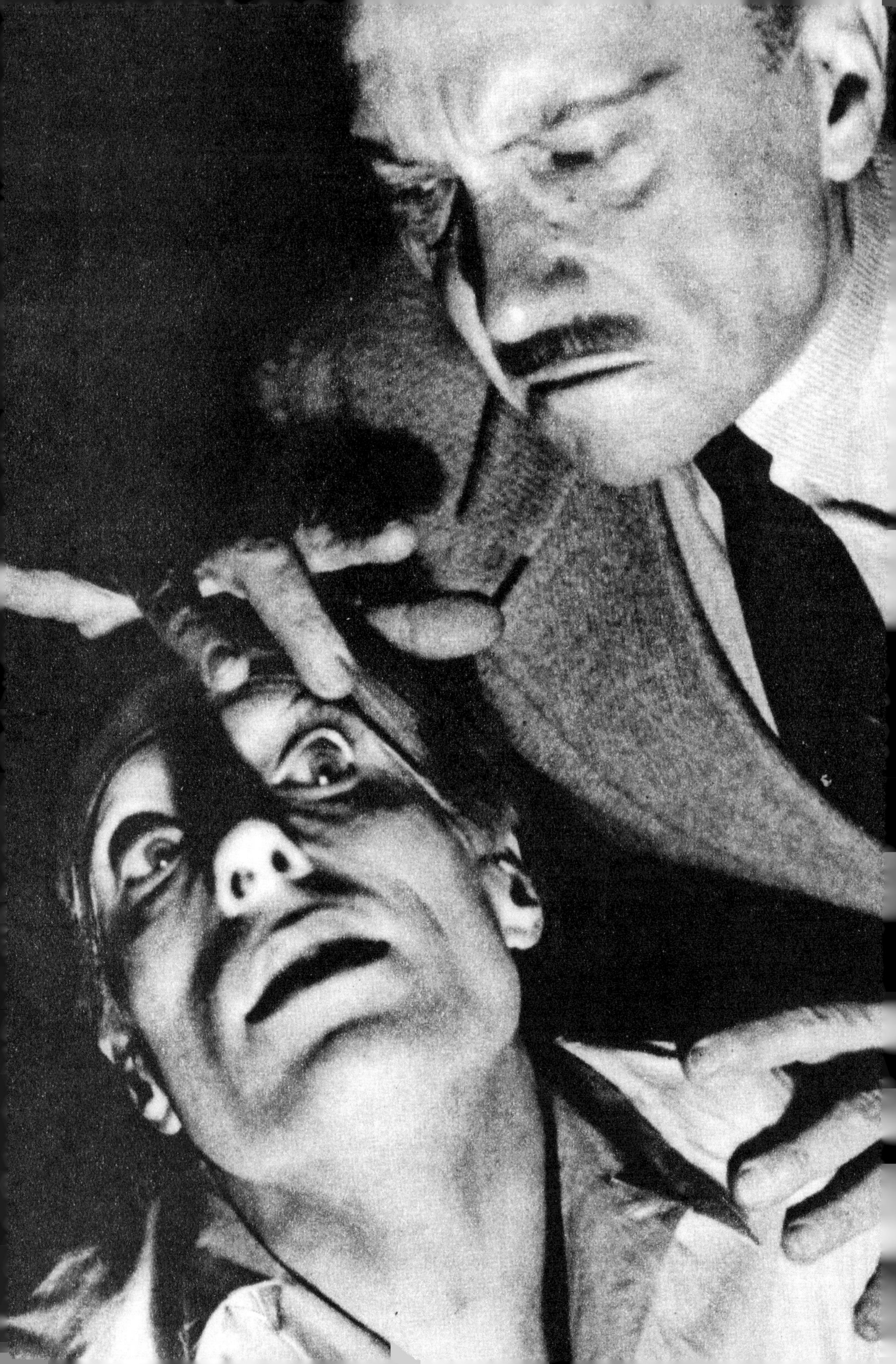

INSANITY

THE MYSTERIOUS MAN
André de Lorde, 1921

A three-act horror play with the additional theme of the Suffering of the Innocent.

Raymound Bercier, head of a successful engineering firm, has suddenly become afflicted with severe and violent episodes of paranoia. His wife (whom he has attempted to strangle) and physician have him institutionalized.

Not knowing about the murderous struggle with his wife, Bercier's brother, a co-founder of the business, persuades the family, including his sister-in-law, to sign a petition for Bercier's release. Bercier cunningly pretends to be cured when brought before a magistrate. The head psychologist of the asylum claims that Bercier is so dangerous that he should never be released. When asked for proof, the psychologist is constantly interrupted by Bercier's brother, which prevents Bercier's madness from being revealed. The judge declares Bercier sane.

Later that day, Bercier returns home and quickly slashes his wife with a knife and strangles his brother to death.

A CONCERT AT THE MADHOUSE
André de Lorde and Charles Foley, 1909

A horror play in two acts.

At an insane asylum run by a cynical and neurotic director, various inmates exhibit their bizarre and comical personas. One thinks that she is made of porceline. Another imagines that he is a railroad. Still another writes modern poetry. An old woman, declared cured, is taken home by her son.

That same evening, however, she returns to the institution, disgusted by her daughter-in-law and grandson's unwelcome reception. Suddenly one of the insane rushes the complaining woman and strangles her to death.

THE CABINET OF CALIGARI
André de Lorde and Henri Bauche, 1925

A popular horror play in seven (later nine) scenes, this was based on the dream-like 1920 German Expressionist film classic. It contains the additional themes of Hypnosis and Mysterious Death.

Alain and Francis plan to break out of an asylum to find Dr. Caligari, a carnival hypnotist, who Francis believes can restore their sanity. As they escape the madhouse, the apparition of the murdered Jeanne, Francis' fiancee, appears. Francis suddenly declares that Caligari killed her as he does to all the beautiful and young people. Later, at Caligari's circus tent, Jeanne volunteers to be hypnotized by Caligari. Francis, knowing of her weak heart, asks to replace her. Under hypnosis, Francis reveals that Jeanne will die before dawn. Alain tries to get Caligari to awaken Francis, who is led into Caligari's stall. That night, the startled Jeanne cannot sleep. From her window, the somnambulant Francis reaches in and carries her away. As police investigate Caligari's booth, he shows them a wax effigy of Francis, which they believe is the hypnotized Francis. After they leave, the real Francis brings in

Jeanne. When Caligari embraces her, she calls out and dies. Francis is instructed to bury her in a cemetery, where Caligari awakens Francis. Later, Francis and Alain are back in the asylum courtyard. Francis convinces the inmates that the head of the institution is really Caligari. Francis is put into a straight jacket and tossed in a padded cell. Seeing Caligari make a strangling gesture at the window, Francis dies.

THE EYES OF THE GHOST

Jean Aragny, 1926

A horror play with the additional themes of Guilt, Imprisonment, and Vengeance.

The chief of a hospital for the mentally ill, Doctor Tardier, a humane physician and gentle person, is concerned for the safety of his patients. One of his inmates has been murdered the previous night at midnight. Tardier increases the number of guards and reprimands one of them for his brutality to the mentally ill. At midnight, another patient is murdered. The patients discover that the murderer is the sleepwalking Doctor Tardier himself. As a storm rages outside, the doctor's patients gouge out his eyes.

THE SYSTEM OF DR. GOUDRON AND PROF. PLUME

André de Lorde, 1903

One of the most celebrated horror plays, this was adapted from Edgar Allan Poe's 1845 short story The System of Dr. Tarr and Professor Fether. *With the additional theme of Mutilation.*

Two journalists, Henri and Jean, visit the office of Dr. Goudron, who is said to have pioneered a humane treatment to cure insanity. As the doctor begins to describe his system, the reporters hear cries and pounding from an adjoining room. Goudron investigates. Another scream is heard and Goudron laughs. The reporters begin to suspect that the doctor himself may be mad. Finally when he parades his colleagues and assistants, who start to behave in an odd manner and then to imitate animals, Henri and Jean realize that they are the ones in danger. A storm increases the mad assistants' insanity. Henri and Jean discover that the insane patients have taken over the asylum and are playing the roles of the attendants. The institution's guards rescue the journalists at the last minute, fighting off the murderous inmates. In the doctor's closet, the real Goudron has been murdered and mutilated. The guards drag out his butchered body as the inmates shriek and laugh in the distance.

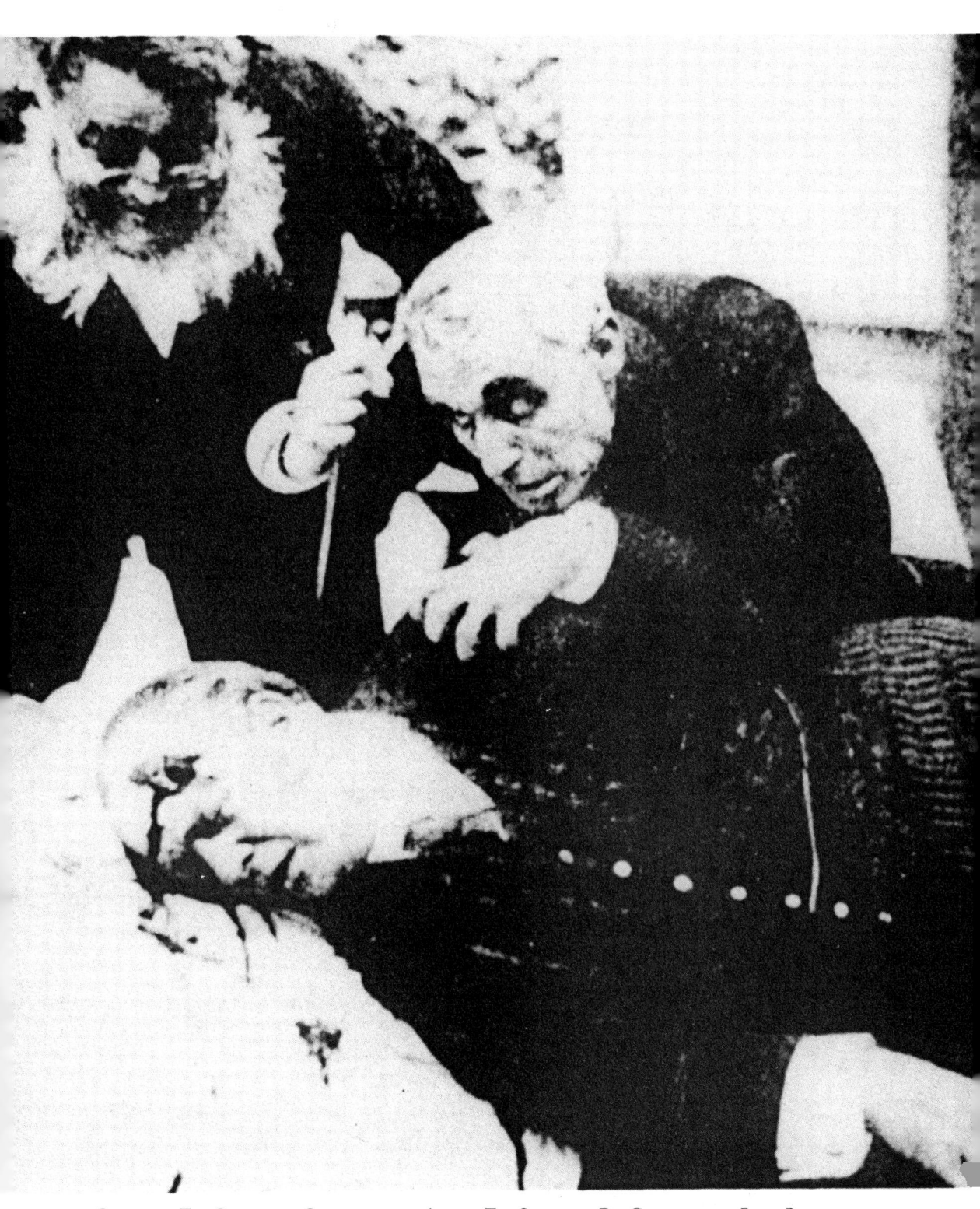

OPPOSITE: *THE CABINET OF CALIGARI*, 1925. ABOVE: *THE SYSTEM OF DR. GOUDRON AND PROF. PLUME*, 1909.

THE NAKED MAN

Charles Méré, 1928

A three-act horror play.

In an old chateau, a woman has lost her sanity since she gave birth to a half-human monster. Her husband keeps their humanoid son chained up in a cage but has managed to teach him basic ideas of obedience and respect. The mother and a friend release the monster, who unexpectedly attacks the woman and is shot and killed by the friend. Finding his son dead, the father goes insane.

MUTILATION

THE LITTLE HOUSE IN AUTEUIL

Robert Scheffer
and Georges Liguereux, 1907

A horror play with the additional themes of Prostitution and Vengeance.

At a small brothel, there is a prostitute who enjoys watching people in pain and suffering. She welcomes a man who soon confesses that he was an accomplice in a murder. The prostitute demands that he describe it and then re-enact the killing with her as the murdered victim so she may enjoy the thrill of terror. The criminal too becomes a kind of victim in the story and has himself tied up. Another sadist, a client of the prostitute, arrives unexpectedly in the room. Seeing the criminal bound to a chair, the sadist rips out his beard, pulls his teeth and nails out, cuts open the man's face with a knife, and burns out his eyes. While the victim screams in agony, the tormentor becomes sexually excited by the sight of blood and savagely possesses the prostitute.

THE MARK OF THE BEAST

E.M. Laumann, 1916

An adaptation from Rudyard Kipling's short story, this horror play in two acts contains the additional themes of Exoticism, Mysterious Death, and Vengeance.

After a drunken New Year's Eve party in a British fort in Northern India, three Englishmen arrive at the Temple of Hanuman, the monkey god. While the Hindu priests chant their morning prayers, the thoroughly-inebriated financier, Fleete, grinds the end of his cigar into the forehead of the red monkey idol. While his friends unsuccessfully attempt to pull him away, Fleete shouts that he has made "the mark of the beast" on the shrine. Meanwhile, amidst the uproar of the local priests, the Silver Man, a naked leper, appears and drops over Fleete, burrowing his flesh-eaten face into Fleete's breast. Suddenly, the priests become calm and one of their leaders tells the Englishmen to leave quickly. Sobering up, Fleete complains about a sharp smell of human blood, which the others cannot detect.

At the house of Commissioner Strickland, one of the three Britishers, Fleete awakens the next morning with a great hunger for uncooked meat. Strickland notices a strange set of black markings on Fleete's chest. During the day, Fleete acts more and more mad, scaring the horses and rolling in the ground, finally turning into a wolf-like animal. Fleete's friends bind him as the Silver Man mews from outside the house. Dr. Dumoise inspects Fleete and announces that he is dying from an advanced case of rabies. The physician departs. Within minutes, Strickland captures the Silver Man as he dances with his shadow in the moonlight. The Englishmen torture him with ropes and a white-hot branding iron. Eventually, the exhausted leper agrees to cure Fleete, which he does by placing his hand on Fleete's breast and inhaling. Fleete opens his eyes, now cured. The Silver Man is released. Dumoise re-enters with a death certificate. He is shocked to see a living Fleete. Fleete sniffs and complains about the "doggy smell" (really, singed flesh) in the room.

A CRIME IN THE MADHOUSE

ANDRÉ DE LORDE AND ALFRED BINET, 1925

This perennially popular two-act horror play was later retitled The Infernals, *or* The Old Women. *It contains the additional themes of Helplessness, Imprisonment, Insanity, and the Suffering of the Innocent.*

In a lunatic asylum, a beautiful girl, Louise, pleads with the head psychiatrist to release her immediately since she has been declared cured. Thinking that she is showing new signs of hysteria, he orders her confined for another night.

In Louise's cell are two hideous mad women, Hunchback and the Normandy Woman. To assuage Louise's fear of them, an unsympathetic Sister is assigned to stand watch through the night. The Sister, however, quickly vacates the cell to attend a funeral service in the asylum chapel. Ignoring Louise's desperate entreaties to stay, the Sister maintains that Louise's morbid premonitions are a product of her hysteria and departs. Suddenly, One-Eye, a madwoman so violent that she is kept in solitary, enters Louise's cell. The old crones believe that a cuckoo bird is imprisoned behind Louise's eyes.

While the first two women pin down Louise's arms, One-Eye gouges out her eyes with a knitting needle. Now fearful of what they have

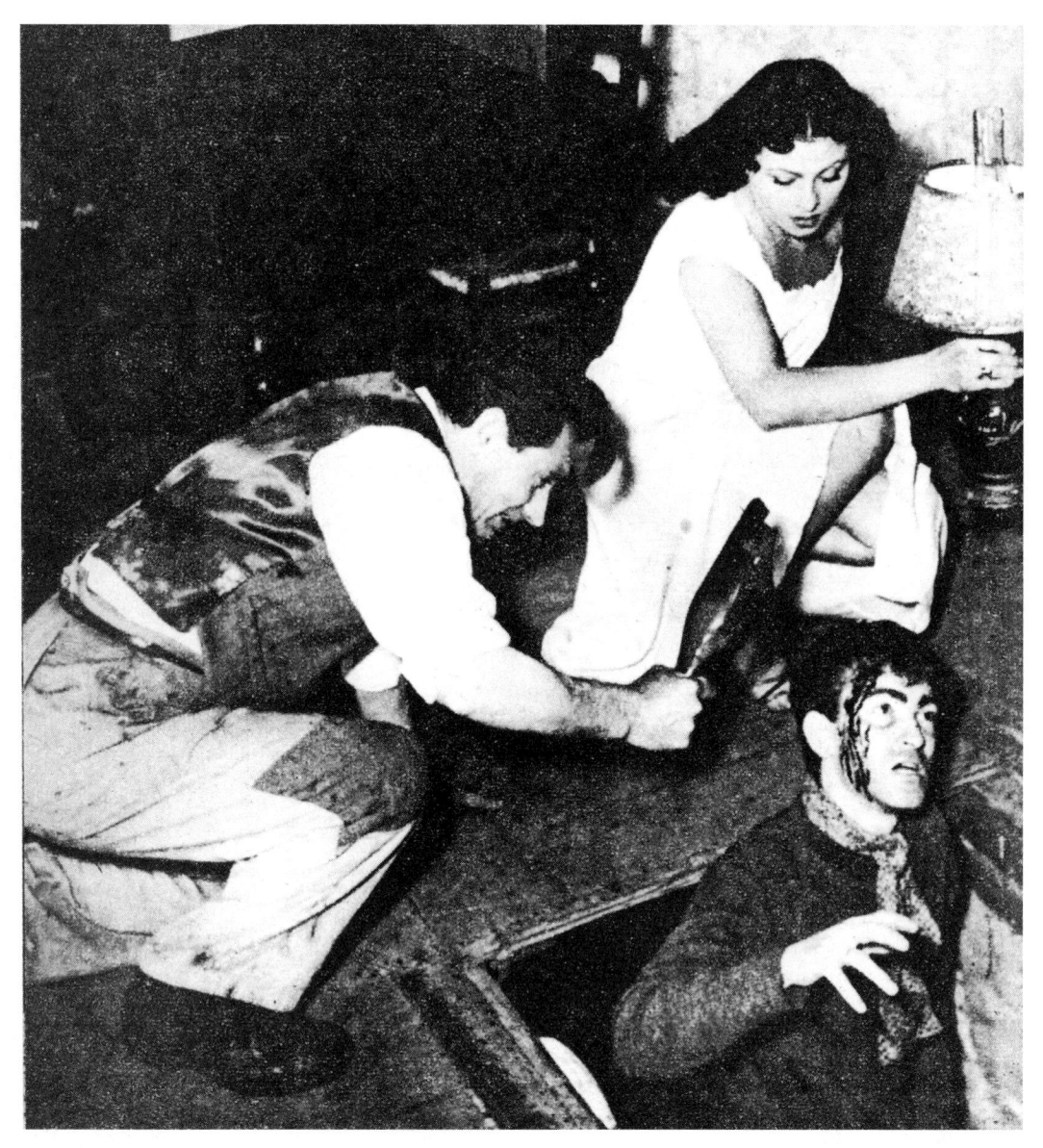

ABOVE: *ABANDONED,* 1953. **OPPOSITE PAGE:** *THE KISS OF BLOOD,* 1947.

done, one of the insane women pushes One-Eye's face against a hot plate that was just used to boil water. The old woman's face is totally destroyed in smoke and flame. It is reduced to an oozing mass of charred and bloody flesh.

THE KISS OF BLOOD

JEAN ARAGNY AND FRANCIS NEILSON, 1929

A horror play in two acts with the additional themes of Guilt, Insanity, Mysterious Death, Surgery, and Vengeance.

Joubert asks his friend Dr. Leduc to amputate one of his fingers, which is causing him horrific pain. Since there is no wound or infection, Leduc pretends to perform the operation, giving Joubert a simple sedative. When Joubert awakes, the pain in his finger is more intense still. He unwinds the surgical gauze and discovers the doctor's trick. Taking a scalpel, Joubert proceeds to amputate his own finger.

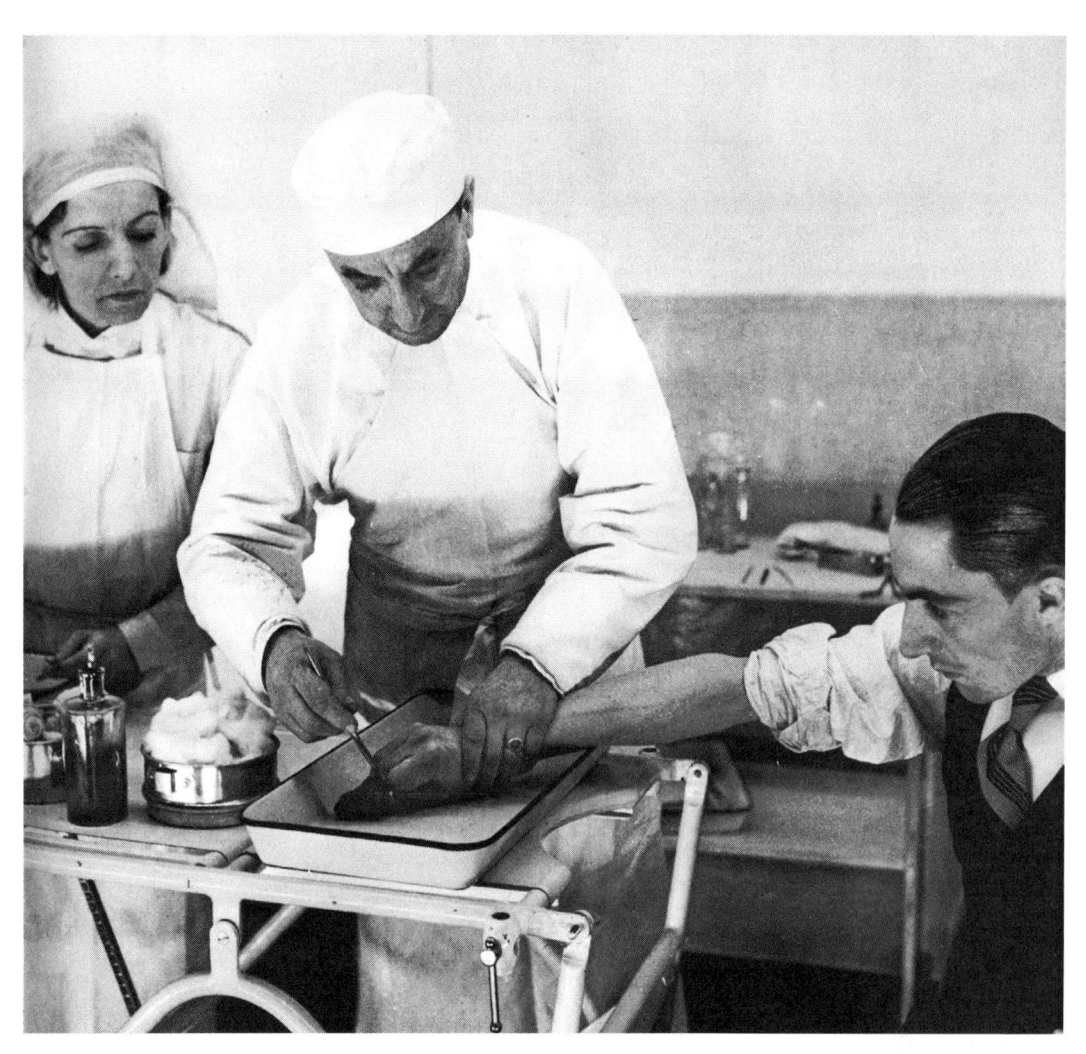

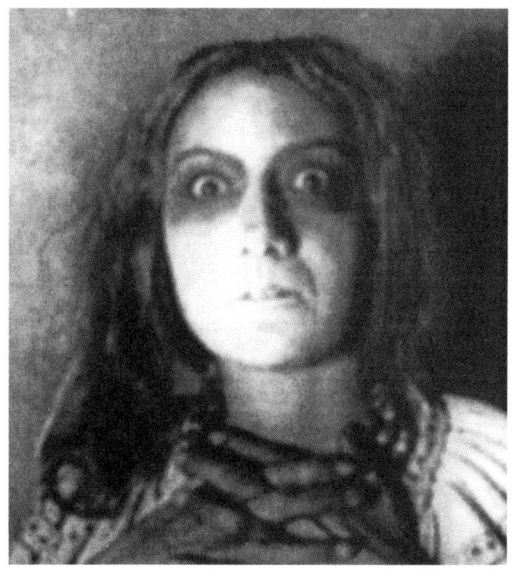

The next day in Joubert's apartment, Dr. Leduc visits him. Suddenly an apparition of Joubert's drowned wife appears, and she kisses Joubert's bandaged hand. The intense pain reappears and the agitated Joubert drops dead. The startled doctor finds out that the ghost was no psychic vision. The real Madame Joubert, now laughing madly at her husband's psychosomatic death, is an escapee from an insane asylum. Previously, Joubert thought that he had murdered his wife by throwing her overboard from a cruise ship. Unbeknownst to him, the woman was rescued by sailors but lost her mind as a result of the murder attempt. They placed her in an institution, from which she escaped.

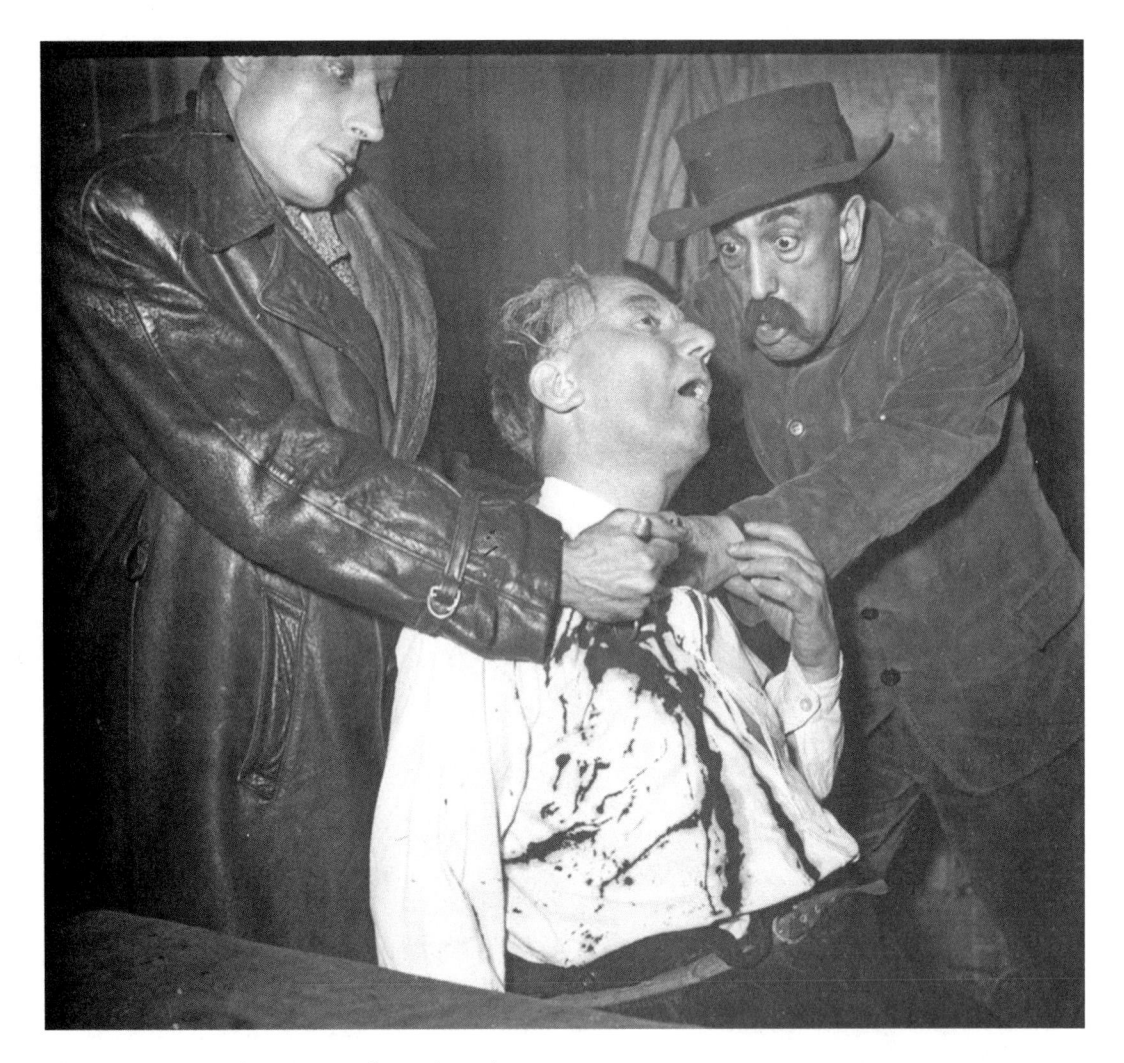

——•——

HSIOUNG-PE-LING, OR THE BLOODY ALOUTTE

CHARLES GARIN, 1911

A "Chinese" horror play in two scenes with the additional themes of Exoticism and Vengeance.

In ancient China, Hsioung-Pe-Ling has been entrusted with her husband's beautiful and superbly trained aloutte while he is away. Master Ling has been called to the emperor's side just at the time of a regional contest, in which his bird would have won first prize. His jealous neighbor, whose bird is second only to Ling's, takes advantage of Ling's absence. He visits Hsioung-Pe and convinces her to show him the aloutte. Promising to teach her the commands needed to control the bird, the neighbor tricks Hsioung-Pe into opening the cage, which allows the bird to fly away. When Ling returns, Hsioung-Pe tells him an obvious lie that someone stole the aloutte.

Ling then invites the neighbor over for a visit. Through clever and suspenseful conversation, Ling confirms his suspicions. He terrifies and then kills the man in front of Hsioung-Pe's parents, who are present as witnesses. "But where is our daughter? Where is she?" they ask of Ling. Ling then lifts the cover of the bird cage to reveal his wife's severed head, her punishment for disloyalty.

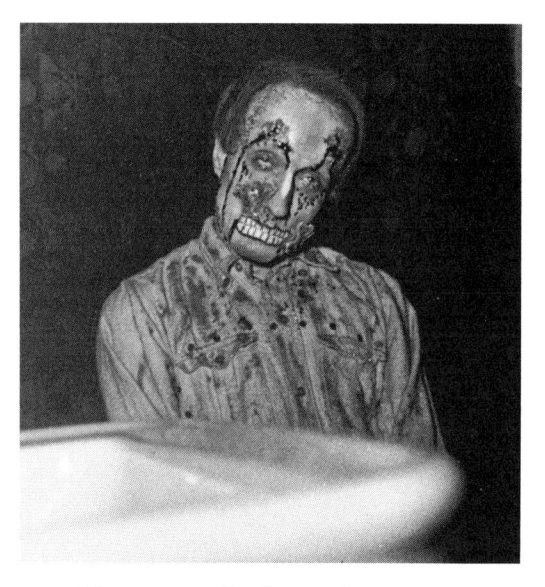

MAKE-UP FOR *THE LIVING CORPSE*, 1937

ORGY IN THE LIGHTHOUSE

LEOPOLD MARCHAND, 1956

A frequently produced horror play with the additional themes of Insanity, Play Transforming Into Terror, and Prostitution.

In a lighthouse off the Breton coast, an elderly marine attendant, Logonadee, and his young assistant, Yann, watch a religious procession taking place across the water during a feast day. A sailor on leave, Yves, Yann's wild brother, unexpectedly appears in the tower with bottles of calavados for the alcoholic Logonadee, and two prostitutes, Rosa and Nini, for his entertainment and that of his somewhat inexperienced brother. While Logonadee proceeds to get drunk, the brothers dance with the whores and become playful. Rosa, the more sexually aggressive of the women, enjoys roughhouse games. Nini reveals that Rosa insulted the priest at the festival earlier in the day. She also offends the respectful Yann by comparing his statue of the Virgin with her whorehouse madame. As an intense storm appears on the horizon, Logonadee retires to the top of the lighthouse with his calavados. In the darkness of the tower, the couples participate in a sexual orgy, which concludes in a drunken slumber. A siren call from a lost boat awakens Yves. The light beacon has gone out and a boat containing the sailors' mother is approaching the treacherous rocks below. Logonadee has locked the door to the beacon, and Yann becomes hysterical, blaming his predicament on the blasphemy of the prostitutes. Yves discovers that one of the women stole the statue of the Virgin. Declaring her the devil, he cuts Rosa's throat and throws her from the window of the lighthouse. The boat with the men's mother crashes against the rocks. In a religious frenzy, the sailors decide to burn Nini to death. After pouring gasoline on her, they incinerate her and pray.

THE MAN OF THE NIGHT

André de Lorde
and Leo Marches, 1921

A horror play.

An artist has developed an obsession with the dead. He finds immense pleasure in digging up corpses and disfiguring them. Their lifeless bodies become the secret of his realistic paintings.

THE GARDEN OF TORTURE

Pierre Chaine, 1922

An adaptation from Octave Mirbeau's decadent novel, this popular three-act horror play contains additional themes of Exoticism, Imprisonment, and Vengeance.

On a French ship to Shanghai, a Chinese man makes advances to Clara Watson, a married English woman. Marchal, a French army officer and the woman's lover, throws the Chinese overboard, drowning him.

At the luxurious residence of the Watsons on the Chinese mainland, Clara persuades Marchal to desert the army to live with her. Secretly in league with the Chinese rebels, Clara attempts to use her position to protect Marchal when they kidnap him. The lovers discover that the Chinese man who Marchal tossed into the ocean was an important figure in the underground movement.

Both Marchal and Clara are brought to the infamous Garden of Torture, where traitors and enemies of the rebels are punished with bizarre and exotic tortures. They see strips of flesh ripped from a young woman's back. The other prisoners describe in obsessive detail the forms of punishment and mutilation that are practiced in the Garden of Torture. Marchal and Clara are tortured and killed. Clara's eyes are pierced with red-hot needles before her execution.

THE BLOODY TRUNK

Maurice Level, 1931

A controversial two-act horror play.

Two penniless students lose all their money—borrowed money—in a poker game. They then kill the young and beautiful Mlle. Soller in order to steal her purse, which is filled with bank notes. They chop up and hide her body in an empty travel trunk.

Just as they start to flee, a creditor comes to reclaim Soller's furniture, including the bloody chest-suitcase. Terrified of being discovered, one of the killers confesses immediately. The second student, furious at his friend's cowardice, shoots him in the head.

MYSTERIOUS DEATH

CRUCIFIED, or THE NIGHT OF THE TWELFTH OF MAY, 1848

A.P. Antoine and
Charles Poidlouse, 1923

A two-act horror play with the additional themes of Exoticism, Guilt, and Vengeance.

William Stone, an Irish patriot, lives with his daughter Ellen and son Billy on Lord Kindlard's farm. Larkin and his son Jack, though Irish, are loyal British subjects. Three years

Eva Berkson backstage at the Grand Guignol, 1946

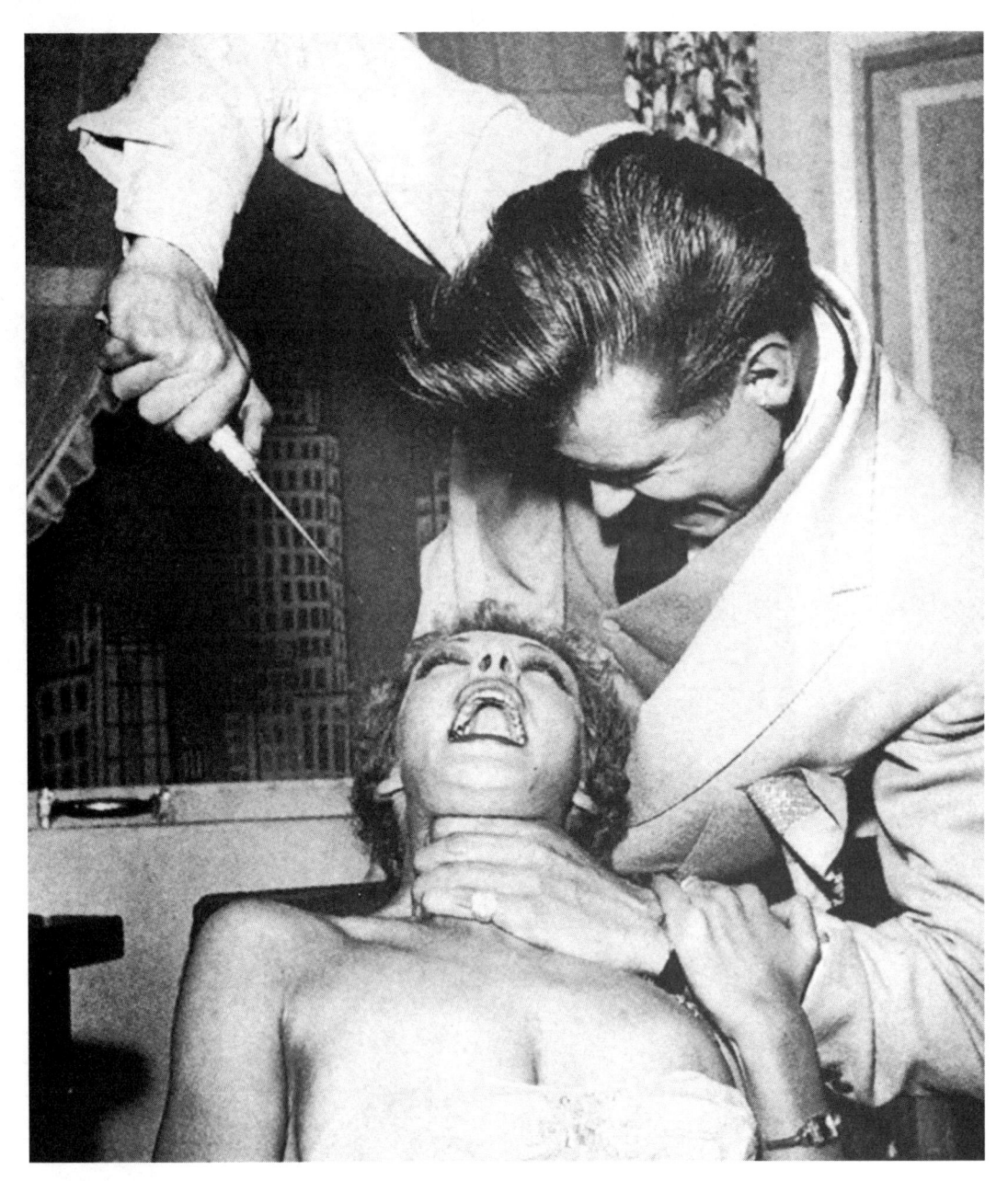

ABOVE: THE SLAUGHTER, 1955. OPPOSITE: SOL HYAMS, THE PAWNBROKER, 1923.

ago in 1845, Jack Larkin called on Ellen and saw three revolutionaries paying Stone a visit. They informed Stone that his son Billy had been captured and crucified. The Irishmen detected Larkin listening to their conversation and crucified him on the door of the cottage.

On each anniversary of Jack's death, one of the four murderers has been killed in a supernatural way. Only old Stone is left. It is the anniversary night. Stone and a friend are about to flee when revenge enters.

SOL HYAMS, THE PAWNBROKER

JEAN BERNAC, 1907

A two-act drama based on the mystery story by British writer W.W. Jacobs. It contains the themes of Exoticism, Guilt, and Vengeance.

Three men have stolen a precious diamond in India. The first thief betrayed his partners and ran off with the gem. After a long pursuit and capture, the other two thieves killed the first and retained his booty. Then the second thief stole the diamond in turn from the third, a Hindu, and escaped to London. In the pawnshop of Sol Hyams, the second thief sells the diamond. Just outside the shop, he is murdered by his Hindu partner.

The Indian then enters Hyams' establishment and attempts to purchase the diamond for Hyams' original price. Hyams refuses to sell it. After much haggling, the Hindu departs, predicting a horrible death for Hyams. As foretold, Hyams dies at the appointed hour in a mysterious and terrifying manner.

GOTT MIT UNS

RENÉ BERTON, 1928

A horror play with the themes of Guilt, Imprisonment, and Mutilation. On its first revival in 1929, it was re-titled The Light in the Tomb *and given an internationalist finale with the German spy praising France as he dies.*

During a First World War engagement, a group of French soldiers take control of a cave from a fleeing German army. As soon as the French unit enters, a German shell hits the mouth of the cave, trapping them inside. The French discover a lone German soldier, Hermann, left behind to spy on the advancing French. Hermann, however, was trying to dig his way out of the cave since a ticking time bomb was secreted inside. As a martyr for his homeland, Hermann refuses to reveal the explosive's location. The French soldiers threaten him with violence and torture, but Hermann will not yield. The French captain, formerly a professor of philosophy like Hermann, finally persuades him to disclose the bomb's where-

NAME OF THIS BIT OF PURE VIOLENCE IS "THE VIOLATOR". PLOT DIFFERS FROM MOST IN CATEGORY IN THAT THE ATTACKER IS A WOMAN WHO LURES UNSUSPECTING ROMEOS TO HER HOME.

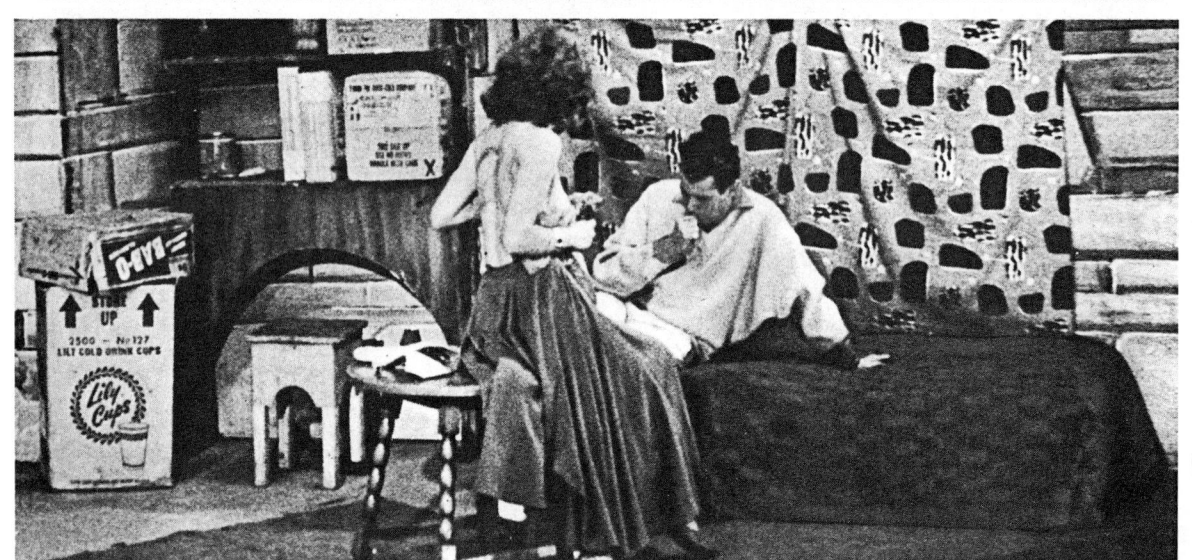

ONCE SHE HAS SEDUCED A MAN, SHE ARRANGES FOR HIS MURDER. DOWNFALL COMES AFTER RELATIONS WITH A BANDLEADER WHO (BELOW) DISAGREES, USES A WHIP. BOTH END UP DEAD

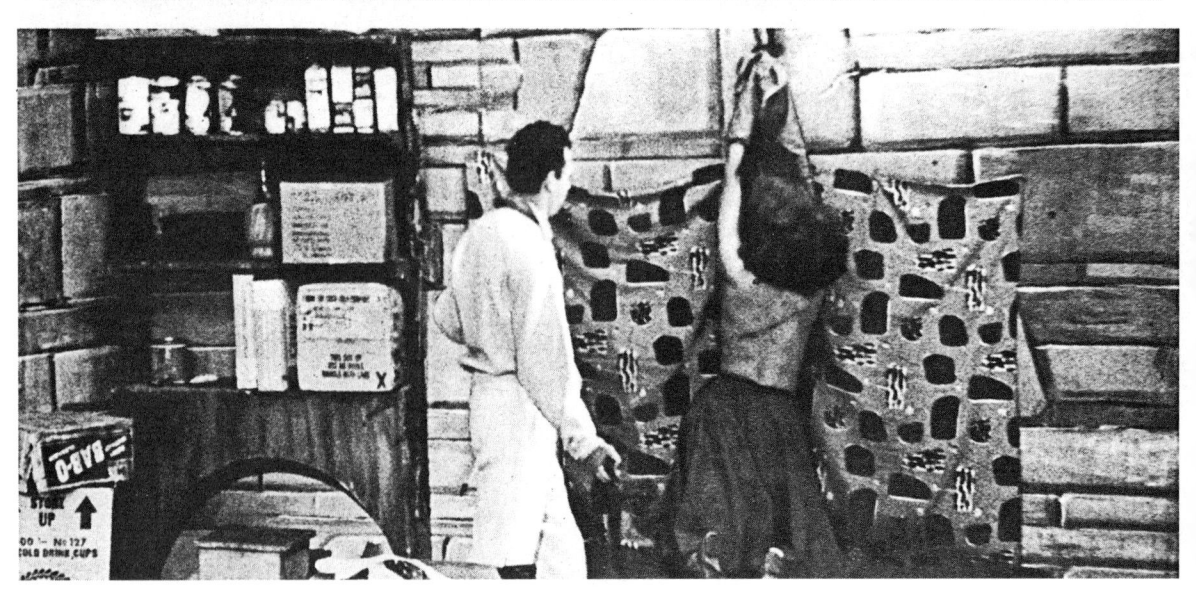

THE VIOLATOR, 1957

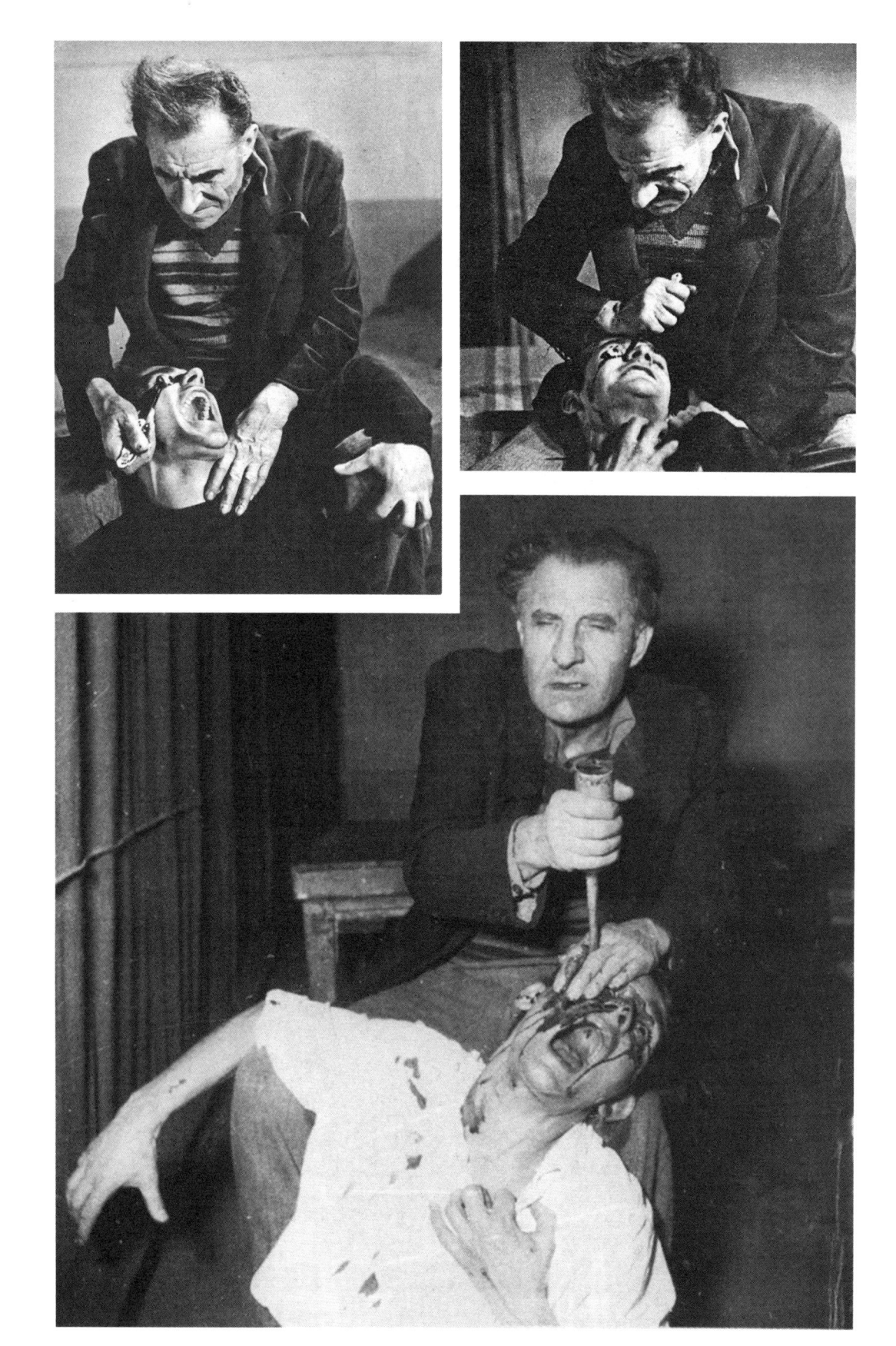

The Rape, 1950

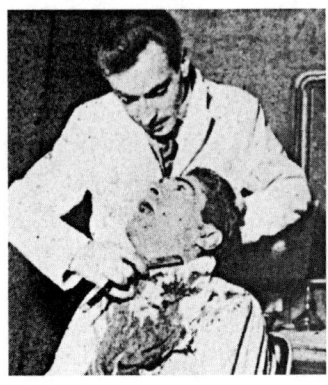

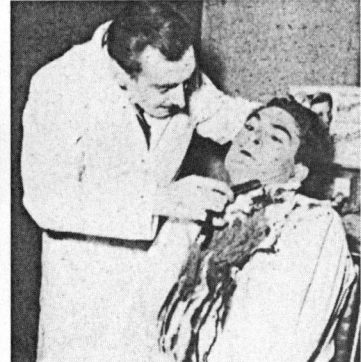

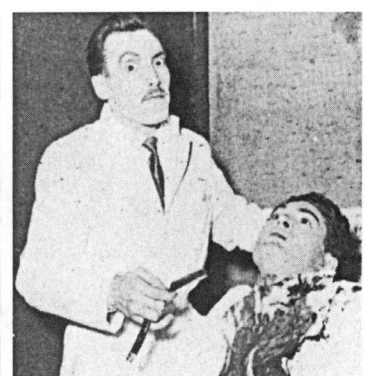

The Lottery of Death, 1957

abouts. It is defused just seconds before exploding. Meanwhile, an engineering unit of the French Army has tunneled into the cave and rescued the trapped soldiers. Hermann runs outside and is hit by a German shell. He returns to the cave with his face blown away. Now once again a loyal German, Hermann shouts, "Gott mit uns!" ("God is with us!") and dies.

THE SIEGE OF BERLIN

CHARLES HELLEN AND POL D'ESTOC, 1914

A horror play with the additional theme of Bourgeois Morality.

In the relic-ladden apartment, eighty-year-old Colonel Jouve, a veteran of the Napoleonic wars, and his twenty-year-old granddaughter, Helene, await the parade of the victors of the Franco-Prussian War of 1870-1. Fearing for his pride and sanity, Helene—along with Doctor Valbert and friends of the colonel—has informed her grandfather over the last two years of fighting that the seemingly invincible French Army has conquered the Germans, its natural enemy. In fact, the opposite is true, and when the military parade passes the apartment, the granddaughter cannot constrain the old man from cheering his heroes. As the old colonel realizes that it is the Prussian Army, not the French, who are marching through Paris, he becomes totally insane for a moment, stiffens, then dies at the feet of his granddaughter.

THE MAN WHO SAW THE DEVIL

GASTON LEROUX, 1911

A two-act horror play with the additional theme of Guilt, by the author of The Phantom of the Opera.

In the midst of the Juas mountains, four tourists find a dilapidated castle. The owner has sold his soul to the devil in exchange for the power to always win at cards. The devil appeared to the old man in a mirror hung on the inside of a closet. The secret lover of one of the female tourists opens the wardrobe and asks the devil for the death of the woman's husband. He then breaks the mirror and faints.

The next day, he aims an unloaded gun at the husband and pretends to fire. The husband drops dead.

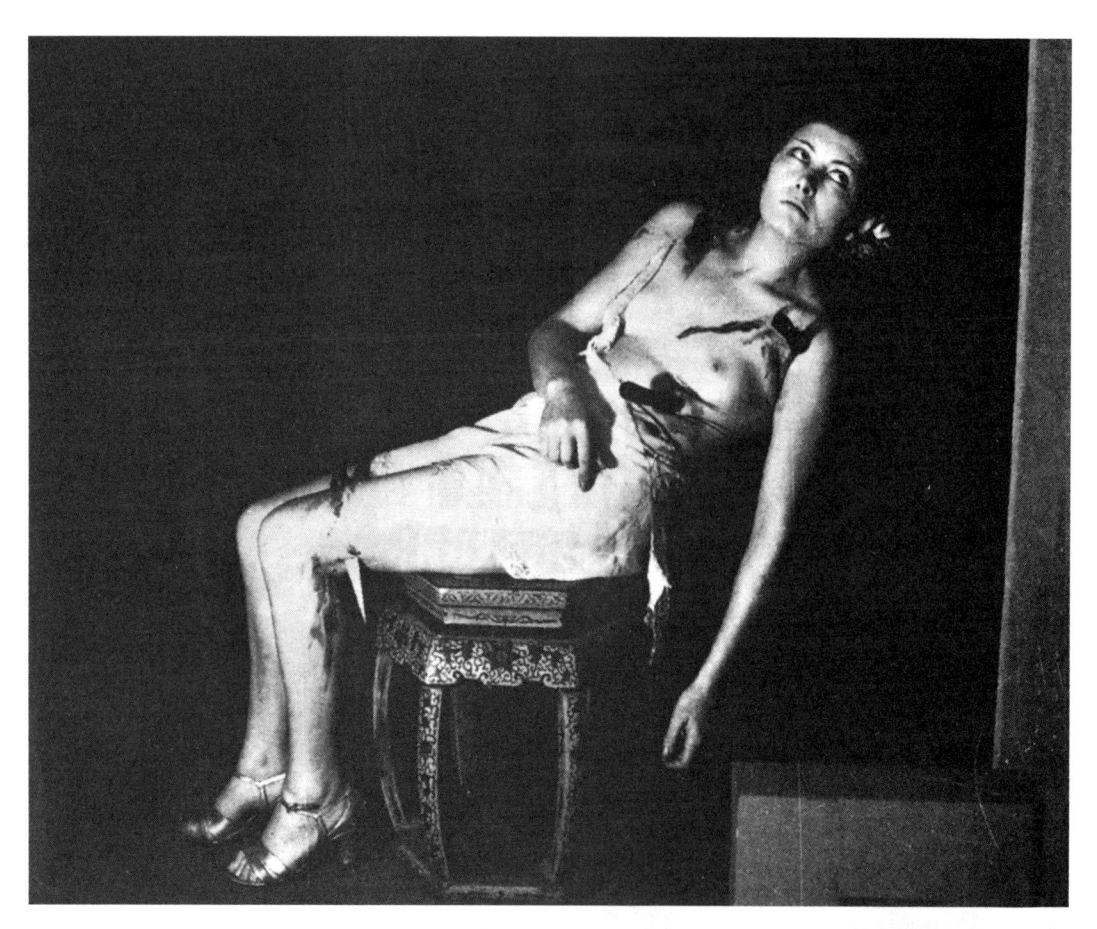

SUFFERING OF THE INNOCENT

THE CASTLE OF SLOW DEATH
André de Lorde and Henri Bauche, 1916

A horror play with the themes of Exoticism, Helplessness, Imprisonment, and Vengeance.

In a luxurious retreat in the Rocky Mountains, where everyone is dressed in cowboy attire, a thief breaks into a wealthy woman's room. She fights to keep the diamond necklace that she is wearing. The thief strangles

This page: *The Embrace*, 1925

her, takes all her jewels and flees. He is stopped, however, by the guards of the asylum. The thief has entered a leprosarium and most likely contracted a highly contagious form of leprosy. In the background, one can hear the mysterious chanting of funeral processions. Now the thief himself must be confined to the resort as both prisoner and patient.

THE MERCHANT OF CORPSES

ANDRÉ DE LORDE, 1940

A horror play in two acts with the additional theme of Guilt.

A mother anxiously awaits her daughter who is late from school.

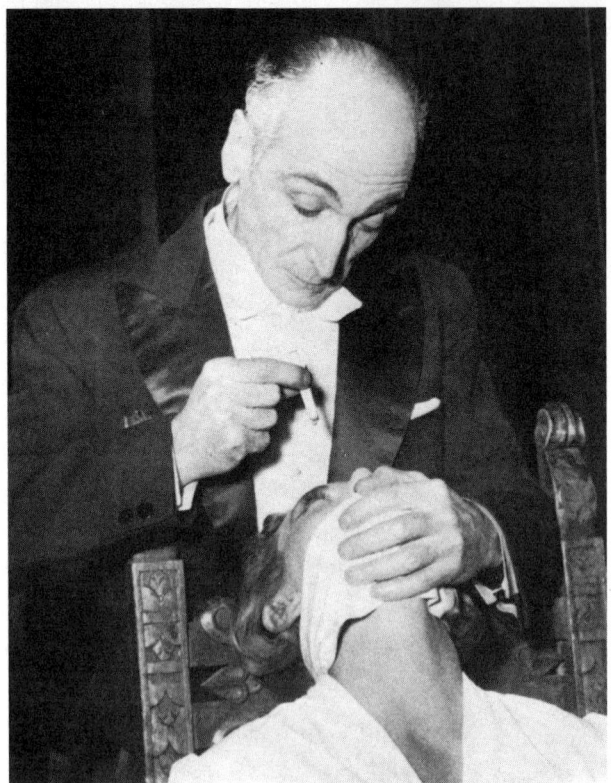

TOP: *THE CLAIRVOYANT*, 1936.
ABOVE: *THE HORRIBLE EXPERIMENT*, 1942.

She has heard about a child-murderer who always reappears at carnival time. In the distance is the growing sound of the music from a street carnival. When her child fails to return home, the mother denounces a carnival employee as the murderer of her daughter. Since there is no dead body, the police can do nothing.

A friend of the woman kidnaps the accused man and plunges him into a vat of acid that is used to prepare skeletons for a medical department. The mother faints when she sees the chemically deteriorating body. She passes out because the dead man was innocent; her daughter has already safely returned home.

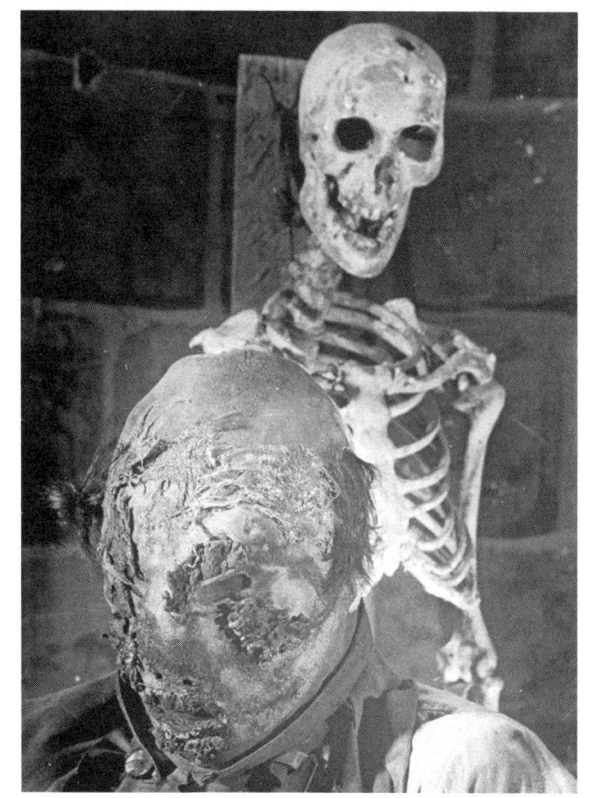

This page: *The Merchant of Corpses*, 1946

This page and opposite: *The Headhunter*, 1960

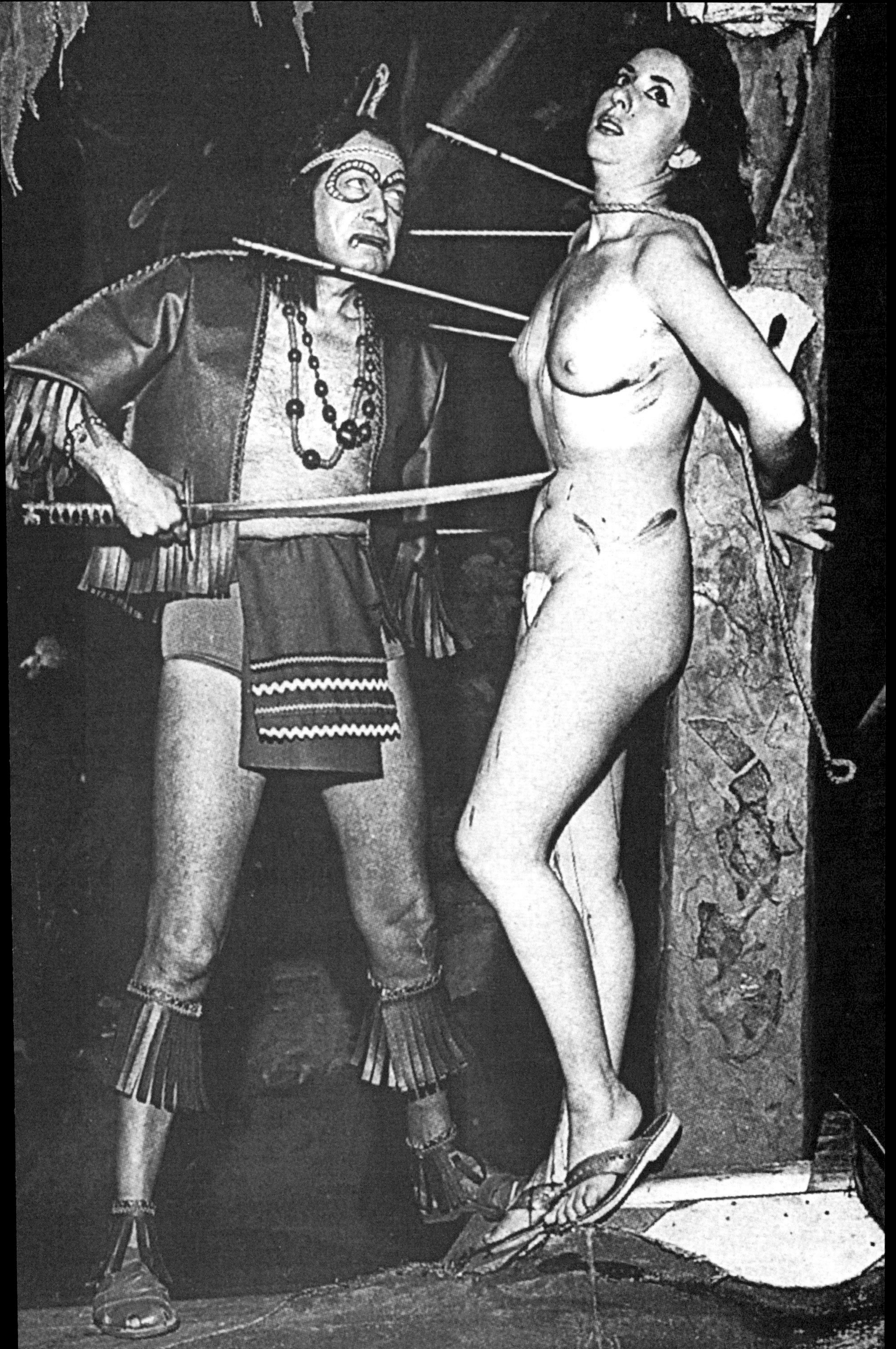

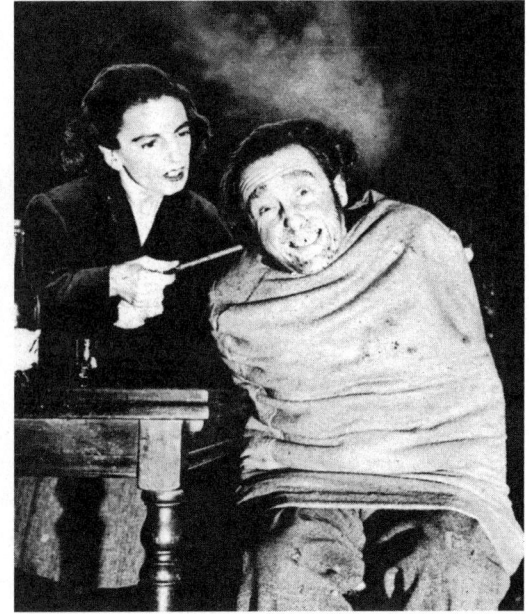

Killer of Children, 1939

THE THREE MASKS
Charles Méré, 1922

A horror play with the additional themes of Exoticism and Vengeance.

A young Corsican, Paolo Delia Corba, is in love with Viola, the daughter of a family that has sworn a vendetta against Paolo's family. Paolo's father, a proud and strict army colonel, refuses to allow the two to marry, even though Viola is now carrying Paolo's baby. His father decides to send him to join the army in France, which will separate the two lovers and keep him safe from Viola's three murderous brothers.

It is Carnival time and, believing that Viola's brothers are out of town, the two lovers make secret plans to put on Carnival costumes and enjoy their last night together. Later that evening, three masked revellers appear at the Della Corba house, dragging a fourth with them who is dressed as a Pierrot. Paolo's father drinks and celebrates with them. The three celebrants apologize for their "drunken companion," who has not moved from the chair he was placed in. The three men depart, leaving the fourth in the chair. Then Viola comes into the house, frantically looking for Paolo whom she says is dressed as a Pierrot. The father lifts the mask of the man in the chair with trepidation and finds Paolo's bloody, lifeless face underneath.

THE NIGHT OF TERROR
Charles Méré, 1919

One of the most successful horror plays with the additional themes of Imprisonment, Parisian Low-life, Play Transforming Into Terror, and Suffering of the Innocent.

Italian Prince Atalonga wagers the Duch-

The Vampire, 1952

esse de Martigny that she will not accompany him to a resort frequented by cut-throats. Together they visit a room in the Cafe Bonnardel, where he plays a practical joke on her, making her believe that he is an *apache* attempting to rob her. Atalonga believes this will give the Duchesse a special thrill. Suddenly real *apaches* storm the room and the prince attempts to explain his joke. But, as the *apaches* break down the door, the Duchesse panics and stabs the prince to death. Thinking that she is a thief like them, the *apaches* hail the Duchesse. After taking the prince's money and jewels, they throw his corpse out the window and thank her, leaving her alone in the room.

THE CELL 13
Roland Dreyfus, 1926

A horror play with the additional theme of Imprisonment.

An innocent man has been convicted and imprisoned. He attempts an escape but is surprised by a prison guard and kills him in self-defense. Just then the prison director arrives to tell the unjustly convicted man that he will be released. A man has confessed to the crime for which he was imprisoned. Now, however, the innocent man is truly a murderer. He will remain in Cell 13 forever.

SUICIDE

NIGHT AT THE HAMPTON CLUB

ANDRÉ MOUËZY-EON AND ARMONT, 1908

A horror play inspired by Robert Louis Stevenson's short story collection, The Suicide Club. *It contains the additional themes of Helplessness, Imprisonment, and Play Transforming Into Terror.*

Herbert Forbes, a British journalist, has managed to gain entrance under false pretenses to the secretive Suicide Club. The sole purpose of the elite London society is to facilitate the suicides of its members. Forbes joins the other members at a card table. Whoever draws the death card that night must kill himself. From the stressful intensity of the game, one member suffers a fatal heart attack. The game continues and Forbes is dealt the card of death. He quickly explains his true intent —to gather information for a newspaper article on the Suicide Club, not to kill himself. The President of the Club is sympathetic to his predicament, but he cannot permit any infraction of the rules: Forbes must kill himself. Now panicked, Forbes draws a revolver on the men. They ignore it, however, and leave the room. Forbes is alone in the bolted suicide room. After undergoing a roller coaster of changing moods, Forbes puts the pistol to his head and shoots himself. The President re-enters and the others carry Forbes' corpse out on a prepared stretcher.

HARA KIRI

JEAN SARTÉNE AND PIERRE DAY, 1919

A horror play with the additional themes of Exoticism, Guilt, and Mutilation.

In a Japanese opium den, Barriere initiates his friend Mainville into the pleasures of the Orient. In the darkly lighted room, Thi Nam prepares the opium pipes while Mara Paiva performs a mysterious and illusory dance. When the Europeans are completely under the drug's influence, Thi Nam rapes and kills Barriere's wife, who is also Mainville's mistress. But suddenly realizing the depravity of his crime, Thi Nam decides to commit suicide and plunges a long knife into his stomach. His blood spurts across the room and he falls. Mara Paiva once again begins her exotic dancing under the protection of veils and multicolored lights.

THE PRISON FOR CHILDREN
André de Lorde and Pierre Chaine, 1910

A social drama that details the cruelty of fathers who abandon their sons to sadistic keepers of children's reformatories. It contains the additional themes of Imprisonment and the Suffering of the Innocent.

One group of brutalized victims breaks out of the reformatory-prison, and one by one are caught by the authorities. Backed into a farmhouse, the young hero Georges decides to hang himself rather than return to the school.

SURGERY

THE HORRIBLE EXPERIMENT
André de Lorde and Alfred Binet, 1909

A popular two-act terror play with the additional theme of Vengeance.

In his laboratory at his country home, Doctor Charrier has discovered how to resurrect human life by electrically stimulating the hearts of corpses. Charrier explains to his illustrious pupil and future son-in-law, Dr. Demare, that he is jealous of him since the young man is able to marry his daughter

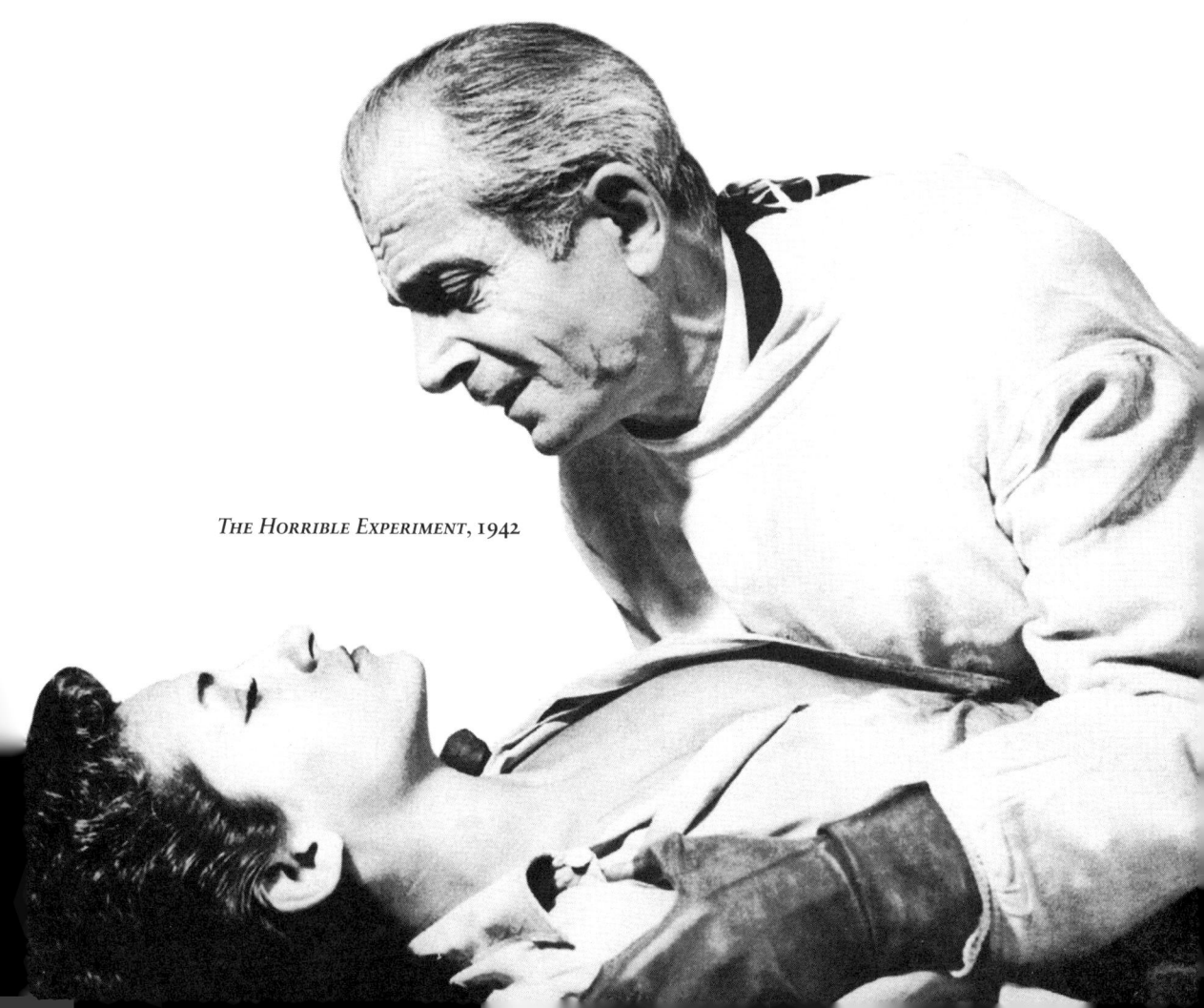

The Horrible Experiment, 1942

Jeanne, whom he raised and adored. Before the young lovers leave on a motorbicycle for Jeanne's grandmothers's house, the daughter announces that the two of them will return sooner than expected since she has discovered a shortcut.

After Jeanne and Demare leave, a stranger in black, the public executioner, enters and explains to Charrier that there will be an execution and Charrier will be able to test his theory of electrical resurrection on the body of the corpse. To caution the delighted Charrier, however, the executioner tells him a story about a guillotined man whose headless body clutched him so fiercely that they had to break the dead man's fingers. The man in black exits and the telephone rings. Jeanne has been killed in an accident with the motorbike. When her body is carried into the laboratory during a storm, Charrier decides to resurrect her, using Jeanne's horrified fiancee, Demare, as an assistant. Charrier makes an incision over her heart and applies an electrode to it. Jeanne begins to hemorrhage. The electricity goes out for a moment. A green light burns faintly as a battery hums. Suddenly there are sounds in her throat. Charrier increases the voltage. His daughter starts to breathe, then her arms stiffen and raise up. Charrier goes to embrace Jeanne's corpse but she strangles him, despite Demare's efforts to loosen her grip.

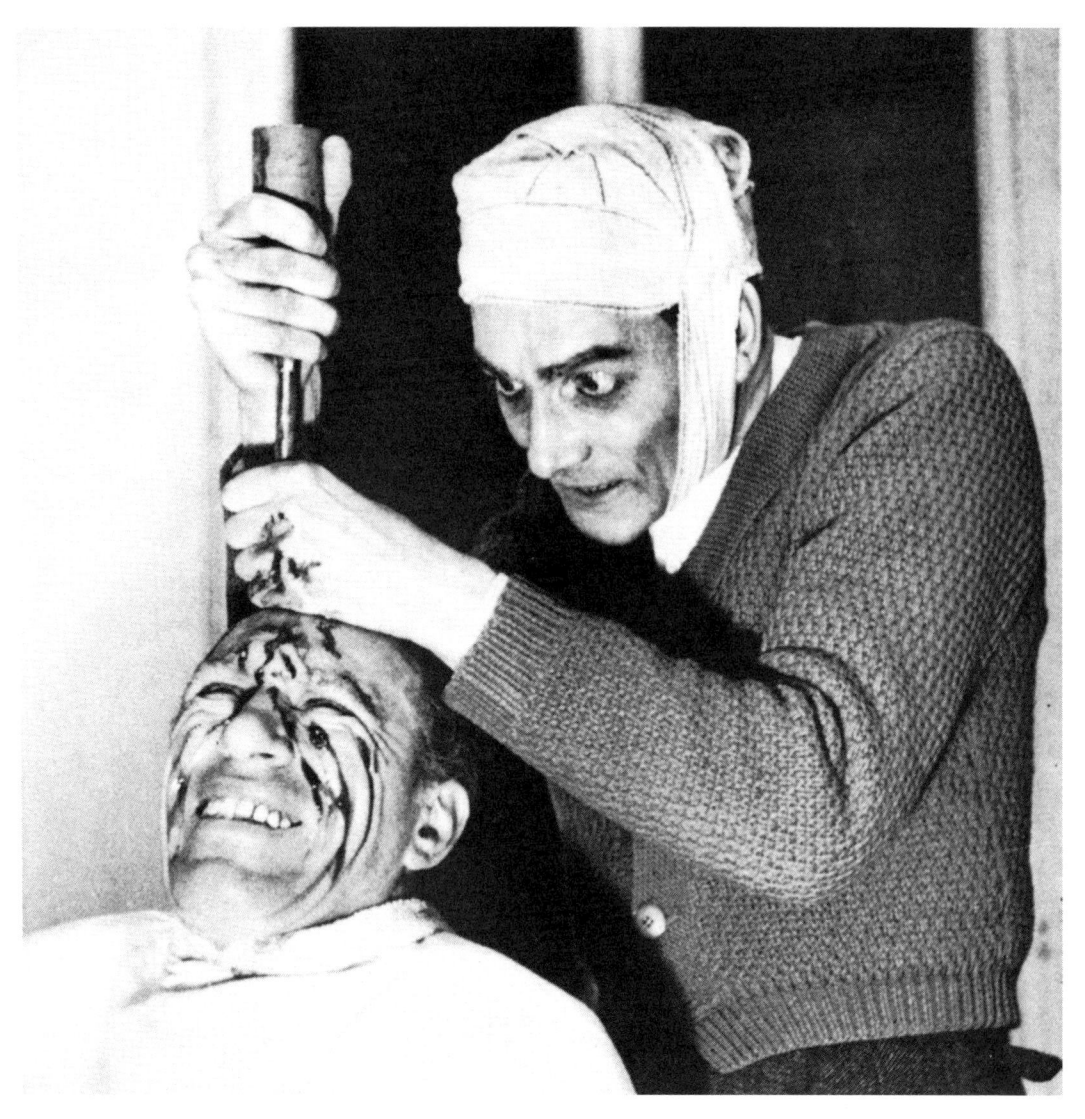

OPPOSITE AND THIS PAGE: *THE LABORATORY OF HALLUCINATIONS*, 1947

THE LABORATORY OF HALLUCINATIONS

ANDRÉ DE LORDE
AND HENRI BAUCHE, 1916

Another popular three-act de Lorde horror play with the additional themes of Cuckoldry, Insanity, Mutilation, and Vengeance.

Sonia, the wife of Doctor Gorlitz, a brutal scientist and head of a sinister health clinic in the country, decides to run off with Monsieur de Mora, one of the doctor's neighbors. She tells her husband that she and de Mora will spend the afternoon innocently with a group to explore a nearby Roman ruins.

While Gorlitz and his assistant engage in torturous experiments with a screaming and bound patient, de Mora is brought to Gorlitz' laboratory. De Mora's car overturned and his skull was fractured. In de Mora's pocket, Gor-

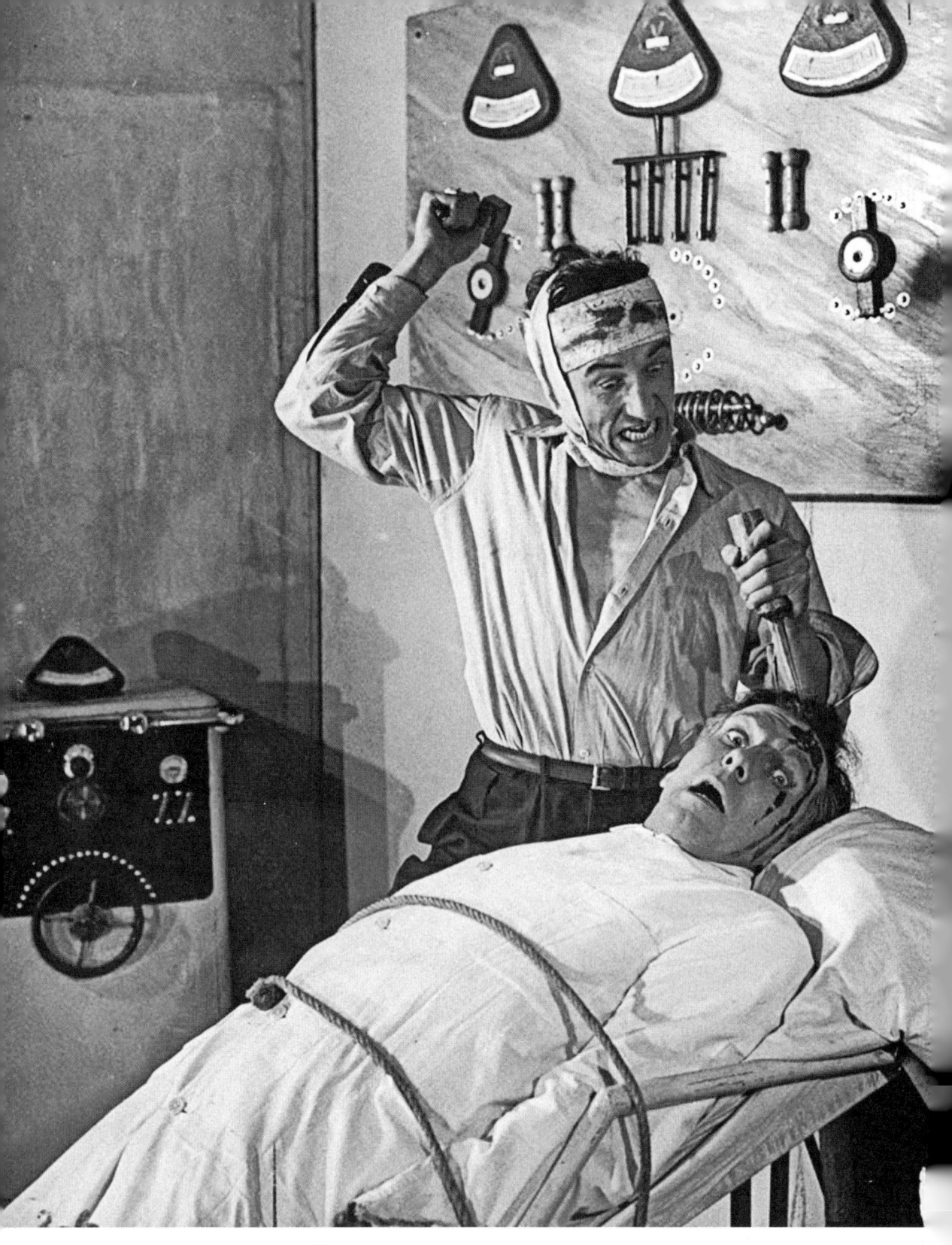

The Laboratory of Hallucinations, 1947

litz finds Sonia's love letter to him. Madly jealous, Gorlitz revenges himself by operating on de Mora, poking and snipping the lobes inside his brain, until de Mora slowly becomes permanently deranged. Gorlitz reveals his plan to Sonia. Soon her lover will deteriorate into a mindless idiot. Gorlitz even shows her de Mora's current dementia.

De Mora overhears Gorlitz and, in a burst of energy, straps Gorlitz to the operating table and cuts open his skull, subjecting him to a fate that was intended for himself.

A LESSON AT SALPÉTRIÈRE
André de Lorde, 1908

A horror play in two acts with the themes of Hypnosis, Insanity, Mutilation, and Vengeance.

At Salpétrière, a medical school within a mental asylum, doctors perform experiments to cure insanity. While the chief doctor, Professor Marbois, conducts his lecture, an intern, Nicolo, executes his instructions. A first patient is cut open. Then a second with a bandaged head and paralyzed arm, Claire Camu, is wheeled in. She maintains that her arm injury was the result of an experiment at Salpétrière. Marbois assures her that she is suffering from an hallucination. Nicolo is ordered to hypnotize her. Under hypnosis, Claire remembers that it was Nicolo who destroyed her nerves with electricity. Grabbing a bottle of sulfuric acid, she hurls it into Nicolo's face, causing him to fall to the floor in excruciating pain. Claire is dragged off by the orderlies while Marbois lectures on the antidotes to sulfuric acid.

THE MAN WHO KILLED DEATH
Renè Berton, 1928

A horror play with the additional themes of Guilt, Insanity, and Mutilation.

Outside a prison courtyard, a celebrated medical scientist, Professor Fargus, prepares the equipment for an experiment to determine whether consciousness remains in a severed human head. A convict is executed by guillotine and his bloody head is rushed in by the prison guards. Fargus places the head on a medical table and attaches electrical annodes to simulate the heart and brain activity. Then he injects beef blood into the arteries. Life returns to the convict's head. The head's eyes and mouth move. The prosecuting attorney, still not free from doubt about the dead man's guilt or innocence, asks him whether or not he was guilty of the crime for which he was guillotined. The head slowly intones, "No!" Inside the room, the guilt-ridden attorney goes mad.

VENGEANCE

THE DEAD RAT, ROOM NO. 6
André de Lorde and Pierre Chaine, 1908

Also called A Pair of White Gloves *in the English-speaking world, this was one of de Lorde's most successful productions, playing on the West End and Broadway in 1912 and 1913. There seem to be two versions of this play: one, where the girl is the sister of a revolutionary; and another, where she is an agent of the Czar sent to kill the philandering general. A horror play with themes of Exoticism and Prostitution.*

THIS PAGE AND OPPOSITE: *A KISS IN THE NIGHT*, 1947

General Gregoroff, a former officer in the Czarist army, is now living a life of dissipation in Paris. He meets an attractive prostitute, Lea, in the Rue de la Paix and falls in love with her. She agrees to dine with him in a private room in the Rat Mort. Unbeknownst to him, Lea is the sister of a revolutionary who has been tortured and put to death under the general's regime as governor of Moscow. During the dinner, as he attempts to undress Lea, the drunken general brags of his cruelty, including the torture of Lea's brother. Just then Lea reveals who she is and strangles him with her white gloves as the general screams for help.

THE CLOSED DOOR

ROBERT FRANCHEVILLE, 1910

A horror play with the additional theme of Mysterious Death.

A doctor's wife died from injuries resulting from a fall. Had her husband operated on her, she would have survived. Her death, however, allowed the doctor to marry a younger woman. Now the dead woman's ghost haunts the doctor's house and entices her replacement into the master bedroom. There, a huge antique mirror falls on the doctor's second wife. The doctor rushes in to save her but the mirror has trapped the young woman and she bleeds to death. The doctor, devastated, declares her dead. The door to the room mysteriously closes.

A KISS IN THE NIGHT

MAURICE LEVEL, 1913

A two-act horror play with the additional theme of Mutilation.

Henri decides to break with his lover, who retaliates by throwing vitriol in his face, disfiguring him terribly. The girl is arrested but promptly freed as Henri refuses to prosecute.

Although forsaken, the girl shows compassion, and visits Henri for a last time. He asks her to kiss him, and she is filled with revulsion as she looks at his scarred features. When their lips meet, Henri strangles her.

This page and opposite: *The Floating Coffin*, 1960

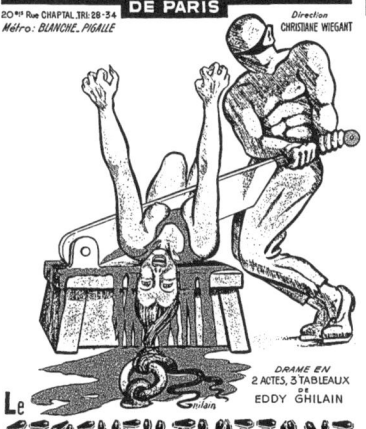

GRAND GUIGNOL DE PARIS
20 Rue CHAPTAL TRI 28-34
Métro: BLANCHE-PIGALLE
Direction CHRISTIANE WIEGANT

LE CERCUEIL FLOTTANT

DRAME en 2 ACTES et 3 TABLEAUX
d'EDDY GHILAIN

ABOVE: *The Leap of Death*, 1958
OPPOSITE: *The Kiss of Blood*, 1947

THE EXPERIMENT OF DR. LORDE

HANESWICK AND WATTYNE, 1916

A horror play in three acts exploiting the name and characterization of André de Lorde. Additional theme of the Suffering of the Innocent.

On the outskirts of Paris, Dr. Lorde has established a "psychological laboratory." There, he has created the means to transfer a soul into the body of another. The subjects of his experiment are a famous English strangler and a young scholar, who is betrothed to the daughter of Lorde's rival. Dr. Lorde transmits the soul (or mind) of the criminal to the young man.

The strangler-in-the-body-of-the-scholar reveals his true identity and begins a series of heinous crimes, ending in the strangulation of his fiancee. Hunted by the police, the monster returns to the laboratory and kills Dr. Lorde.

THE CARGO FRAUD

ANDRÉ DE LORDE
AND MASSON-FORESTIER, 1906

A horror play in two acts.

The owner of a cargo ship, *The Gladiator*, Le Hertel has knowingly overloaded its container compartments, intending the boat to sink. Le Hertel does this to collect a large insurance premium despite the fact that the husband of his god-daughter is the captain.

When news of *The Gladiator's* fate—and the drowning of the crew—becomes known, relatives and neighbors of the crew storm Le Hertel's office. He attempts to calm them but only in vain. They throw him out of the window and his body smashes against the pavement below.

HOT EARTH

HENRI-RENÉ LENORMAND, 1913

A horror play with the additional themes of Exoticism, Guilt, and Mutilation.

In a jungle clearing in French Equatorial Africa, an African native, Maelik, is being lashed on his bare back. A French visitor, Prefailles, realizes Maelik is clearly innocent of any crime. The French commander, Rouge, insists this is white man's justice. Later Maelik's wife comes to the camp requesting medical help for her husband. The wife of one of Rouge's officers, Madame Le Cormier, goes to assist. A short period after Le Cormier's exit, the Africans return with a large bloody box. It contains Madame Le Cormier's head. Prefailles becomes hysterical about the madness of it all. Rouge reminds Prefailles that twenty years before he learned about "white man's justice" from Prefailles' behavior.

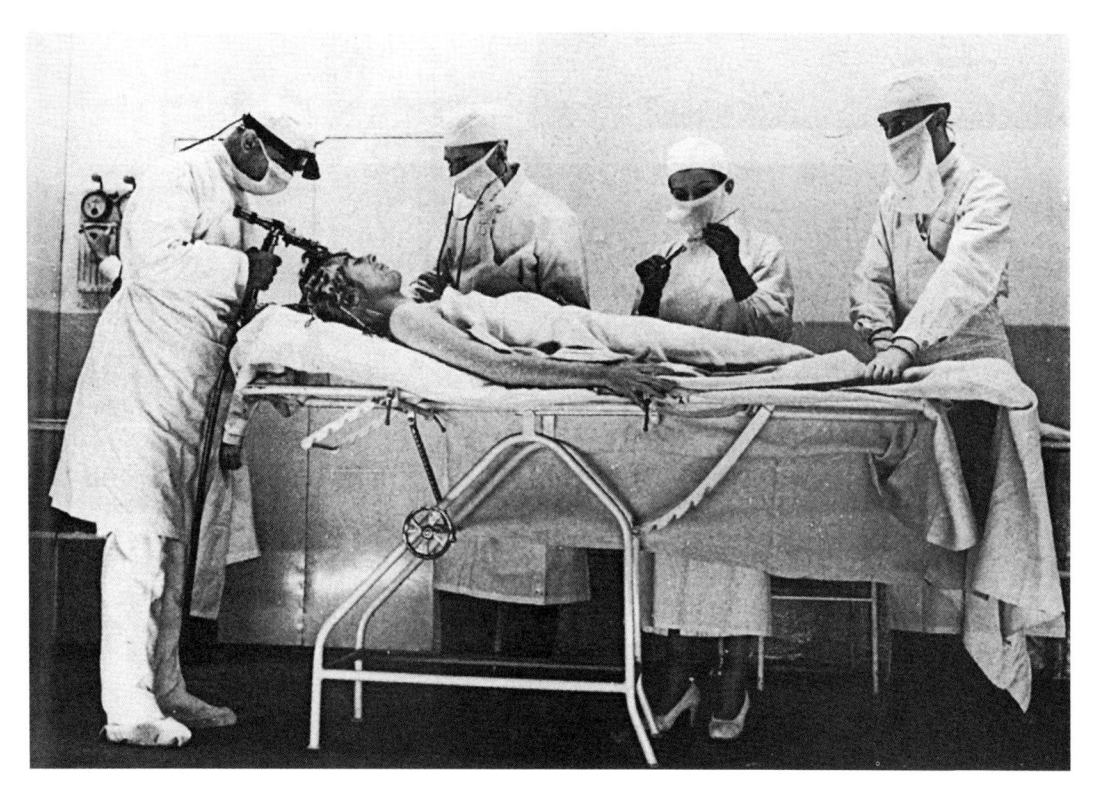

AT THE BREAK OF DAY
André de Lorde and Jean Bernac, 1921

A horror play with the additional themes of Guilt, Imprisonment, and Insanity. The original ending, showing the main character guillotined on the stage, was changed on the order of the High Commissioner of Police after much debate in the Parisian press.

A murderer awaits his execution in a prison cell. In a fit of jealousy, he strangled his girl friend. His cellmate turns out to be the girl's father. Everyday the old man torments the condemned man with elaborate descriptions of the guillotine's preparations. Finally the half-crazed murderer is led to his beheading.

CATHERINE GOULDEN
E.M. Lauman, 1917

A horror play with the additional theme of Mysterious Death.

A servant of a cruel master who has mysteriously disappeared, Catherine Goulden is suspected of his murder and interrogated. Although she denies the charge, under questioning Catherine admits that she had once dreamed of killing her master with a hatchet. Just then her master returns, furious that his servant dreamt of murdering him. He throws her out of the house and strikes her with a cane. It is winter and Catherine's anger and hatred are fanned into flames.

duce her. The caged gorilla becomes jealous and interrupts the doctor's undertaking with grunting sounds. To punish both the gorilla and Lina—for her resistance to his lovemaking—Brockau announces that he will disfigure Lina's beautiful face. Although terrified, Lina manages to maneuver Brockau into the corner of the tent where the gorilla can reach out of his cage and strangle his tormentor.

THE MASK

JESSE AND H.M. HARWOOD, 1916

A horror play adapted from an English drama with the additional theme of Cuckoldry.

THE MAKER OF MONSTERS

MAX MAUREY, CHARLES HELLEM, POL D'ESTOC, 1929

A horror play with the additional themes of Helplessness, Insanity, and Mutilation.

A mad scientist, Dr. Brockau, has created a menagerie of freak animals, which he has given various human traits and physical resemblances. He exhibits them in a traveling circus show. His great project is to transform a gorilla, which he keeps in the corner of his tent, into a man. One night, Brockau invites Lina, a circus woman, into his tent and attempts to se-

A victim of a mining accident, James Glasson has to wear a mask in order to shield others from the sight of his grotesquely disfigured face. He suspects his wife, Vashti, of being unfaithful and plots to catch her with her lover. Pretending to leave the house, Glasson secrets himself in the room where he quickly discovers Willie, his wife's lover. Glasson overhears that Vashti and Willie plan to run off together. When his wife leaves the room, Glasson attacks Willie, who murderously pushes Glasson to the floor. Vashti returns and, thinking that her husband has been killed, cold-bloodedly advises Willie to dispose of her husband's corpse in the old mine shaft. She even provides Willie with a mask for the perfect disguise as her husband. Once again, Glasson, seemingly lifeless, waits for Vashti to exit and he attacks Willie. This time he kills his rival and drags the body to the mine shaft. When Glasson returns, he immediately climbs the stairs to Vashti's room, removing his mask. Seeing his disfigured face and realizing what has happened, Vashti screams for help. Glasson strangles her.

THE COFFIN OF FLESH
ANDRÉ DE LORDE AND HENRI BAUCHE, 1924

A horror play with the additional themes of Cuckoldry, Hypnosis, Mysterious Death, and Surgery.

Four English doctors have formed a club to determine whether the soul can live without the body. At one of their seances, Henderson's dead mother appears, which causes Henderson to have a stroke. Murphy, whose wife is Henderson's lover, decides to use this occasion to hypnotize the weakened Henderson into a novel physical state between life and death. The remaining doctors prepare for a surgical operation. But when one of them cuts into Henderson, no blood flows from the incision. Before they can draw any conclusions, an arm from the drapes reaches out and strangles Murphy. The corpse of Henderson then falls from the operating table with a clenched hand.

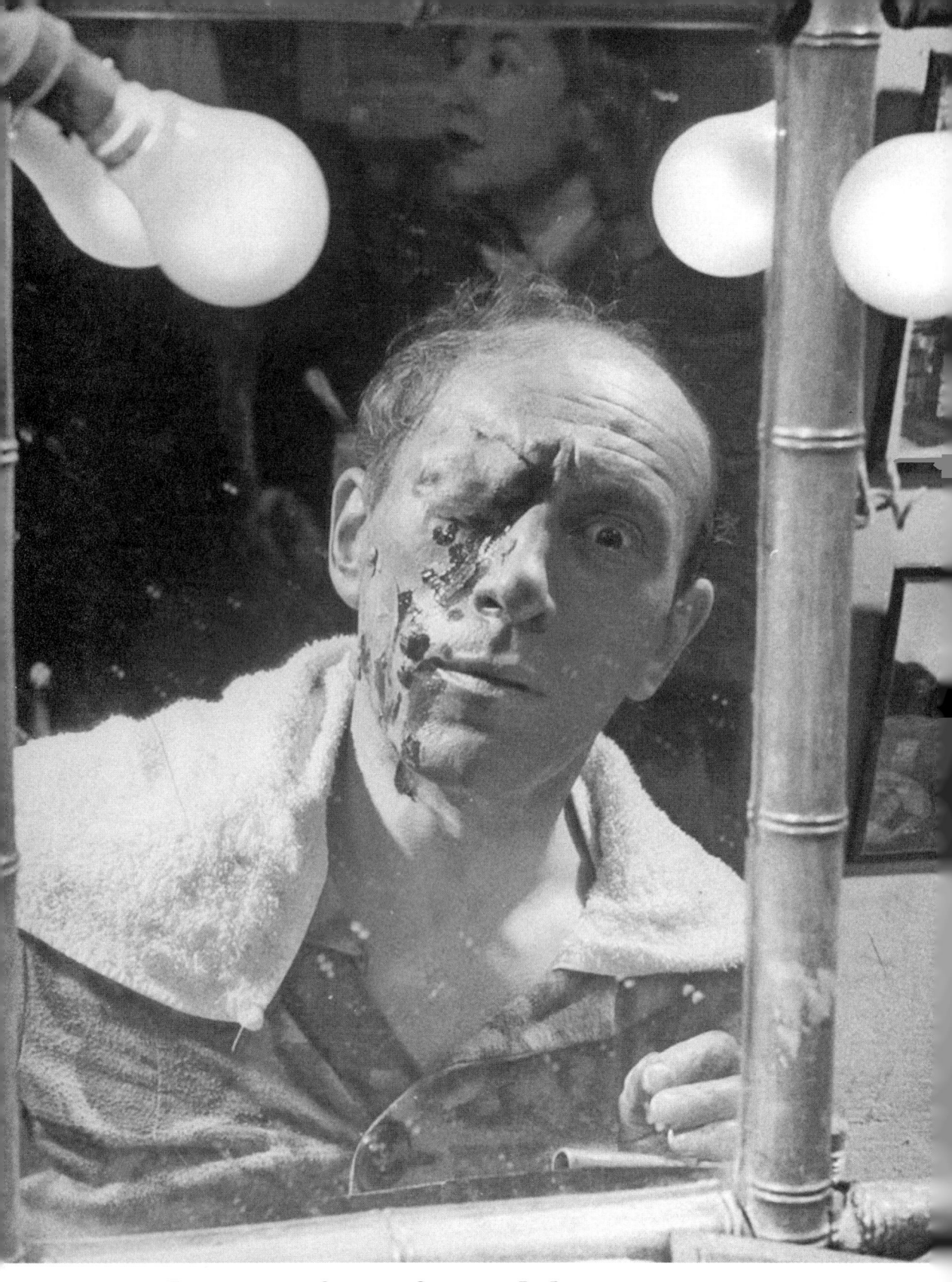

Facial effects for *Carnival of Ghosts*, with Eva Berkson in reflection, 1947

The Lover of the Dead, 1925

His Post, 1901

The Three Masques, 1922

GRAND GUIGNOL THEATRE OF FEAR AND HORROR

CHARLES MÉRÉ

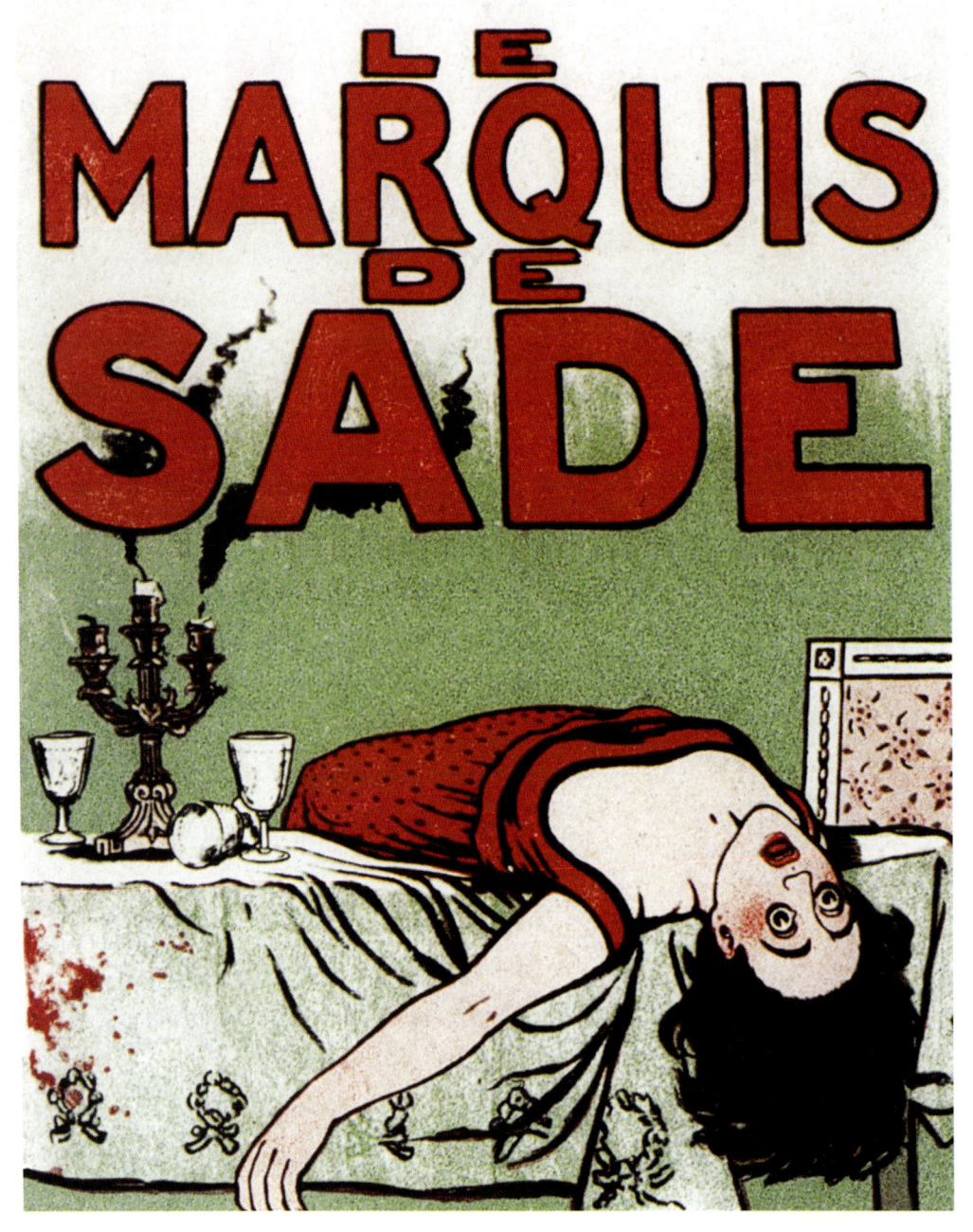

LE MARQUIS DE SADE

The Marquis de Sade, 1921

The Garden of Torture, 1922

Gott Mit Uns, 1928

The Puppets of Vice, 1929

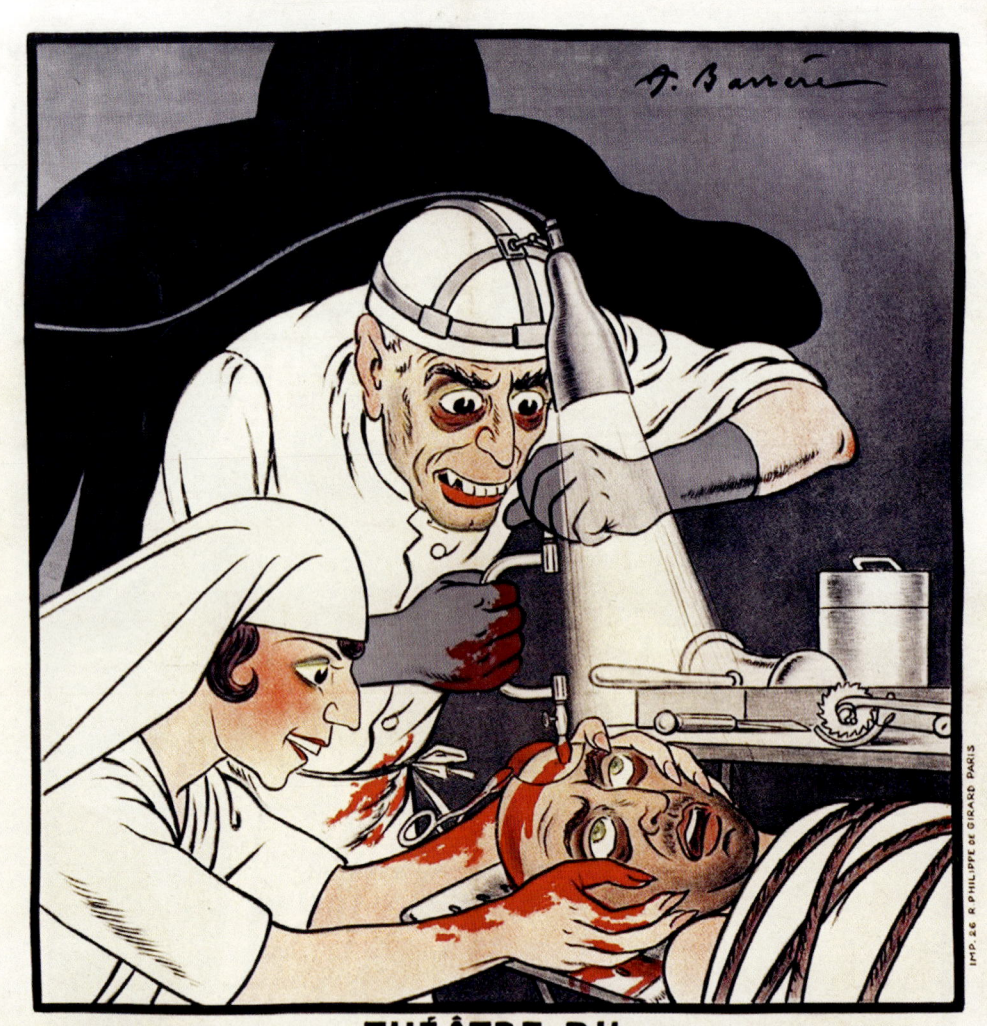

THE KISS OF BLOOD, 1929

At the Telephone, 1902

Montreal Touring Poster, 1923

On the Slab, 1923

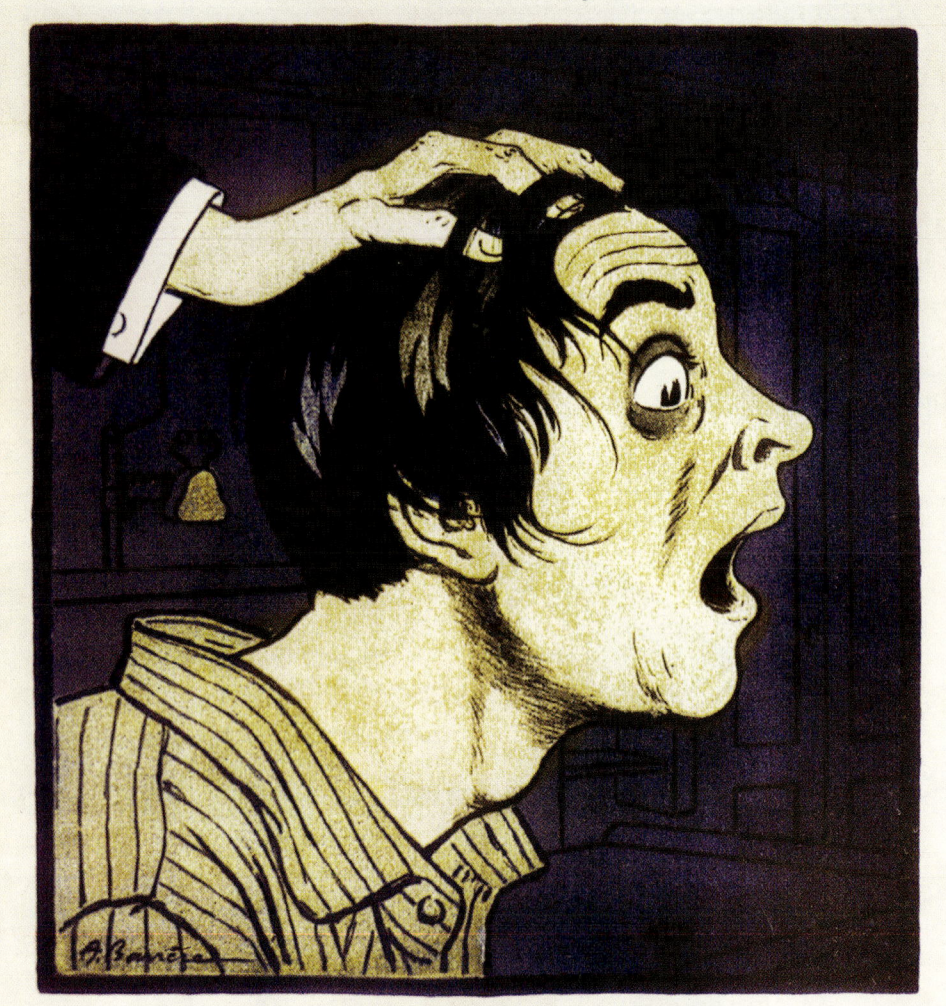

The Laboratory of Hallucinations, 1916

The Man Who Killed Death, 1928

The Embrace, 1925

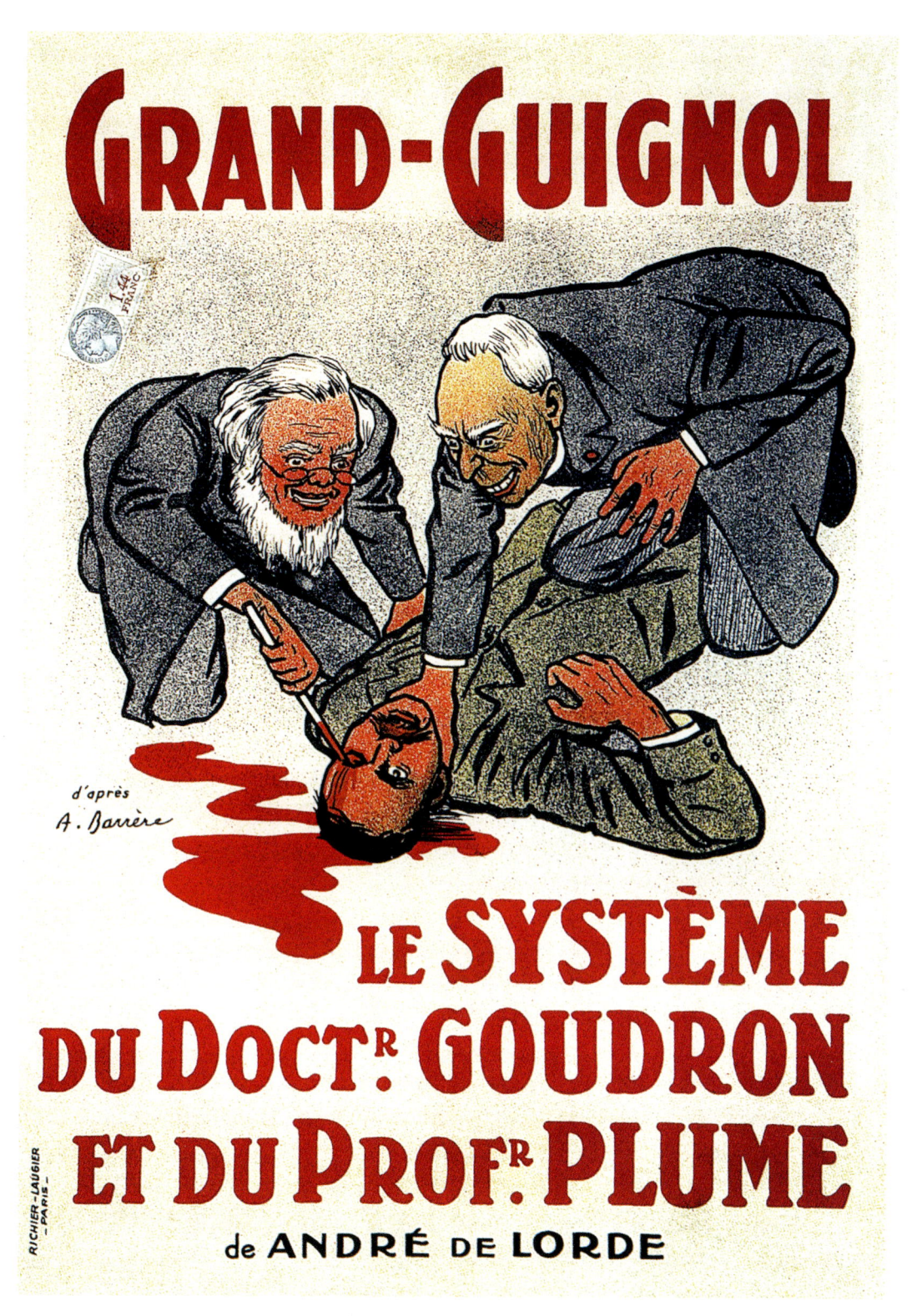

The System of Dr. Goudron and Prof. Plume, 1909

Photograph of a Grand Guignol prop table, 1957

Me, Napoleon, 1957

COMEDIES AND FARCES

BOURGEOIS MORALITY

LED BY THE NOSE, OR NOUNOUCHE

Henri Duvernois, 1919

A farce.

Benjamin is married to a thoroughly disagreeable wife, Bichette, who "leads him around by the nose." Rather than work for such an unpleasant mistress, their current servant quits. Bichette refuses to cook and Benjamin has to patronize cafes that he can ill afford. Benjamin's old nurse appears and is hired on as the new cook. The nurse bosses Benjamin around mercilessly, but places the house in order, and puts Bichette into her proper place.

AN AMBITIOUS MAN

Miguel Zamacois, 1906

A farce.

Georges, a struggling young doctor, begins his practice by unethically finding patients in the waiting room of an eminent doctor. All of Georges' remedies are ridiculous. A man who complains about a stomach disorder is told to remove his tie clip. Another whose rheumatism will not allow him to reach to the top of his closet is advised to lower his shelves. A wealthy widow who wishes to ask the doctor about the wisdom of remarrying becomes convinced to wed Georges. When the real doctor's valet comes into the waiting room, he asks for some medical advice from Georges, although he knows that he is a phony. Since the young doctor was about to pay the valet his agreed bribe, Georges merely deducts an amount from the valet's fee.

SCRUPLES

Octave Mirbeau, 1902

A comedy.

Late at night, a highly sophisticated thief and his assistant have broken into the house of a connoisseur of art. The victim discovers the thieves and calls the police. While they wait for the authorities, the thief praises the tastes of the owner and explains how an intelligent man like himself becomes a house thief. He had tried many other professions, including business and politics, and found that stealing was the most honest and gentlemanly. The victim becomes so taken with the thief's style and philosophy that he waves away the chief of police when he arrives and invites the thief and his valet to breakfast. Exiting, the thief declines, saying that, in his silk hat and dress suit, he is improperly attired for the morning meal.

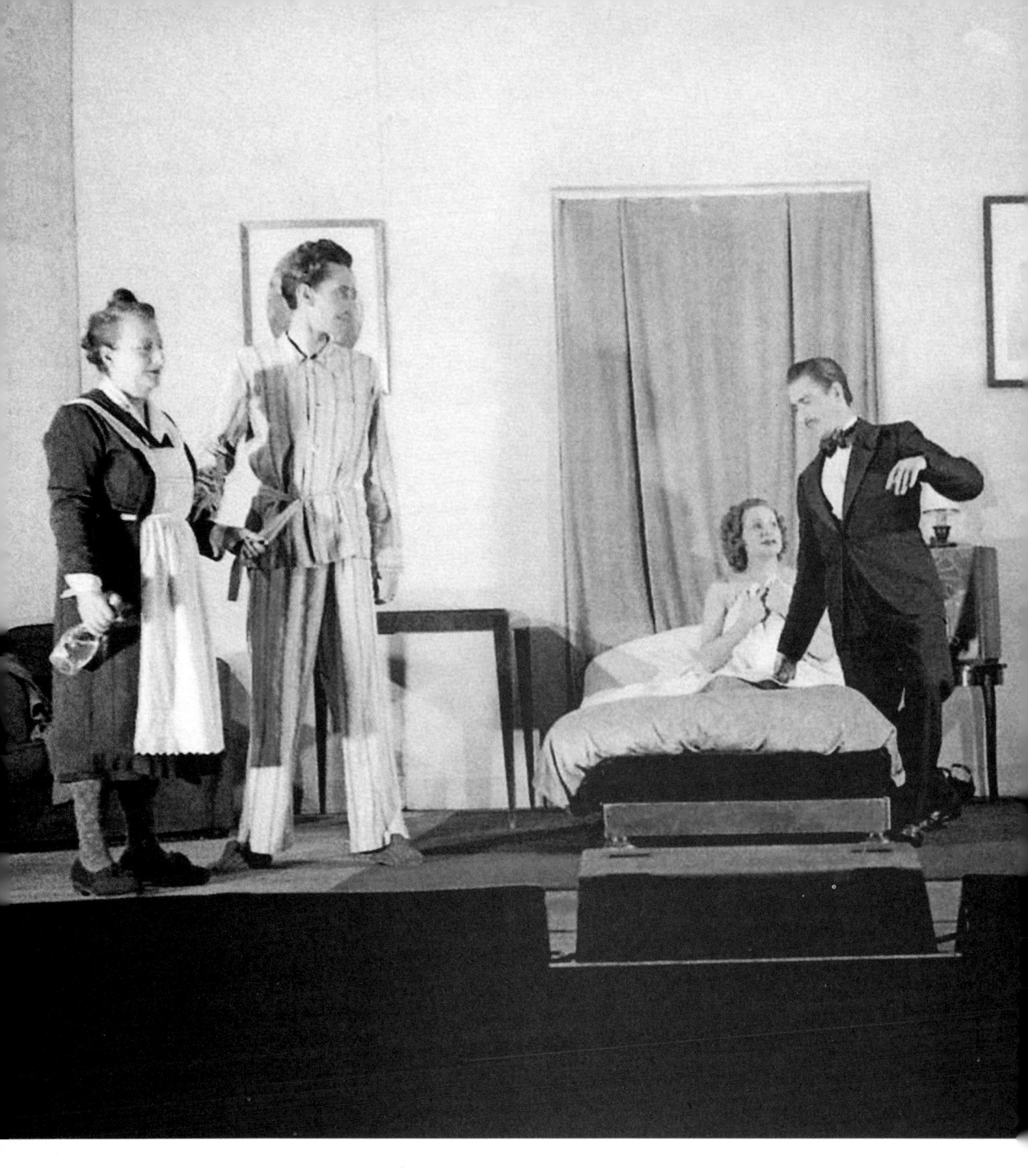

THE SERIOUS LITTLE MAID

Timmory and Manoussi, 1904

A farce with the additional theme of Prostitution.

An old provincial couple are looking for a maid servant. They read an advertisement in a Paris newspaper of an agency that provides girls. In response to their answer, the agency man brings a very pretty little prostitute. There is a misunderstanding when the woman of the house speaks to the girl, who inquires if the service in the house is hard. The woman, who is old and haggard, tells her they have so many guests in the house that she helps out with the service. The young prostitute is amazed.

The Star Role, 1921

THE CHAUFFEUR

Max Maurey, 1908

A classical Grand Guignol social farce about employers and modernity.

Monsieur Nock has purchased an expensive automobile but does not know how to drive it. Nock hires Alcime, a gardener, to be his chauffeur. Alcime, who does not know how to drive either, is supposed to pick up Monsieur Filfer, a prospective buyer. Terrified, Alcime declares that the car is not operative. Nock and his wife look under the automobile and Alcime hands them tools. A crooked mechanic comes and takes away the steering wheel. Finally, Filfer arrives angry that no one has come to meet him. Filfer decides to buy the automobile only with the condition that Alcime be his personal chauffeur.

THE RECOMMENDATION

Max Maurey, 1920

A farce.

A poor man calls on the Director of a Paris bank to ask for a job. He brings with him the usual letter of recommendation. An underclerk takes the letter but hides it in his own pocket. The confused applicant has to explain to the banker his quest of a job. The official asks for the letter of recommendation. The job-seeker does not know how to tell the Director that his underclerk has stolen it. But because the applicant is the first person to come to the Director without such a document, the banker shows keen delight and hires him for a high position.

Sauce for the Goose, 1921

AT THE COSY CORNER

Frederic Boutet, 1913

A farce.

Twenty years ago, the owner of a café outside Paris was murdered. Since then the owner's son has taken over and the cafe has prospered. Now the murderer has returned to the sight of his crime and confesses to the son. The son is distraught for two reasons: here he has discovered his father's murderer but also news of the crime will once again hurt his business. He makes a deal with the murderer.

SAUCE FOR THE GOOSE

Robert Dieudonné, 1921

A sex farce.

André Galoyer has been engaged for four years to Henriette. He is now preparing to confess that during this time he has already married someone else. When Henriette arrives, he is hardly able to get a word out before she confesses that she is now engaged to another man. André becomes furious and reproaches her for her outrageous behavior. André now claims that it is in order for him to marry another. For the life of him, the upset André cannot understand how Henriette would leave him for another man.

Take My Lady, 1922

ON THE BENCH

CHARLES HENRY HIRSCH, 1920

A popular curtain-raiser farce.

A young man from the provinces falls in love with a Parisian dressmaker. They rendezvous on a bench in the Luxembourg Gardens. The youth begs the girl to spend Sunday with him in the country—and not to worry about catching the last train home. An old man beside them overhears and asks why they do not marry. The girl is willing. The young man is unwilling since the dressmaker is not of his station in life. The old man tells them of a similar situation from his own youth, which ruined both his life and his sweetheart's. Reacting to the story, the dressmaker decides not to go to the Sunday outing and lose her virtue.

THE FOX

PIERRE WOLFF, 1925

A farce.

An ex-drama critic turns thief and is caught in the act of robbing a playwright. His charm and endearing melancholy win the playwright over. The thief uses flattery to capitalize on the moment. The mediocre playwright, delighted with the compliments of his plays, offers the critic a meal. Then, by acting out a scene of a work-in-progress—in which a father is sweet-talked into giving his son-in-law money—the foxy thief walks off with 1,000 francs.

Jealousy, 1923

I WANT YOU TO GO TO SLEEP
GEORGES FEYDEAU, 1940

A farce with the additional themes of Hypnosis and Vengeance.

The young master Boriquet has been hypnotized by his evil valet Justin into doing all the household work. Before Boriquet's fiancee, Emillienne, and her father, Doctor Valencourt, come to visit, Justin hypnotizes Boriquet into insulting them so his power can continue uninterrupted. Valencourt, however, suspects something and hypnotizes Justin into confessing. Boriquet's trance is broken and he is reunited with his Emillienne. Justin is punished by repeating endlessly that he is bad.

CUCKOLDRY

TICS
RENÉ BERTON, 1908

A sex farce.

A man confesses to his host, a doctor, that after intercourse he always suffers an embarrassing twitch. The doctor assures him many people develop such tics after making love. Afterwards the guest accompanies the doctor's wife into her bedroom, while the doctor "examines" the man's wife in his private office. The chauffeur and maid also go off together. When they reassemble in the living room, all struggle to conceal their nervous tics. At a loss, the doctor blames the maid and fires her.

A THIRD ACT
Serge Veber, 1921

A farce with the additional theme of Vengeance.

Two young authors are collaborating on a play. Robert is courting Marcel's wife, Madeleine, who feels Robert has much more talent than her husband. As she plays with great spirit a love scene that Robert is reading to her, Marcel enters the room to discuss the ending of the third act. Marcel wants a strong ending; Robert and Madeleine wish a happy ending. Marcel, quick to understand, leaves them alone and returns with a new scene, in which the deceived husband abandons his place to his rival. He plays the scene himself and goes out of the room leaving the lovers alone. Robert, with no desire to marry, finds himself alone with Madeleine and realizes what is ahead of him. He is now not so sure of a happy ending after all.

MADAME AURELIE
Yves Mirande, 1909

A sex farce with the additional theme of Bourgeois Morality.

Madame Aurelie, a bearded lady in the circus, is having an affair with an effeminate young man. Her husband, leading a police escort, rushes into the room to expose her deceit. As the naked Aurelie hides behind the window drapes, an appreciative audience gathers outside the hotel. Sensing an advertising coup, Aurelie's husband drops the charges and plans to integrate the unfortunate scene into a circus sketch.

TAKE MY LADY
Max Girard, 1922

A farce with the additional theme of Vengeance.

A man about town has just broken up with his lover. He awaits his next conquest, a married woman. But, instead of the woman, her husband appears in the room. The husband drones on, smoking and moralizing, as the anxious lover listens for the wife's arrival. Finally the husband beats the lover at checkers.

SEX FARCE

NIGHT ATTACK
André de Lorde
and M. Masson-Forestier, 1903

A farce in two acts with the additional theme of Cuckoldry.

A woman comes to a police station late at night, distraught that her lover has just had a heart attack in bed. She asks the police chief to help move the body before her husband returns from a business trip. Since she is pretty, he agrees and they return to her home.

At the house, they attempt to move the lifeless body but the man awakens. As soon as the policeman starts to care for the sick man, the telephone rings. It is the woman's husband calling to tell her that he will be arriving on a later train. With the approval of the woman, the officer attacks the ailing lover and drives him out of the house. The policeman takes the woman to bed.

A LITTLE MUSIC, 1923

THE SEDUCTRESS

ROBERT DIEUDONNÉ, 1914

A farce in eight scenes.

A woman invents stories of men pursuing her in order to incite her lover to jealous rage and action. The man's nephew is about to come to dinner. The woman tries to make her lover believe that this harmless and sexless relative is after her. To prove it to him, she convinces him to hide under the table when the nephew arrives. She practically forces the nephew to kiss her. The lover sees through her ploy, but when she accuses the unsuspecting delivery boy of attempted seduction, the lover finally pretends to be jealous and chases the boy out of the house. At last, she is content and begs her lover not to make such a fuss.

THE SHORT CIRCUIT

BENJAMIN RABIER AND EUGENE JOULLOT, 1916

A farce with the additional themes of Cuckoldry and Vengeance.

A star of the music hall, Nina de Coursac, has captivated the attentions of Prince d'Inertie. The prince asks his secretary to arrange an interview with the singer at her apartment. Unfortunately, Nina's lover Robert is arriving the same day, so Nina must get rid of him before the prince's interview. An electrician has been called to the apartment to repair a short circuit. There Robert bribes the electrician to impersonate the prince, while he disguises himself as the electrician. The fake prince seduces Nina so easily, that the lover and later the prince give up on her.

Alone, 1922

THE FLASK

Max Maurey, 1918

A farce.

Pierre's valet Louis gives his master, who is normally reserved and shy, a flask of a powerful aphrodisiac solution. Before Pierre can drink it, Lucette, the object of his seduction, arrives. Suddenly Pierre is called out of the room and the unsuspecting woman drinks the liquid, thinking it is a sedative. Pierre returns and frantically searches for the flask. Meanwhile Lucette has grown amorous and sexually aggressive. She cannot understand why Pierre is ignoring her for a missing bottle. Pierre then realizes what has happened and becomes horrified. Unsatisfied with his physical response to her, Lucette leaves, vowing never to return.

ALONE

Henri Duvernois, 1922

A two-act farce.

A charming and decadent poet, Eugene, tells a friend about Mme. Hellaf-Deleponte, a woman of the world who became infatuated with him and his poetry but whom he has not seen since their meeting six months ago.

Mme. Hellaf-Deleponte arrives when Eugene has stepped out of his studio. She hides in order to surprise him. Eugene returns and, thinking he is alone, acts accordingly, revealing innately gross behavior and the fraud beneath his poetry. Then, noticing Mme. Hellaf-Deleponte behind the curtains, he launches into an effusive apology. The woman, however, has suffered no offense or disillusionment. She knows an artist needs a great freedom of expression. As she is about to leave, Eugene asks her to stay and sleep with him. She takes off her hat in wordless assent.

THIS PAGE AND FOLLOWING: CAST MEMBERS OF THE GRAND GUIGNOL, 1947

TO KILL TIME

MAX MAUREY, 1923

A farce with the additional theme of Prostitution.

Two old ladies have opened up a "salon," or brothel, and advertised to attract clients. While waiting for guests to arrive, they sit and knit and read and drink. The bell rings. One exits to change, and the other woman greets the man at the door. He is gruff and obviously uncomfortable. The man demands to see the "women." The hostess offers him just one—her crony—who struts in dressed like a twenty-year-old, complete with wig and garish makeup. At first, he refuses her but lets himself be talked into taking her. After a brief conversation, they suddenly recognize each other: she was his nurse when he was a boy. He explains that he was merely killing time in order to appease his sick wife, who wants him out of the house, despite his desire to care for her. He entered only because it started to rain. The old nurse pats his hand and sends him on his way with admonishments to button up against the weather.

A NOT-SO-SERIOUS CLIENT

SERGE VEBER, 1923

A farce.

With a heist on his mind, a thief enters a jewelry store. He is so captivated with the beautiful eyes of the salesgirl behind the counter, however, that he forgets about his plan and buys her a piece of jewelry.

ONE HOUR OF LOVE

Charles Hellem and Pol d'Estoc, 1920

A comedy with the theme of Prostitution.

After a night out, a drunken man takes Flora, a prostitute, back to her room, promising to pay her two weeks of rent. As an aside, he tells the audience his plan to pay her with a counterfeit bill. He tells her that he only has one hour free before he returns home to his wife. Unfortunately, he has a habit of falling asleep right after sex. Flora promises to wake him in time, but before she can do more than loosen his clothes, the man falls asleep on her bed. While he sleeps, the landlady comes in and reminds Flora of her rent due. Flora has an idea. She wakes the man up, pretends that they have already made love, and compliments him strongly on his performance. He is so happy to be told that he is a great lover that he gives her 100 real francs and runs home to his wife. Flora exclaims that being a chaste liar pays better than being an honest whore.

THE SNOWS OF D'ANTAN

André Mouëzy-Eon, 1926

A two-act comedy.

An elderly bachelor and astronomer, Rozier-Perlot, receives a telephone call from his old schoolboy chum Sauveterre. Amazingly, Sauveterre challenges the astronomer to a duel. Forty years ago, it seems they secretly shared the same mistress and Sauveterre wants to settle that score. It was so long ago, however, that neither can even remember much about her.

Rozier-Perlot and his maid, Hermine, attempt to discourage Sauveterre's foolhardy idea. To calm down the old man, Hermine tells a story about the time in life when she had two lovers. The men realize that Hermine was their mistress in school. Sauveterre calls off the duel. Hermine assures each of them privately that he was her favorite lover.

SUFFERING OF THE INNOCENT

THE CORNFIELDS
Georges Courteline, 1898

A celebrated farce with the additional theme of Bourgeois Morality.

An elderly bachelor in New York City, Herring desires nothing so much as absolute peace and quiet. He enters the house of the Cornfields, who at a party had invited him to spend his winter evenings. The Cornfields, however, are not the pleasant and agreeable couple he thought they were. From the first, they argue about everything, with Herring always the innocent object of their fights. Each of the Cornfields grabs him and pulls him in the opposite direction. One after the other put so many pillows under his seat that the chair collapses. Fighting between themselves, the Cornfields inadvertently destroy his clothing, kick him in his wooden leg, throw soup in his face, shoot his artificial leg, set fire to their apartment, toss a bucket of water at him, and, as Herring exits, they invite him for a glass of champagne.

INTERVIEW

Octave Mirbeau, 1904

A farce.

A reporter invades a poor wine merchant's shop and submits him to a remorseless, crazed interview, inventing the most horrible and sensational stories around the man's half-uttered answers. Eventually, it becomes clear that the reporter has mistaken the merchant for a wife-killer with the same last name. Refusing to believe that he could have the wrong man, the reporter goes to great lengths to get the merchant to confess and divulge the horrid details of his lurid crime. The reporter finally exits in a tirade, leaving the shop in a shambles, and the innocent merchant a nervous wreck.

THE ROOM NEXT DOOR

Robert Dieudonné, 1911

A sex comedy.

After a long night of cards, Jules Toussaint, a traveling salesman, is about to collapse into his hotel bed. Suddenly, he hears a knock at the door. His neighbor in the adjoining room, Dodo, begs Jules to take in his female companion, Gisele, since Dodo's wife has followed him to the hotel. Reluctantly, Jules consents, especially since Gisele has taken sole possession of his bed. When Dodo and his wife leave, Jules sends Gisele into the next room. She immediately returns, however, because she is afraid to sleep alone. Finally, Jules decides to make love to Gisele, and as soon as the light is put out Dodo comes to claim the girl. After the ruckus that quickly erupts, a man from the card game enters to pay his debt to Jules. It turns out that he is Gisele's husband. The police are brought in and Jules, the accused, is asked to leave the hotel.

THE NEGLECTED

Max Maurey, 1928

A comedy.

A young man announces to his wife that he has been embezzling funds from his company and he cannot replace the money. Valiantly, she offers to sell her jewels to help replace the funds. Her diamonds, he tells her, are fakes. The concierge enters the rooms and tells them to be quiet. (It becomes apparent that they are rehearsing a play.) The couple begin to rehearse the scene again when it breaks into a real family argument. This time both the concierge and the landlord enter in a furious mood. Months shy of paying their rent, the young actors now fear that they will be thrown out of their apartment. But the landlord reassures them that he is just practicing being angry for throwing out the house guests that he is expecting next week.

THE CHEMIST

MAX MAUREY, 1910

A farce with the additional theme of Guilt.

A woman comes to the apothecary's to buy medicine for her sick child. The chemist by mistake gives her a poisonous potion. Discovering this when the woman has gone, the chemist is frightfully upset. He turns all his customers away, including a little girl who keeps reappearing. The chemist is in terror. Again, the girl, refusing to be driven out, returns and finally succeeds in making the distracted chemist listen. It is her little brother who is the sick child. The sister returns the vial, which the chemist forgot to fill.

THE BRONZE LADY AND THE CRYSTAL GENTLEMAN

HENRI DUVERNOIS, 1921

A popular farce in two acts with the additional themes of Helplessness, Imprisonment, Insanity and Play Transforming Into Terror.

Monsieur Sourcier, now retired, is married to a most unpleasant wife. To gain relief from her nagging, he pretends that he is insane and has himself locked up in a private sanatorium. Now he is free to paint and be happy. Sourcier pretends that he believes that on even-numbered days he is made of delicate crystal and may break at the slightest jar; on odd-numbered days, he is tinder. Either way, absolute quiet is mandatory or he will shatter.

His wife, however, visits him twice each week. Being lonely without his company, she decides that she will pretend that she is made of bronze, a Statue of Liberty, so she can be placed in the asylum near him. Realizing that he has been outwitted, Sourcier confesses his secret to the head of the sanatorium. The doctor now is certain that both Sourciers are truly mad and has them placed under permanent confinement.

DRAMATIC PLAYS

"CRASS" MANNERS

LITTLE BUGGER

Oscar Méténier, 1897

An ironic and humorous depiction of working-class life (rosse, or "crass" play) in two scenes, adapted from Méténier's short story. Also the themes of Cuckoldry, Parisian Low-life, and Vengeance.

In the backroom of a wine shop, Eugenia tells her lover Jean, a day laborer, that he has gotten her pregnant. Jean accepts the news gleefully and attempts to cheer her up, talking of raising the "little bugger." The whining Eugenia then confesses that years ago she has married a cabinet maker, Leon Grelu. Eugenia wants to leave the shop because Grelu has reappeared in her life; she just saw him in the wine shop. Jean explodes and decides to goad Grelu into violence so Eugenia will be granted a divorce. Eugenia agrees to the plot and leaves.

Jean invites Grelu into the room for the confrontation. Instead of fighting, Grelu, a freedom-loving anarchist, toasts to Jean's proposal and leaves. Alone in the room, Jean sits confused.

MEAT-TICKET

Oscar Méténier, 1897

Another rosse play in two scenes, adapted from Méténier's short story, with the additional themes of Parisian Low-life and Prostitution.

In the backroom of a wine shop, the Pichard family and a friend celebrate the communion of the Pichard's second daughter, Nini. The older Pichards bemoan that their first daughter, Louisa, gave them much trouble at Nini's age, running away from home. Eventually, she decided to settle down at Madame Trollon's brothel and get a "meat-ticket," a prostitute's card.

Suddenly the successful Louisa enters the room, to her family's delight. Louisa is encouraged to tell the story of her decision to become a whore: the parish priest told the Pichard children never to disobey the wishes of their parents, no matter what they are. Nini explains that she too will get her "meat-ticket" when she becomes of age. The mother Pichard concludes that even parish priests can have a good influence on the family.

MADEMOISELLE FIFI

Oscar Méténier, 1897

Produced over two thousand times, this adaptation from Guy de Maupassant's short story was one of the most popular plays of the Grand Guignol. A drama with the additional themes of Bourgeois Morality and Prostitution.

In a French provincial town during the Franco-Prussian war of 1870, German officers and French prostitutes engage in a wild party.

In a cheap Parisian hotel, a prostitute, Violette, and her madame are reading a story aloud from the newspaper. A brutal killer, Martinet, is on the loose. After robbing an old woman in her apartment, he murdered her in a grisly fashion, nearly severing her head from her body with a huge knife. While the two read a list of the items that Martinet has taken from the woman, a customer arrives for Violette. The madame departs. As the the man undresses and begins to take out the contents of his bag, Violette slowly realizes that her client is the sadistic Martinet. Eventually, with the assistance of her madame, Violette gets the murderer drunk and into bed. Meanwhile the police are notified and come to arrest Martinet.

THE MICROBE MERCHANT, OR THE GIRL WITH THE OVARIES

HENRY CÉARD AND H. DE WEINDEL, 1898

This was the first of offensive Grand Guignol dramas that truly shocked newspaper critics.

A well-meaning doctor sets himself up as a charlatan. One client comes to buy a poison to kill his father, and another man buys poison to kill his son. The charlatan sells them both harmless potions. Next a young woman arrives who has been told by a lover that she must have her ovaries removed for her to be "safe for love" and demands that he perform the operation. He refuses. The two clients return, complaining bitterly and threatening to inform the police of his quackery. The young woman realizes the doctor's good intentions, falls in love, and decides to marry him.

In the midst of the celebration, a prostitute, Rachel, stabs a young German officer with a dinner knife. As the blood pours from his chest, Rachel escapes, knocking over a candelabra. In the cast of strange shadows, the Germans quietly and ritually place their dying fellow officer on the champagne-laden table. It is an ironic moment. Suddenly, the once silent bells of the town church ring. The murderer Rachel is now a heroine. France has defeated Germany.

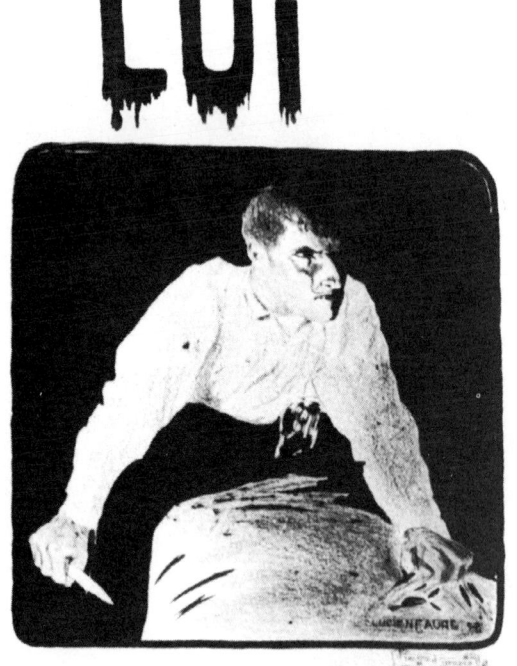

HIM

OSCAR MÉTÉNIER, 1897

An example of the early genre of dramatized news tabloid items that featured macabre or shocking stories (faits divers). A play with the additional theme of Prostitution.

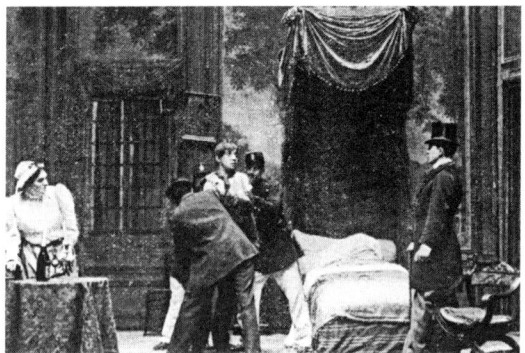

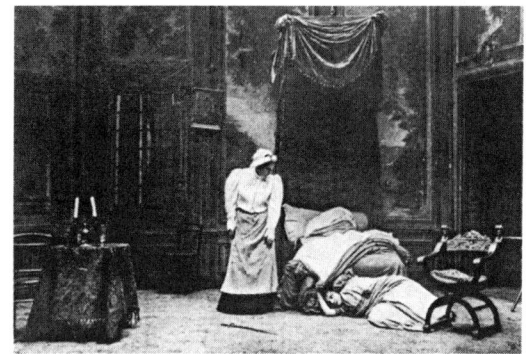

This page and opposite: *Him*, 1898

AN AFFAIR OF MORALS

CHARLES ESQUIER, 1902

A drama with the additional themes of Prostitution and Vengeance.

A highly-successful judge is having a private dinner party with two prostitutes. One of the women, whose lover has been sentenced by the judge, threatens to expose him. The judge suffers a fatal heart attack. The waiter brings in a doctor who has been carousing in the cafe below. The young doctor is aghast: the judge was his father. Since there is no backway, the only solution to avoid a scandal is to carry the dead judge out as if he were drunk. The waiter and doctor support him by his arms as the prostitutes hysterically sing the "Firemen's Anthem."

GUILT

THE WHITE MADNESS

HENRI-RENÉ LENORMAND, 1905

A two-act drama with the additional theme of Helplessness.

Marc and his fiancee are about to scale a difficult Alpine slope. They discuss what would happen if the other one fell from the mountain in the morning. Marc's fiancee says that she would cut the rope between them to save herself. Marc maintains the opposite: he would never sever the rope; he would rather die with her.

The next day they climb the mountain during a storm. On the hotel's terrace, Marc's parents nervously watch them through a telescope. Marc's fiancee slips and falls off the slope. He cuts the rope and lets her hurl through space. Then in remorse, Marc jumps off the slope into the "white madness."

UNDER THE RED LIGHT

MAURICE LEVEL AND ETIENNE REY, 1911

A drama in three acts with the additional theme of Insanity.

The mistress of Philippe Garnier, Therese Vaugeois, has died of influenza after only two days of sickness. A hurried medical examiner advises that she must be buried immediately to prevent the epidemic from spreading further. Garnier blames himself for her death since he allowed Vaugeois to go to the countryside where she contracted the disease. As a final memento, Garnier takes a photograph of his mistress' face.

After the funeral Garnier's friends, Suzanne and Didier, attempt to comfort him, but Garnier is inconsolable. He must see Vaugeois' face again. Using a photographer's red light, Garnier develops the negative that he took. In the photographic image, Vaugeois' eyes are open. The magnesium flash produced a living response in her. Insanely, Garnier shouts that Vaugeois was not dead.

At the cemetery, Vaugeois' corpse is exhumed before Didier and the medical examiner. Her face is bloody from a violent struggle to rip open the coffin. Evidently, Vaugeois awoke from a coma after the burial and died only a few hours ago. When Garnier enters the graveyard, Didier sobbingly tells his friend that his mistress was truly dead.

ON THE SLAB

ANDRÉ DE LORDE AND
GEORGES MONTIGNAC, 1923

A psychological drama with the additional themes of Insanity and Parisian Low-life.

A young *apache* is arrested for killing a soldier. He is taken to the Paris morgue, where he sees the soldier's body on a slab. Still he denies having committed the crime. Knowing the young criminal is an alcoholic, the detective Poirel locks him in the room with the covered cadaver and a bottle of whiskey. Once the *apache* has polished off the bottle, he begins to hallucinate that the body has moved. Immediately, the street tough attacks the corpse with the empty bottle, screaming, "This time, I'll really kill you!" Listening from outside the room, the police come in and arrest him.

THE RED INN

SERGE BASSET, 1934

A psychological drama with the additional theme of the Suffering of the Innocent.

A young French officer has been accused of murdering a traveling German salesman. The basis of the evidence against him has been supplied by a night watchman who saw the killing through a window. Just as the soldier is being led away to a firing squad, the watchman realizes that the military emblem on the condemned man's sleeve is of a different sort. Actually, one of the officers who helped the watchman convict the soldier is the murderer. The watchman attempts to inform the head of the firing squad. He is too late. The innocent soldier has been executed.

THE VISITOR

ANDRÉ DE LORDE
AND HENRI BAUCHE, 1916

A psychological drama with the additional theme of Bourgeois Morality.

Two women, the wife of a soldier and his secret mistress, await news of his safety. There is a strained atmosphere as each plays out her assigned social role. Finally, a strange woman arrives, who reveals the man's death on a battlefield.

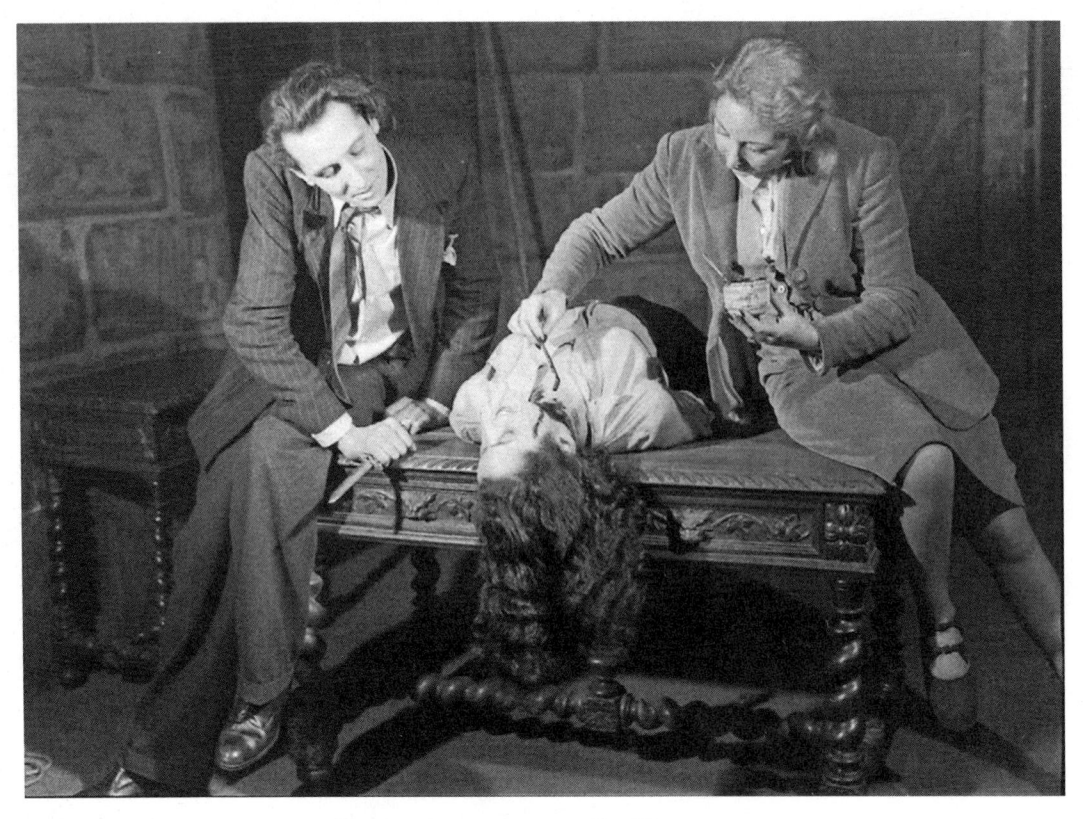

This page and opposite: The Hussy, 1947

INJUSTICE

THE WOMAN WHO WAS ACQUITTED

ANDRÉ DE LORDE, 1919

A drama with the additional themes of Bourgeois Morality and Hypnosis.

In his chamber after a trial, the Judge complains to his friend, the Doctor, about the jury's verdict. They have acquitted a governess who was a suspect in the strangulation murders of three children in three different families. The Judge believes that Madame Menard was guilty, but he has no proof. The Doctor urges the Judge to ask Madame Menard into his chamber. She is brought in almost against her will. Looking into her eyes and holding her wrists, the Doctor hypnotizes her. Although she will not answer any questions, Madame Menard hypnotically re-enacts the murder of the last child. Since hypnotism holds no sway in a French court and since the trial is over, Madame Menard is allowed to walk out into freedom, where the Judge predicts she will continue to strangle children.

THE SOUND OF THE GONG

JACK JOUVIN, 1931

A psychological drama with the additional themes of Bourgeois Morality and Guilt.

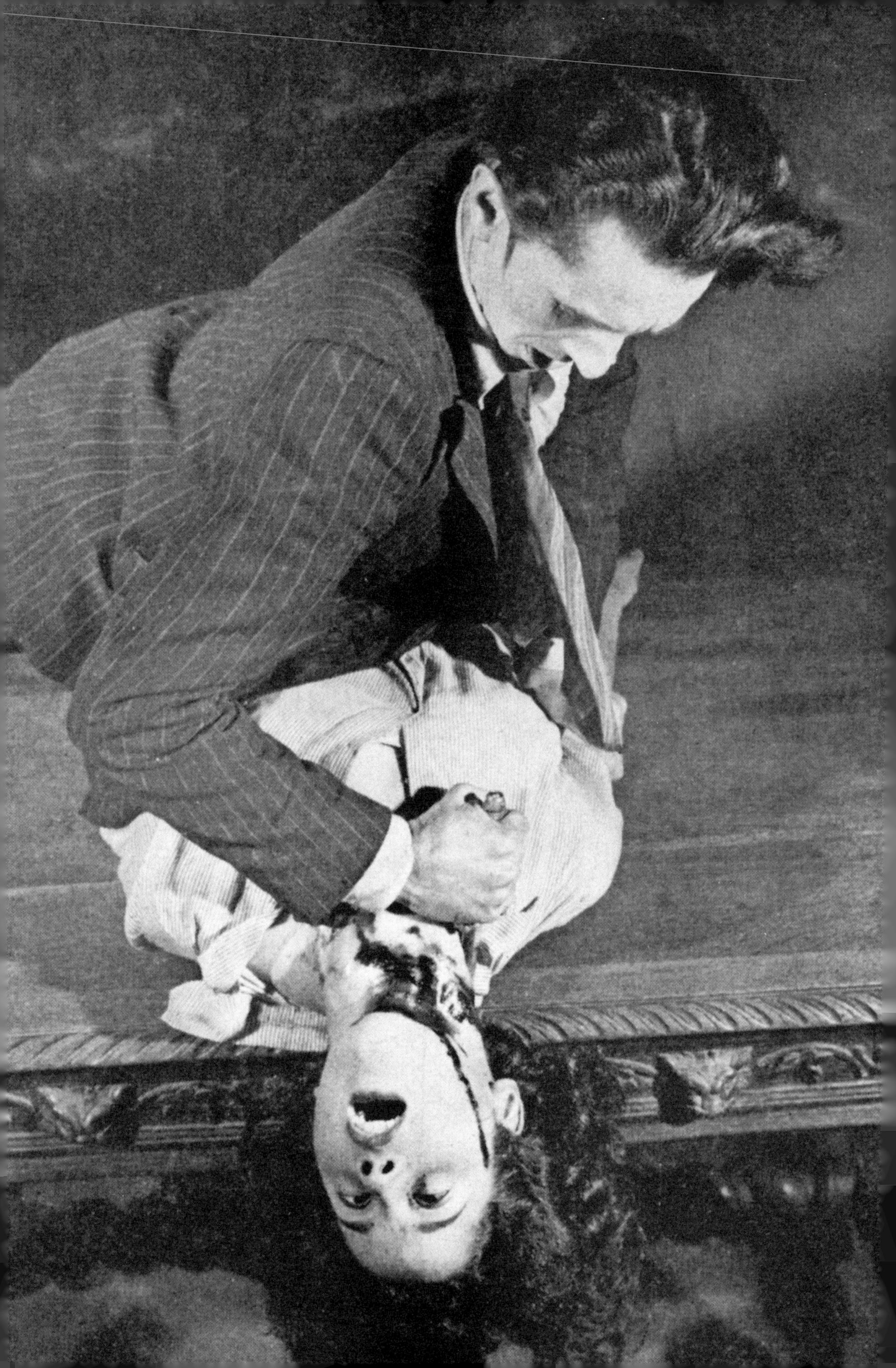

The Gangster's Return, 1949

The naive and innocent governess of a bourgeoise family returns to their household after spending a year in prison for neglect of duty. Answering her mistress' bell, she temporarily left the two children alone. During her absence the younger of the two children, a favored little girl, was found drowned in a reflecting pool. The governess' reappearance after the year of the drowning and trial causes Robert, the dead girl's brother, to confess that it was he, out of jealousy, who drowned his sister. The grandfather in the family, however, rejects the boy's confession and convinces him that it was all really an accident.

THE CATWALK

Robert Francheville, 1913

A drama with the additional themes of Bourgeois Morality and Imprisonment.

A prison guard is having an affair with a female convict. Thinking that someone is about to catch them and expose their illicit relationship, he takes out his gun and fatally shoots her. When the prison authorities rush in to investigate the gunplay, the guard maintains that he fired at the prisoner to prevent her escape. Satisfied with his explanation, they promise him an immediate promotion. ⚜

FEAR
IN
LITERATURE
BY ANDRÉ DE LORDE

NEITHER ACTOR nor director, André de Lorde was the dominant figure in the Grand Guignol's history. Dubbed the "Prince of Terror," de Lorde wrote many of its most popular plays, which he quickly anthologized together with important statements and analyses on the genre of theatrical horror. An intellectual and amateur scientist, de Lorde articulated and coyly justified the Grand Guignol's exploration into such taboo and artistically lowbrow subjects as insanity, incest, race hatred, murder, and bodily mutilation. Beginning with Dr. Goudron and Professor Plume *in 1903, de Lorde's dramas* were staples of the Grand Guignol's predilection for unexpected violence and sexual hysteria. In de Lorde's seemingly naturalistic world, madness was a human constant that had the power to overthrow any social contract at any time, be it bourgeois authority or familial bonding. De Lorde's plays achieved an enormous following in Paris and beyond because they reminded their audiences and readers that torturous thoughts and brute violence are always lurking behind the most innocent of relationships. Nothing in life is really certain.

AN ENTIRE LITERATURE of Fear exists.

Why should this be astonishing? Each one of us has in his innermost being a secret longing for violent emotions. At all times, in all parts of the globe, horror shows have drawn large audiences. The huge amphitheaters in Rome were too small to hold the citizens eager to see the gladiators slaughter one another and the Christians thrown to the lions. If the Inquisition had made public its interrogations conducted on the rack, they would have had to turn people away. To witness the hideous torture of Damiens, the crowd surged toward the square as though to holiday festivities.

"Bah!" you will say, "Times have changed; in our days, the progress of civilization has made such barbarous pastimes unthinkable." True enough. Still, set men, bulls, and horses at one another in an arena, and excited spectators will shriek with joy; at break of day guillotine some human wreck half-dead with fright, and there won't be enough soldiers, their bayonets fixed, to hold back the pushing throng of those who want to see. And don't those tender hearts, who are revolted by such spectacles, seek out at fairs the most violent and horrific "attractions"? Don't they derive acute pleasure at the circus or music hall from watching the most dangerous feats? If I perspire with anxiety as I follow the movements of the dancer along the tightrope, if my breathing stops with the music when this young person in pink tights is about to attempt what she herself calls the death leap, it is because

> *At all times, in all parts of the globe, horror shows have drawn large audiences.*

I actually imagine an atrocious death for her, her battered corpse bloodying the sand in the ring. No doubt, if I were sure that the accident was going to happen, I would be the first to rush forward to prevent it; but if, on the other hand, I was certain that it would not happen, I would lose interest in the show. A most curious compromise on the part of our consciences is at work here. If my sensibility steps forth to reproach me for the odious satisfaction that I find in thus anticipating a calamity, I immediately assuage these scruples by involving the law of probabilities. There is only one chance in a thousand that the accident will happen precisely today; but as soon as this reassuring thought runs the risk of dulling my pleasure, I revive it again by calling up in my mind's eye the image of the fall, despite what seems possible. I would not be as ferocious as that Englishman who went to every show of a wild animal act in order to be present when the lion tamer would get eaten; but, by going once quite by chance, I have the slight hope, without admitting it to myself, that today will be the day, more or less in the same way that I dream—without daring to believe it—that my lottery ticket will be the winning one....

Fear has always existed, and each century has stamped upon its literature the mark of the fears that tormented it, but the primitive caveman and the contemporary businessman have not shuddered for the same reasons. The sources of fear have varied, but not fear itself, which is eternal and immutable....

Feeble as they are, the Gothic novels had a real vogue; not only were Anne Radcliffe and Monk Lewis imitated by a host of minor writers, they also had the honor of inspiring two of England's greatest writers, Walter Scott and Lord Byron, to write many a picturesque descriptive passage. In France, *The Monk* and *The Mysteries of Udolpho*, translated in 1797, were read, appreciated, and plagiarized; the novelists, from Ducray-Duminil to Eugene Sue, went to them for stirring subjects for many, many years, and the playwrights along the Boulevard of Crime brought to the stage the principal episodes of these works.

As early as 1799, Guilbert de Pixérécourt, the father of melodrama, staged at the Ambigu his *Chateau des Appennins*, borrowed from Anne Radcliffe's novel, but where the horror is considerably attenuated. This astute dramatist knew how to turn a famous novel to good profit in the theater; he neglected no "effect" capable of moving or astounding the spectators: *Victor, Ou l'Enfant de la Foret, L'Homme a Trois Visages, Le Monastere Abandonne*, quite like *Le Chateau des Appennins*, are full of ingenious situations. In one of his plays, *Christophe Colomb, ou la decouverte de Nouveau Monde* (1814), whose action in part unfolds in the Antilles, Pixérécourt, on the look-out for novelties, was even convinced that he should, "for the sake of greater verisimilitude," have his savages speak the language of the Antilles taken from Father Breton's Caribbean dictionary. The results are not without savor, as witness this piece of dialogue between King Oranko and his subject Kavaka:

ORANKO:
> Cati louma.

KAVAKA:
> Amouliaca asackia Kereber

(Oranko hesitates).

ORANKO:
> Inolaki … Chicalama …

KAVAKA:
> Hava a moutou Koule Ouekelli.

ORANKO:
> Areskoui, azakia, kavaiti avou.

ALL:
> Anakilika!

KAVAKA:
> Ouallou hougousou!

And so it goes on and on… for whole scenes the actors carry on the dialogue in Caribbean….

The true genius of fear is, in actual fact, incarnated in Edgar Poe, and his work brings together all the seeds of terror that can blossom in the human soul: physical horrors, moral anxieties, painful apprehensions of the other world, and even this sensation previously unrecorded in literature, *the fear of being afraid*, that tortures the unfortunate Roderick Usher. The dominant trait of this exceptional talent is the conjunction of unbridled imagination and imperturbable logic, the fusion of nightmare and truth. In the midst of his most hallucinatory dreams, Poe always keeps one foot firmly planted in reality. In his work, macabre fantasy and meticulous precision conducive to verisimilitude become intertwined, overlap, and grow inseparable. There results from this union an impression of dread that no one else, not even Dante, has ever produced. As the reader enters into contact with Poe, a secret terror softly steals and glides into his soul, then takes possession of him, clasps him tightly, makes him shudder. The strongest nerves can offer no resistance; willy-nilly, we follow Poe into Hell, to which his art has been able to lend a semblance of life. First he rocks us on the waves of a raging sea, and then he suspends us on the edge of a bottomless abyss; vertigo seizes us, anguish makes our throat contract. "Panic-stricken" genius is the phrase that Barbey d'Aurevilly has used in speaking of Poe: no epithet could be more fitting….

> ***The true genius of fear is, in actual fact, incarnated in Edgar Poe, and his work brings together all the seeds of terror that can blossom in the human soul…***

Poe's literary influence has been immense. Strangely enough, it was felt in France before showing any signs in his native country. In the second half of the nineteenth century, while Charles Nodier, Gerard de Nerval, Theophile Gautier, and Erckmann-Chatrian continue the Hoffman tradition and write fantastic rather than terrifying works, we see the example of the American master inspire numerous disciples….

His influence can be seen on many writers, including some of the greatest: above all on Baudelaire, who translated almost all of Poe and who is indelibly marked by his work; there are many poems in his

Les Fleurs Du Mal where we catch reminiscences of Edgar Poe, and it can be asserted that without him, Baudelaire would not have realized all his capabilities.

Poe's mark is no less visible on Barbey d'Aurevilly and Villiers de l'Isle-Adam. Both read Poe (Barbey even devoted some magnificent pages to him), both have been subject to his authority; but *Les Diaboliques* and *Contes Cruèls* are very far removed from Poe's *Tales of the Grotesque and Arabesque*. That is because Barbey and especially Villiers are unrepentant romantics. They can only conceive fear with a stately train of situations and antithesis in the style of Victor Hugo; the veiled figures, the funeral processions, the cloistered leper in Villiers' *Duke of Portland* are scarcely more believable than the coffins in Hugo's *Lucrece Borgia* or the drowned bodies in Dumas pere's *Tour de Nesle*. All of this literary satanism is hardly frightening; it has the musty smell of old bric-a-brac and the property room.

Much more realistic in their sober precision, Merimee's novellas achieve effects of terror that strike you with unexpected rapidity like a gypsy girl's dagger. *Colombia, Lokis,* and *La Venus d'Ille* surpass by far in emotional intensity the best of the *Contes Cruels*. The true spiritual heir of Edgar Poe is incontestably Marcel Schwob—with the difference that separates talent from genius. Strange affinities exist between these two spirits: the same sarcastic and terrifying imagination is characteristic of each of them; they both possess the same "meditative facility" which Poe bestows upon Egaeus in the tale "Bernice." The painful anxiety of the one, and the Jewish sensibility of the other, reach by different routes the same goal. There is in Schwob's *Sur les Dentes* a ferocious irony that closely resembles Poe's "Loss of Breath" or "The Man Who Was Used Up," and *L'Homme Voile* equals in phlegmatic horror "The Cask of Amontillado."....

Writers could not simply go on imitating Poe indefinitely, still less could they outdo him. They were obliged to renew the genre. This is what has been attempted by the creators of the scientific-marvelous, a rich source of terror and delight. The progress of the sciences, the quasi-fabulous discoveries of the past thirty years, and the publicity given to research accomplished by inventors have contributed to arousing our minds to new objects of curiosity. Science has gone from the laboratory to the novel.

Jules Verne confined himself to considering as accomplished certain discoveries that already exist to all intents and purposes. Wells, Rosny the elder, and Maurice Renard go much further still: they are not concerned with what will be, but with what could be, and, boldly wielding the hypothesis, they venture out into vast expanses of the unknown. Here, it should be observed, there is no question of the supernatural, which for science does not exist. At most, they propose for our scrutiny facts susceptible to a dual interpretation, the one miraculous, the other rational (Wells' *Pollock and the Porroh Man* and Maurice Renard's *be Singe*); the true domain of these storytellers remains the uncertain and the not-yet-known. That is how Wells imagines perilous journeys through time; that is how Rosny supposes the intrusion onto our planet of one of those invisible worlds that fill the emptiness of infinite space; that is how Maurice Renard makes us perceive the diabolical experiments conducted by Dr. Alexis Carrel. Pure imagination? No, certainly not, since such tales offer us, as applied to the study of imaginary phenomena or of monsters, the most rigorous methods of investigation. We find in Wells the study pursued with perfect logic—except in one point—of what would happen if a man succeeded in making himself invisible by the discoloration of his blood. Thus these authors create new subjects of terror, which are addressed less to the nerves than to the understanding, and which answer our desire for truth while at the same time giving sustenance to the need for shudders which is a part of our nature. ⚜

—*Translated by Daniel Gerould from* La Revue Mondiale *(March 15, 1927)*

GRAND GUIGNOL THEATRE OF FEAR AND HORROR

I AM THE MADDEST

MAXA
Fantastic beyond belief are the roles Maxa plays on the stage, but macabre as they are they cannot match her private life. Haunted by her grisly roles, tormented by memories of violent love affairs, torn by strange tortures, her life has become a nightmare in which only pain is real.

WOMAN IN THE WORLD

by Maxa

STAR OF THE GRAND GUIGNOL

STAGE LOVE
In the first act alone is Maxa permitted romantic love roles. After that her stage lover develops sadistic tendencies, brings down the curtain in a finale of horrible torture and bloodshed.

THEY witnessed the last spasms of life in her nude tortured body. There was tense silence as hundreds of eyes looked on that grim spectacle. The wound in the left breast had stopped bleeding. The quivering limbs grew still. Slowly death took possession of the beautiful form. Dark spots began to appear around the eyes, the throat. Greenish shadows etched themselves on the lower part of the body. Slowly the corpse turned black....

With consumate skill, Maxa, the Princess of Blood, had died again. Nightly, season after season, Maxa died a thousand deaths for the patrons who haunt the weird theatre known to Parisians as the Grand Guignol. The title "Princess of Blood" is not an idle misnomer. In all her ghastly roles, Maxa is exposed, violated, tortured. Paris has given her still another title—"Priestess of Sin and Horror."

Maxa calls herself the "maddest woman in the world." It is her strange destiny to carry into her private life the same horrors and tragedies she must portray in the Grand Guignol. Just as unseen lights discolor her undraped body on the stage, painting it livid, then green, then yellow, so do wierd influences of her roles discolor her life, casting bizarre shadows over a haunted, tragic existence. For Maxa is no ordinary tragedienne. It is not enough that she die dramatically. She must die in torment, tortured beyond endurance that her sensation-craving audience be provoked to bizarre desires, their sadistic instincts whipped to furies of perversion. And when her fellow actors have removed their makeup and gone their ways for the night, living counterparts of their roles step into Maxa's life and carry her on to anguish that is real.

Her story deserves to be told with unbiased frankness. It might be a warning to all parents. Science will find in it many points of interest. The perversions exposed in this story often can be found in apparently normal people in the form of inhibitions and repressions. A better knowledge of the hidden manifestations of sex would avoid so many tragedies caused by demented criminals. Maxa's story tells of these barbaric atavisms and bestial perversions, of sex torture and blood lust.

Here is the story as Maxa, Princess of Blood, tells it herself.

I WAS born in ordinary surroundings. My parents were well-off, but by no means were they to be considered "modern" parents at all. I guess they hardly knew what "modern" meant.

We lived in the famous Montmartre quarter of Paris. But don't get the wrong idea when I say Montmartre. It is true that this part of Paris is the district of night-life and vice. The beat of street-walkers and drug-peddlers where tourists

15

GRAND GUIGNOL   THEATRE OF FEAR AND HORROR

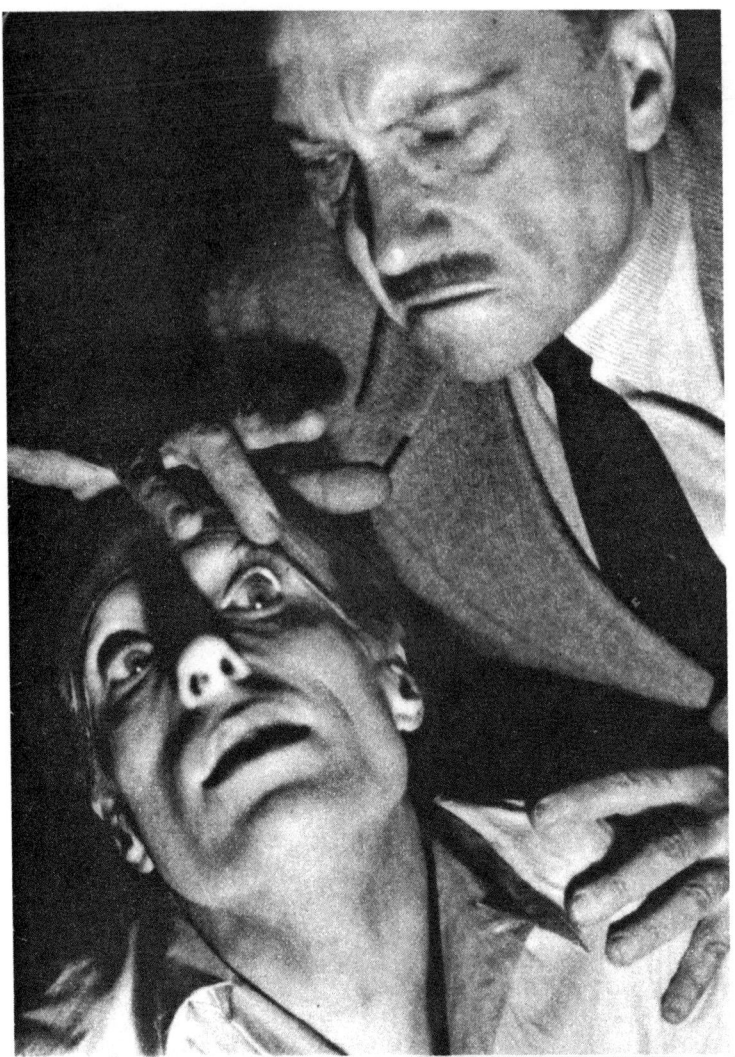

are accosted by 14-year-old girls selling obscene photographs—especially tourists of Anglo-Saxon appearance, because everyone in Paris believes that all traveling Americans and Englishmen are millionaires. This wicked part of Paris, however, has provincial and unexciting corners where hard-working middle-class people lead a quiet and sound life.

At the highest point of Montmartre glimmer the white towers of the Church of the Blessed Heart. With the faint pink of each new dawn, candles are lighted on the altar, and the pure toll of the tower bell calls the people to prayer. The peaceful little church is a symbol of the life I led as a child in this neighborhood of orgies and commercialized vice...

My mother was a school-teacher. She gave me all the care a loving mother could give her child. I learned perfect manners and foreign languages, and took piano lessons. I revealed an early talent for music and dreamed of becoming a famous concert pianist.

I was a premature child. At the age of 12, I had the figure of a grown-up girl. I was tall and slender, well-shaped, and had graceful legs and large expressive eyes.

Across the street from my parent's home stood an office building. The young men working there noticed me quickly. They made signs or wrote huge invitations on large pieces of card-board. I was only a child then, despite my mature figure, and hardly understood what they wanted from me. I knew nothing of rides out to moon-lit lovers' lanes and of necking-parties. I still liked to play with dolls, of which I had several beautiful ones. I kissed and adored them naively, and behaved like all little girls in which the first impulse of the loving and child-bearing woman manifests itself in childish play.

A year later I began to change and other interests developed. I no longer liked to play with my dolls. I enjoyed the company of young boys much more.

ACT MACABRE
No comedy rears its head in the Grand Guignol theater of Paris, only gruesome tragedy. Above, Maxa submits to examination in a weird drama involving leprosy, mad doctors and tainted gold.

PRELUDE TO MURDER
Starred for years in the Grand Guignol, Maxa has drawn a strange following from the ranks of Parisian cultists. In this scene she commits a gruesome murder under the spell of a hypnotist.

16

I was sometimes subject to strange feelings.

My favorite playmate at that time was a boy three years older than I. Whenever my parents left home, I invited him indoors. Then we played a game that we used to call "Doctor and Patient." He was the "doctor" and I the "patient." The "doctor" knocked on the door and I answered in a faint voice.

Then he began "treating" me. He took my pulse, felt my body, pinched me with tweezers from mother's dressing-table, stuck me with needles and put hot-water bags on my stomach. He did everything he could think of to give me pain.... I resisted a little, but secretly I felt a strange satisfaction in the physical agony. Childish play of sickness and helplessness turned into an early sex-aberration. It was the first sign of the curse that should mark my life later on with hideous tragedy.

When I was 15 years old I still wore childish clothes as most girls in Europe do. About that time I met John, a tall handsome boy of 17, who liked to punch and fight, and play truant with me. He was an excellent musician. For hours I listened to his piano playing, exuberant with rhythm and joy.

Because we were such close companions his parents asked my mother to let me go with them on a vacation. She gave us her permission and we left for the country where we spent delicious days. Only city children can enjoy country life as we did. Lingering for hours in the woods, we listened to the murmur of the brook, chased butterflies and picked berries. In the evening we came home, arms enlaced, tired, sleepy and ready for bed.

A few days before the vacation finished, I went with John on a long hike to the mountains. We were allowed to stay over night in a scout camp. Night fell before we arrived at our destination. We became fearful as the long shadows of the mountains descended and the night closed in. We clutched each other closely like the frightened children in the fairy tale. But we didn't get discouraged. Finally, after a two hour search we found the camp.

When we left early the next morning, only the first glow of the new day was rising above the mountain peaks. The guide of the camp took a lamp and went with us a short way. He was a handsome fellow with strong features and a tanned skin that looked golden in the flickering light of his lantern. When I looked at his almost stripped body, I was overcome by a strange feeling of excitement I had never known before. I couldn't explain it. I was frightened. I think I must have looked silly and up-set. The young guide noticed my emotion. I saw a slight smile on his face. Meanwhile we had reached our trail. The guide said goodbye and walked away briskly. I was alone with John. It was a chilly morning. But an inner fire was burning me. I felt drawn to John. I leaned against him and put my arms around his shoulders....

All that happened then will stay in my memory for ever.

While we walked, holding each other closely, I felt John becoming strangely agitated. His hands trembled. Perspiration broke out on his forehead. He pressed his body against mine. I had no clear consciousness of what was happening. When I looked at his face I was terrified. I wanted to scream for help. But he put his hand brutally over my mouth. He stared at me with a bestial expression. I had never seen such an insane look on a human face. He tore my clothes off and threw me on the ground. I cried for help and struggled desperately. My resistance aroused him to new furies. He choked and hit me viciously to beat me into unconsciousness. The sight of blood on my exposed body destroyed what he had left of self-control. I saw a blade flashing through the air. He struck blindly. Three times he slashed my throat. I fainted....

When I came to I was lying in a hospital bed. The injuries were serious. I had lost much blood. But my life was not in danger. I asked for John. I didn't want him to be punished for his crime. I feared for him. The nurse hushed me.

"You mustn't talk," she said, "John is all right."

A few days later I was told he had shot himself. He thought he had killed me.

THAT was my first "romantic" experience. Love became violence, desire turned into blood lust, and boyish foolishness led to suicide. My first lover had been a sex criminal....

This experience marked me forever. Sex torture, violence, physical pain became a sinister destiny I never could escape. Later on I had to endure perverse brutality so often that I got used to it and liked it. The time came when I couldn't live without love torture and longed for it in morbid desire if I didn't get it. Blood lust followed me as a curse. I attracted all sorts of cranks and madmen. Even in my stage career I felt this curse. From the beginning I was given roles of victimized women. It is no wonder that most of my fan mail dealt with murder, sadism and fiendish perversions. The men who were drawn to me followed a tragic course. They became insane, killed in lust and killed themselves.

I believe my parents are to blame that I followed this road. They didn't want to know that even a child's soul may be an abyss of unconscious passion and pre-

TRAGEDY
"But he is dead, madame. They killed him before my eyes, like this!" It was parts such as this that deepened Maxa's morbid outlook, caused her to lose faith in happiness.

SCANDAL
Opium is the motivating force in this bizarre drama of passion in the Parisian underworld. The role is not strange to Maxa who has seen the curse of drugs on herself.

mature morbidness. Had they been less hypocritical they probably would have warded off the tragic events that marked me.

I FELT early the strange power I had over men, and even over degenerate women. I think sometimes those poor witches burned at the stake during the Middle Ages had the same sex fascination. I didn't however, use this power delibately. It was a part of myself that unleashed hidden impulses in many men and women who approached me. They ceased to be civilized, conventional and normal people. They turned to perversion. Their nights were filled with black and scarlet dreams. They conceived love in deathly embraces. It was my bad luck that love never was for me a romantic longing. Virginal dreams had been chased when the first man forced me to do his will, stabbed me in blood thirst and, fearing punishment, killed himself.

AT THE age of sixteen I married the French Count C——. He gave me all the luxuries wealth could offer. He loved me deeply. I should have been very happy if I had been capable of enjoying normal happiness. Home life soon tired me. The theater began to interest me and I longed to become an actress. The inevitable happened. After several months of married life I left my husband and went on the stage.

My first contract was with the Grand Guignol in Paris. It is probably the strangest show house in the world. All plays presented there deal with torture, murder, madness, rape and suicide. They are given with unrivaled realism.

I was already familiar with the Grand Guignol since I had seen several plays there before. I remember especially an adaptation of Stevenson's Suicide Club. The story is known. The members of the Club gamble for life or death with cards. The loser has to kill himself. But this time the "low man" is a coward. When it comes to his last minute, he gets panicky. He tries to run away. The exits are all locked. He beats the doors furiously and shrieks in deathly fear. The laws of the Suicide Club, however, are inexorable. Steps are heard. . . It is the killer of the Club. The steps are coming nearer and nearer . . . Frantic, the looser whips out his gun and shoots himself.

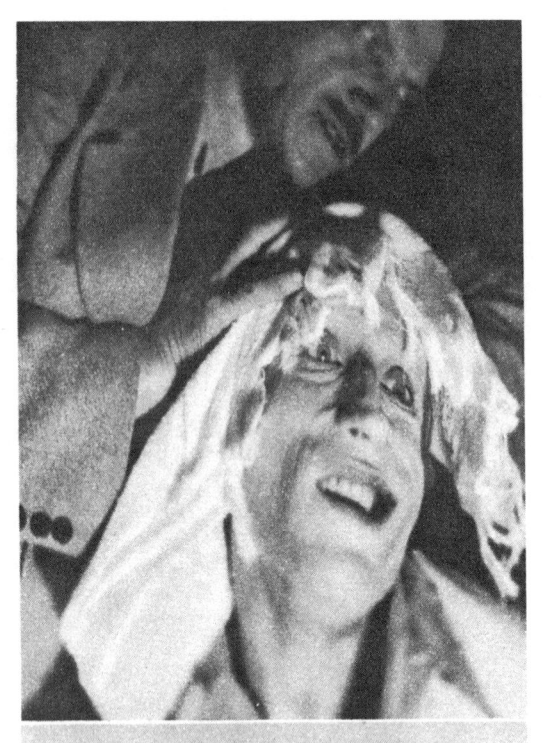

HIGHLIGHTS AND SHADOWS
Ghastly lights that cause bodies to turn black, dark shadows that partially conceal menacing action, weird red and greens that seem to make living flesh decompose, these are a few of the artifices resorted to by the Grand Guignol. Lights impart half the horror in the picture of Maxa above, clarify action in picture of her below.

MELODRAMA
Scarcely an act goes by without violence, torture, or murder. Strangers to the theater have been known to faint before the end of the first scene. Veterans cannot get too many gruesome details.

REAL-LIFE IN THE UNREAL
Although this picture of Maxa is a still from a stage production, her own life was filled with bitter parallels of the scene from which it is taken. Emotional abnormalities have haunted her since childhood.

This is the sort of play shown at the Grand Guignol. They are given with such realism that the nerves even of the most resistent spectators break under the strain.

The Grand Guignol is situated in a dark, narrow street of Paris. No one would suspect a theater in such a sordid, dingy neighborhood. It lies at the end of a roughly cobbled court. In earlier centuries the building sheltered a monastery. The vaulted church-like ceiling with the iron chandeliers hanging from the beams are still to be seen. The interior is of old oak carved with rare angel figures. Costly tapestry covers the walls. The atmosphere is severe and fear-inspiring.

My throat was parched and my pulses tingled with excitement the first time I went to this theater. My husband accompanied me. Strangely, the horrors on the stage didn't crush and frighten me as they did other people. The exhibitions of cruelty and perversion made me almost happy. It was the first time I felt clearly my relationship to physical torture.

My first assignment under the contract to the Grand Guignol was to understudy a player in the Laboratory of Hallucinations. I had to take part in two gruesome operations. In the first one my jealous surgeon-husband pushed long needles into the skull of my lover to drive him insane. He became subject to macabre visions, imagining himself wandering nightly in a cemetery amidst half-rotten corpses emerging from their graves. He avenged himself by tying his torturer to the operating table and crushing his head with murderous hammer strokes.

My morbid passion for unusual excitement found thorough satisfaction in this play. Soon I had an opportunity to take over the role when the actress I understudied became ill. It was an unexpectedly great success. The dramatic critics of Paris put my name in headlines. The public was raving about my performance. My realistic acting won me the title "Princess of Blood." They didn't know how close they came to the truth.

In all my following roles I had to shriek in torture, wade in blood, disembowel people and descend to the profoundest depths of madness.

Little by little, these half insane roles affected me like a potent drug. The famous Italian playwright, Pirandello, wrote a play in which the actors identify themselves in the end with the personalities they portray. I, too, became a victim of fiction. I began to live my roles. My former life seemed to be only an illusion, a mask, an error... My roles became my real life. I now was a true creature of horror, a woman whom degenerates and cranks dream of violating and torturing, and whom all sane people avoid as obscene and dreadful.

But the strangest of all, I was not exactly morbid by nature. My constitution is sound. I like the feeling of physical strength and fitness, am able to enjoy the beauty of an early summer morning. It is only in my emotional life that I am poisoned, corrupted, condemned.

SINCE the first day I stood on the stage of the Grand Guignol I have died thousands of violent deaths in every imaginable manner. There isn't a spot on my body that hadn't been exposed in spasms of torture and trembled in weird paroxisms. I had been shot, burned, poisoned, flogged in the nude, bitten by snakes, dismembered on a butcher's table, strangled, left bleeding to death—all at the whim of the playwrights.

I probably received more insane, weird, and abject letters than any other actress in the world. In my private life dopefiends, sadists, flagellants, homosexuals hang around me. I met some good souls too, however, who wanted to save me from the vicious hallucinations that had become my very existence.

I remember one of these "saviors" especially, Marcel...

At the time I knew him I was playing in the *Marquis de Sade*, a melodrama full of the customary horrors. The actor taking the part of the perverted French nobleman forced me to crouch on all fours and to lick his hands like a dog. He chained me in irons and slashed my breasts; in the end he locked me in his house to drive me insane. In a fit of madness I strangled his daughter who shrieked and moaned horribly in her death struggle.

One must be pretty much insane not to find such a series of atrocities simply ridiculous. But—there are many people insane to that extent. I, myself, found great pleasure in the horrors as long as I was on the stage.

Marcel was unhappy to see me pursuing such a career. But he loved me so much that he tried to put up with it.

One evening before we left for the theater I conceived a satanic idea. I told Marcel to get several thousand francs in bills. I managed to arrive earlier than usual.

"Put the bills on the seats all over the house!" I told him.

He did it reluctantly, thinking it was a quite unnecessary publicity stunt. I asked him to join me on the stage as soon as he finished.

We stood behind the peep-hole and watched the arrival of the spectators.

The first to come grabbed the bills, turned them around skeptically and couldn't believe that they were genuine. Then a woman cried excitedly:

"But they're real ones!"

A wild rush followed. The smartly dressed audience scrambled, pushed and jumped over the seats to collect the notes. They fought on their hands and knees, tore the bills away from each other... Women lost their hand-bags and jewels in the brawl. Fists flailed and clothes were torn off in the free-for-all of the bill-hunting. Dignified gentlemen in tails and white ties knocked each other around, kicked women and twisted their wrists to make them release the money... The bejeweled ladies of Paris' society were [*Continued on page* 99]

GRAND GUIGNOL   THEATRE OF FEAR AND HORROR

true   **I Am the Maddest Woman in the World**
[*Continued from page* 19]

not showing any more restraint than their escorts, as they bit and scratched and screamed... The refined, sophisticated and always well-mannered public of Paris was unleashed. It showed its true face: that of a beast. Most of us have such a second face, I think. The face of a beast.

We were standing behind the curtain to watch the savage spectacle. The shameless exhibition of human depravity gave me extreme satisfaction. I glanced at Marcel, my good angel, my zealous savior. His features were distorted. Perspiration ran down his face, his breath was heavy.

He was intoxicated by the sight. I had made another victim. Now he was watching the progress of the muddle with feverish eyes. He felt the same sadistic pleasure I felt.

When the uproar quieted down and the performance started, the audience was still in a feverish mood. Applause and booing rose for no particular reason. The horror scenes on the stage provoked a reaction that any physician would call pathological. I was so overwrought that in the scene in which the Marquis de Sade tortures my breasts I knew an intense voluptuousness impossible to describe.

The rest of the evening Marcel was entirely changed. He sat silent and brooding in my dressing-room. He made me fearful, but at the same time curious and expectant.

When we came home, he forced me to lie down on the couch. His face had a dreadful expression. In a coarse, choked voice he said:

"You are a perverted girl... I'm going to punish you for your sins."

He flogged me unmercifully Using his belt, he brought out huge welts on my soft skin.

"Well, my darling, my little pigeon... It isn't a pleasant feeling now... You don't play a role any more... Sing, my dear, sing!... Cry, weep... weep my sweet, my dear little sweet!..."

Thus talking in a gasping voice, he struck me again and again, this time with the buckle. Soon my whole body was an agonized, bleeding mass.

The intense pain drove me frantic. Purple flames danced before my eyes. Then everything went black. I heard faintly a strange, unrecognizable voice whispering into my ear:

"I'm good to you, darling... my darling pigeon... This purifies your soul and chases other temptations... Weep my sweet, weep.... I love your tears, my little vampire... Suffer, you will become a saint... You're so beautiful when you writhe in suffering... I love you, my little demon..." Psychologists will recognize in this the rapture of a flagellant.

The next day I left Paris to escape
[*Continued on page* 106]

99

I Am the Maddest Woman in the World
[Continued from page 99]

Marcel. Later I learned he was sent to a sanitarium for nervous disorders.

I went to the country for some time. My nerves were shattered. In the peace of a little village I could think over my last adventure calmly. The tortures I had suffered had been frightful, but again I had found sensual satisfaction.

In the beginning of my country exile I went daily to the little village church. I took long walks in lonely lanes and tried to cast off all thoughts of my former life. I wanted to start anew. A month went by calmly. One day I met the schoolteacher of the village. He was young and handsome, and when he talked to me, I felt my old sinister passions arising. It was as if evil forces would drive me to corrupt and destroy this nice chap. I wanted to prove to myself again that I had unlimited, ruthless power over men. Another victim, more and more victims!... What did it matter?

I asked the young man to come over. When he arrived I was dressed in a flimsy negligee. I leaned back on the couch as I had been taught to do on the stage. In his eyes the fire of lust was lighted... He got up suddenly. He scared me. He came nearer and nearer. Frightened, I tried to ward him off, but I had carried my power too far. He threw himself against me and assaulted me. In lustful cruelty he hammered my face and body with his fists.

I shouted for help. A servant saved me from the hands of this maniac who a short while ago had been a calm and timid young man. I had played with fire and been burned. But I liked it. I knew then I would find no peace in that village, or any village.

My next play at the Grand Guignol was the *Garden of Tortures*. In it I had to portray a sadistic female who avenges herself by scientifically contaminating her rival with leprosy. In another scene I had to find sensual satisfaction in gazing upon chained slaves dying from hunger. At the end my lover burned my eyes out with a red-hot iron.

The public acclaimed this as a sensational rôle. None of the perverted sentiments, however, I had to act out on the stage were strange to me. Not even the sensation of being burned... I had become an easy victim for maniacs who liked to scorch the soft white flesh of women with glowing cigarettes.

I LIVED only a few blocks away from the Grand Guignol and usually walked home alone after the performance. The streets I had to pass through were dark and tortuous.

I was always afraid of the walk home. The fever of my performance still burned within me. I was frightened by the passersby and was suspicious of everything and everybody. Nightmares gripped me, and I had visions of all the roles I had played in the last few years. I saw the insane asylum set again where they inoculated me with the virus of hydrophobia; the coffin in which I was buried alive, the sinister frame of the blood-smeared guillotine on which my head fell, the laboratory in which sex-crazed maniacs tortured me scientifically... I lived all over again these imaginary horrors when I walked through the dim, shadow-strewn streets. That I had a new admirer was no appeasement of the situation.

Maurice was a successful businessman from Paris. He was in love with me. He begged me continually to marry him. But I only laughed at him. In a few weeks he spent a fortune on me.

It wasn't long before he was poisoned by my own morbidness. He transformed my apartment into a death chapel. Walls and ceiling were covered with black velvet which made a striking background for the blood-red furniture. Huge candles in massive candelabras shed an eerie light. In the house I wore rough clothes, cut like monk's frocks.

For reasons I never understood clearly Maurice was arrested one day. I suppose he hadn't been cautious enough in his calculations and had spent more money in satisfying our costly whims than he could afford. I sold my jewels to pay a lawyer. We chose a prominent member of the bar in Paris. This lawyer was a cold, intelligent and distinguished fellow, husband of a charming woman. From my first interview with him I felt he might become another victim. I didn't want to be unfaithful to Maurice who was languishing in a dank French jail. But finally the temptation proved stronger than my scruples. My charm worked fast and thoroughly. The lawyer fell in love with me.

DURING this time I received many heartrending letters from Maurice. He complained about postponements in the trial, but hoped he could soon prove his innocence and be released.

"Why is the lawyer so slow?" he asked several times in his letters.

My position was rather complicated. As much as I had fought against it, I had fallen in love with the lawyer. When I asked him to hurry the case he answered evasively. I tried vainly to cool his passion, but coldness had only the opposite effect. Even when his wife found out about our affair and made countless scenes, he didn't let anything interfere with our hours of passion.

The letters from Maurice became more urgent and alarming every day. One night when the lawyer was in my dressing-room at the theater the door was suddenly flung open. Maurice, whom I believed in jail, stormed in. His face was distorted by rage. He roared at me and smashed everything in sight. He called me a bum and a tramp and lots of other names. He slapped me and threw things at me. The lawyer hid like a coward behind my wardrobe. I put up a despairing resistance. Maurice grasped my throat and dug his fingers into my flesh. I lost my breath and fainted. Stage hands rescued me. Maurice never saw me again after that, but in my wild, turbid dreams I saw him often.

My suspicions about the many postponements of his trial were confirmed. The lawyer had double-crossed us both for love of me. Another lawyer whom Maurice had hired secretly, obtained a quick release.

One night some friends came to see me at the theater. A stranger I had never seen before accompanied them. He was a tall, dark and very attractive man. His eyes had a strange, immobile expression. There was a mysterious air about him, an inexplicable vagueness and aloofness that allured and intrigued me from the minute we met. I let him see my interest for him. But he remained cool and very indifferent.

When he left he said abruptly:

"I'll call for you tomorrow night after the show."

Before I had time to answer he was gone. I had no desire to escape this meeting. I was very much attracted by him. Maybe I was hypnotized by his strange green eyes which made me dream of secret pleasures and new sensations.

I shouldn't be disappointed!

HE CALLED for me the next night. We drove to his house. On the way we spoke very little. I was fearful and tense. When we arrived at his luxurious home he said in an emotionless voice:

"Get undressed!"

He pointed to the door of another room and added:

"You'll find Chinese gowns and pajamas there.... Put on whatever you like."

I didn't answer. I obeyed as a slave obeys his master. When I came back, wrapped in a perfumed Oriental gown, he lay on the couch.

A sweet odor filled the room.

My pulse was beating furiously. What was going to happen? I had terrible apprehensions.

A little brass lamp was burning on the couch beside him. He held a long oddly formed pipe over the flame. Little sizzling noises were heard and spirals of bluish smoke rose from the pipe as he started to smoke... His face was marked with happiness. He stared with fixed eyes which were lost in a strange dream-world...

"Smoke," he said and handed me the pipe.

I began to smoke opium and new horizons of dangerous happiness opened before me.

More and more phantoms of death haunt me. I invent new tortures, suffer deeper pains than my distorted imagination has ever dared picture. Life becomes a dance of shadows. Between my roles on the stage, and the opium-scented hallucinations that follow me to my room, my life has ceased to exist. The boundaries between dream and reality have vanished gradually. I know I'm a lost soul. My warped nature has made me the maddest and most sinful woman in the world.

A famous fortune-teller told me once I would die a violent death. She might be right. I would deserve such an end. I always killed people—in my own way, of course. I toyed with horror and torment. I drove my lovers mad. They became criminals or killed themselves. It was always my fault. Only in unspeakable tortures could I find real happiness. Fiends often tried to kill me. Some day one will succeed. Death will be my last love affair....

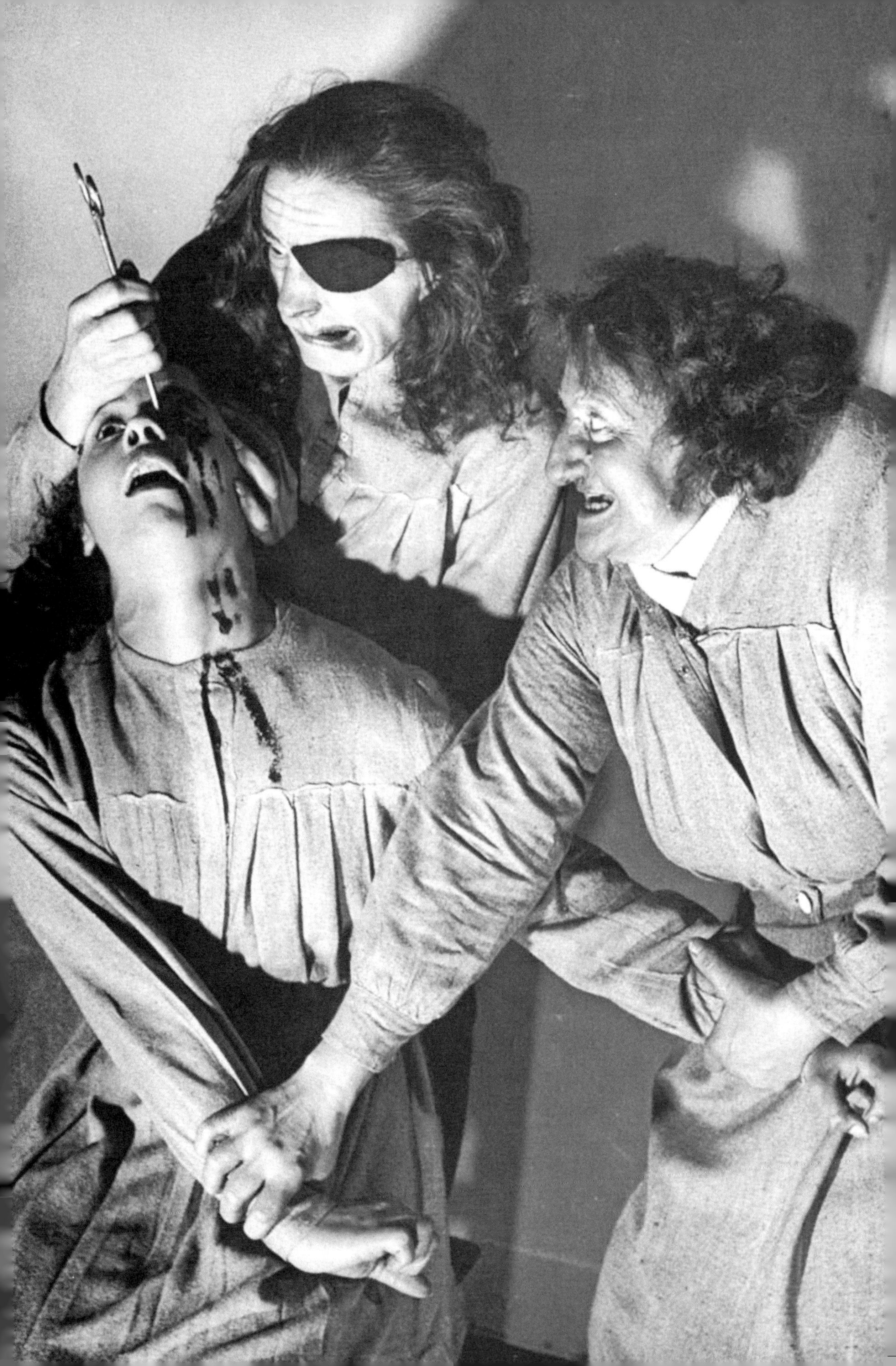

A CRIME
IN THE
MADHOUSE
OR
THE DIABOLICAL ONES

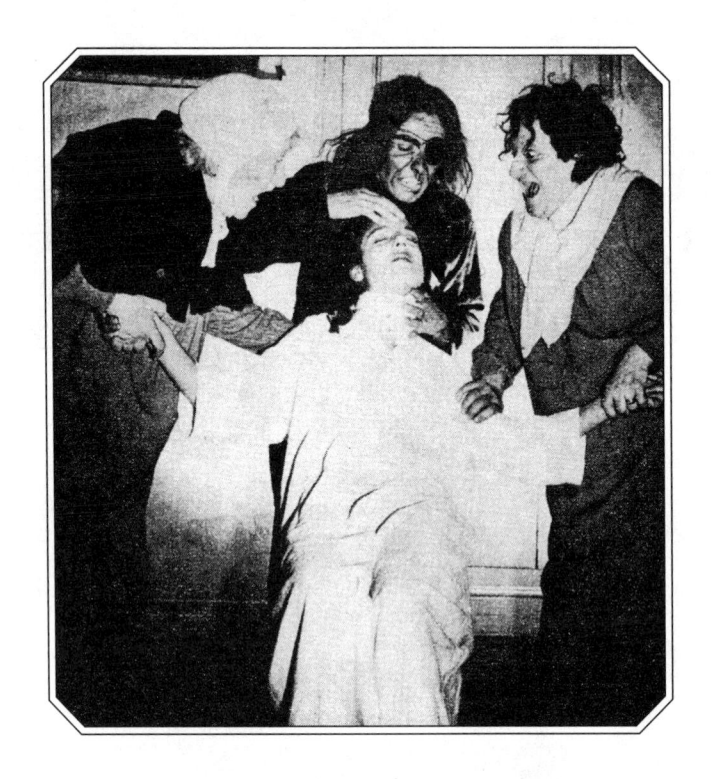

A CRIME IN THE MADHOUSE
OR
THE DIABOLICAL ONES

A Drama in Two Acts

BY ANDRÉ DE LORDE AND ALFRED BINET (1925)
TRANSLATED FROM THE FRENCH BY ANDRÉ GISIGER
WITH ADDITIONAL STAGE DIRECTIONS FROM THE ORIGINAL PRODUCTION.

CHARACTERS:

The Sister
Madame Robin
The Normandy Woman
Hunchback
Louise
The Doctor
The Intern, Lebrun
One-Eye
Second Sister, Sister Agnes

(The play unfolds in a small room of a madhouse in Saint-Léger in Normandy. The asylum walls are whitewashed with doors on each side. A window faces the left side and a black crucifix sits on a wall shelf. There are three beds, each with a small table on the side. A cast-iron stove stands between the second and the third beds.)

ACT I

(When the curtain rises, the Sister, sitting in one corner, prays with her rosary. A bell chimes in the distance.)

(Madame Robin enters from left.)

MADAME ROBIN:
Sister!
THE SISTER:
(Finishing her prayer) One moment!
MADAME ROBIN:
(Mysteriously) Excuse me, Sister! Please excuse me! I didn't know you were busy.
THE SISTER:
(Puts down her rosary and makes the sign of the Cross.) Well, what is the matter?
MADAME ROBIN:
The doctor told me that he'll be here shortly with the intern.
THE SISTER:
Good. Thank you. Is the dinner meal finished already?
MADAME ROBIN:
No, Sister, but I wasn't very hungry tonight. I left before the others.
THE SISTER:
(Putting on her glasses) Then pass me my knitting box. Over there, on the shelf.
MADAME ROBIN:
Yes, Sister. *(Hands her the box.)* I am going to prepare the beds and evening lamp.
THE SISTER:
Remember to put everything back in its place, so things aren't scattered about!
MADAME ROBIN:
(Arranges the beds.) You don't have to tell me that. No one is more organized than me. Ever since I was given a private room, I spend most of my time putting things in order. That is my pleasure. And I have been here quite a long time. Là là!
THE SISTER:
(Walking around) How long have you been in this asylum?
MADAME ROBIN:
Forty years. *(Thinks.)* Forty years! That was the time of Doctor Delbec. He died. His intern's name was Monsieur Bernier. He died, too. And then, there was also a Sister, Sister Félicité. She died. Everybody is dead. How very funny!

(She fixes the bed lamp and gets the evening materials from the wall shelf.)

THE SISTER:
Why do you stay here when you are cured? Have you no family?

MADAME ROBIN:
    Oh, yes, Sister! Just, you know, when one has been in the asylum for so long, it is difficult to get used to the outside world. Family look strangely at you. They fear that your sickness will return. When people know that you've come from the madhouse, you are treated as if you are contaminated. Therefore, one is quite happy to return to Saint-Léger. If only to die.

    (At that moment, distant cries of anguish are heard.)

THE SISTER:
    What was that?

MADAME ROBIN:
    (Looks through the window.) Nothing. It's that Marie with her episodes! *(Takes back her thought.)* If I were that girl…

THE SISTER:
    What girl?

MADAME ROBIN:
    (Points to the bed by the window.) Well, the girl who sleeps there, little Louise. She has more fortune than I have had. She's young! She can still achieve happiness. Sister, when she is completely cured, can she return home?

THE SISTER:
    (Disinterested) That's what people say.

MADAME ROBIN:
    You know, Sister, her family are good people. I know them from the countryside.

THE SISTER:
    (Contemptuously as she places the box on the table) Puhh! They raised their daughter in strange ways.

MADAME ROBIN:
    Ah!

THE SISTER:
    She's a child who knows nothing.

MADAME ROBIN:
    Yet she knows how to read.

THE SISTER:
    She knows how to read, but she doesn't know her prayers. I even question if she believes in God!

MADAME ROBIN:
    Don't be angry at her, Sister. It's not her fault that her parents have raised her … *au naturel.*

THE SISTER:
    Not believing in God, you call that *au naturel!*

MADAME ROBIN:
    Sister, there are certain things you don't know outside of Mother Superior's teachings!

THE SISTER:
    Stubborn as a mule! And she already has the soul of the madwoman! Twenty times I begged her to go to the chapel. But no such luck! When she leaves here, she shall behave like a good Catholic, that little nothing! And if she doesn't… People without religion are merely beasts of the field!

(A bell rings.)

MADAME ROBIN:
(Looks through the window.) Ah! Now it's the end of the meal. I must go. There are faces I would not like to see here.

THE SISTER:
Of whom do you speak?

MADAME ROBIN:
(Pointing at the two beds) The two dirty mad ones who sleep here: Hunchback and the Normandy Woman. What bitches!

THE SISTER:
That does it! Listen, Madame Robin!

MADAME ROBIN:
Excuse me, Sister. Excuse me! It slipped out. The thought was stronger than me.

THE SISTER:
What do you have against them? They are two poor crazed women.

MADAME ROBIN:
Two dangerous crones. Malicious madwomen.

THE SISTER:
I have never noticed anything like that. With me, they are obedient and gentle.

MADAME ROBIN:
In front of you, Sister. Crazy people are like everybody else. There are bad ones, mean ones, and ones who concoct evil plots. One has to be on one's guard always with them! Where do they come from, those two witches?

THE SISTER:
I don't know.

MADAME ROBIN:
I heard that each one went mad from grief, after losing a daughter. Is that true?

THE SISTER:
Yes.

MADAME ROBIN:
Well, nowadays they can't even look at a young girl without becoming envious, without having the urge to hurt her. As if they are reliving an episode!

THE SISTER:
Whom do they wish to hurt?

MADAME ROBIN:
(Pointing at a bed) Her!

THE SISTER:
Little Louise?

MADAME ROBIN:
Yes. While cleaning the rooms I have realized certain things. In the next room, the old woman who has just one eye, you know the one who sleeps behind the door there?

THE SISTER:
Ah, yes! One-Eye!

MADAME ROBIN:
You can't maintain, Sister, that she is a good Catholic! She was condemned to die for having murdered children. They have even given her a nickname: the Ogress!

THE SISTER:
> She is a poor demented woman. The doctors already declared her legally insane. And the courts acquitted her of any criminal responsibility!

MADAME ROBIN:
> In any case, accused murderers should never be incarcerated with mad people. They have to be placed in separate asylums. Otherwise, there are unfortunate possibilities!

THE SISTER:
> The woman has been paralyzed for six years. For six years she has not moved from her bed. There's nothing to fret about.

MADAME ROBIN:
> You claim!

THE SISTER:
> How anxious you are! Nobody's in danger here. The asylum is well guarded. There are ten Sisters alone for the women's wing.

MADAME ROBIN:
> Yes, during the day. But at night, the patients are alone.

THE SISTER:
> That is the regimen.

MADAME ROBIN:
> I understand. It's not your fault. You have enough work during the day so you need to rest during the night.

THE SISTER:
> At night we pray. We pray for you.

MADAME ROBIN:
> Nevertheless, there are asylums where they do nightly rounds. But not here.

THE SISTER:
> Nothing bad has ever happened here.

MADAME ROBIN:
> It needs to occur only once!

(Shuffling can be heard from the left and right. The insane are returning to their rooms.)

THE SISTER:
> Would you stay here for a moment to watch the patients, Madame Robin? I will inform Sister Placide about the Mass tonight.

MADAME ROBIN:
> What Mass?

THE SISTER:
> Sister Sulpice died this morning. The whole Order will hold a wake for the body, tonight in the chapel. *(She exits left.)*

MADAME ROBIN:
> *(Alone)* Poor Sister Sulpice! She was the one good Sister.

(From the right, the Normandy Woman and the Hunchback enter. They are two small old malicious-looking women, with diabolic expressions on their faces.)

MADAME ROBIN:
> Ah, here they come there, the crones!

NORMANDY WOMAN:
(Looks around.) Psst. She isn't here yet!
HUNCHBACK:
(In a low voice) She has to pass through the courtyard.
NORMANDY WOMAN:
Right. Then we have to go see One-Eye.
HUNCHBACK:
She's waiting for us.
NORMANDY WOMAN:
She's in charge.
HUNCHBACK:
And when she screams …
NORMANDY WOMAN:
That's the sign of death!
MADAME ROBIN:
What are you mumbling about? *(The Normandy Woman laughs.)* Why are you laughing?
NORMANDY WOMAN:
Are you the Bastard of Chambourcy?
HUNCHBACK:
He gave a bribe to the caretaker of the cemetery. The porter told him: "It is closed from nine o'clock at night until eight o'clock in the morning. By the grave of my mother." Amen.
NORMANDY WOMAN:
Amen.

(Both of them make the sign of the Cross.)

MADAME ROBIN:
(Lifts her shoulders and laughs.) They are completely mad! There are times when they make you giddy even though you don't feel like it!
NORMANDY WOMAN:
(Crosses to Louise's bed and turns to Hunchback.) Here. Look!
HUNCHBACK:
The head over here.
NORMANDY WOMAN:
The feet over there.
HUNCHBACK:
Ha! Ha!
NORMANDY WOMAN:
Ha! Ha!
MADAME ROBIN:
Are you done yet? Go to sleep! That would be healthier still for the two of you. What do you have against that girl? What has she done to you?
NORMANDY WOMAN:
There are some things one cannot talk about. Do you understand?
HUNCHBACK:
And if one talks about them, that person is cursed!
MADAME ROBIN:
Yes. That's right! So, listen: if you continue to frighten her with your gestures, to make

her miserable.... I saw the other day how you tried to trip her. I may tell the doctor about that! Perhaps he will put the restraining jacket on you again. *(To the Normandy Woman)* Like the other night!

NORMANDY WOMAN:

(Frightened) Ah! Shut up! Shut up, stupid wench! *(She exits left.)*

HUNCHBACK:

(Following her) Toad! Slimy toad!

MADAME ROBIN:

(To herself) Nothing else makes them afraid. Now where did they go? *(She looks through the open door.)* There! They went to One-Eye's bed. What could they be talking about, the three of them? They're looking at me. And what evil eyes they have! They even make me afraid, the nasty crones. *(She slams the left door as Louise enters from the right.)* I refuse to sleep in this wing!

(Louise, an eighteen-year-old girl, pretty, with blonde hair; but timid and sickly-looking, enters.)

LOUISE:

(Happy) Ah! Good evening, Madame Robin. I am delighted to see you. Why are you still here?

MADAME ROBIN:

I'm waiting for the Sister. She's returning soon. Good evening, my darling. How are you?

LOUISE:

Fine!

MADAME ROBIN:

It's fitting that you depart from here ... that you leave soon.

LOUISE:

It is over, Madame Robin! I am finally cured.

MADAME ROBIN:

But are you happy?

LOUISE:

Oh! Yes. There is no one I am going to miss when I leave here except for you. You were so nice to me!

MADAME ROBIN:

The feeling is mutual! It was the least I could do. You are so gentle, so good-hearted! Every time you received something from the outside, you always shared it with me.

LOUISE:

It's so tedious, the asylum. One has to share the little bits of pleasure.

(She looks around.)

MADAME ROBIN:

What are you looking for?

LOUISE:

They haven't returned yet?

MADAME ROBIN:

Yes, they're over there, on the other side, with One-Eye.

LOUISE:
Ah!

MADAME ROBIN:
I don't know what they're up to. They are always conspiring.

LOUISE:
Yes. Listen, Madame Robin, I need to confess to you. Those three women there, they frighten me every time I go near them. When they look at me, they stare strangely. Especially One-Eye. I get the chills. What do they want from me?

MADAME ROBIN:
Nothing. They are sick people. Don't pay them any attention.

LOUISE:
I try, Madame Robin. But I just don't feel safe with them!

MADAME ROBIN:
If it bothers you so much, why haven't you spoken to the Sister about it?

LOUISE:
She doesn't listen to me. We don't have a good "rapport."

MADAME ROBIN:
Then make your good rapport with God. That's what I say. Go see the doctor. You can tell him about it. He's a fine man!

LOUISE:
Yes, but I don't dare to. I have only—

MADAME ROBIN:
(Hearing noise) Quiet! The Sister!

(Both are silent.)

THE SISTER:
(Entering from left, she sees Louise.) Ah, it's you! I have been informed that the doctor has decided to release you prematurely.

LOUISE:
Yes, Sister. I believe …

THE SISTER:
He has to make a new examination.

LOUISE:
Sister …

THE SISTER:
Yesterday was Sunday. But you were not at the chapel. Why was that? *(Silence)* There is no reason now, is there? I met the Monsignor and he asked me: "Sister, in the entire asylum there is only one patient who has never taken confession. She is on your wing!" Do you think that I was pleased to hear this reprimand?

LOUISE:
No, Sister.

THE SISTER:
You have been very sick. Twice you nearly died.

LOUISE:
That's true.

THE SISTER:

Suppose your illness reoccurs and you have finally lost the power to recuperate. Then Death will surely appear, knocking at your door to take you with him, and you'll be terrified. You'll wish you had confessed. But then it will be too late, my little pagan!

LOUISE:

My God!

MADAME ROBIN:

(In low voice to Louise) Look, agree with her! You know, the Sister means well. That's her job. *(Loudly)* So, until tomorrow, good night, my little one. You're not going to be here for a very long time. Everything will go by quickly. Good night, Sister.

THE SISTER:

Good night.

(The bell for the dead rings in the distance.)

MADAME ROBIN:

(As she exits right) Listen how that rings! That poor Sister Sulpice!

LOUISE:

(Shuddering when hearing the bells) Those bells! So frightening!

(The doctor enters from left with the intern.)

THE DOCTOR:

What is the bell for the dead all about? Did somebody die?

THE SISTER:

Yes, Doctor. Sister Sulpice, this morning, at eleven o'clock, during the Saint's Mass. The entire Order sat at her deathbed.

THE DOCTOR:

(Ironically) And the sick, during that time, what happened to them? Who took care of them?

THE SISTER:

We weren't absent very long!

THE DOCTOR:

I hope not. And here, anything new?

THE SISTER:

No, Doctor. Everything is quiet ... as usual.

THE DOCTOR:

No fever, no eruptions, no convulsions?

THE SISTER:

Nothing at all.

THE DOCTOR:

Okay, wonderful. *(To the intern)* Are you coming, Lebrun?

They prepare to leave.

LOUISE:

Sister!

THE SISTER:

What do you want?

LOUISE:
> I would like to talk to the doctor!

THE SISTER:
> The doctor has no time.

THE DOCTOR:
> *(Returning)* But yes, Sister, but yes. Do you have something you want to ask me, my child?

LOUISE:
> Yes, doctor. Oh, yes.

THE INTERN:
> *(Aside to the doctor)* She is pretty, that little one.

THE DOCTOR:
> Isn't she?

THE INTERN:
> With her blond hair and her pleading behavior, makes you think of Ophelia. Isn't that true, Sister?

THE SISTER:
> *(Disinterested)* I don't know.

THE DOCTOR:
> Now, my child, what is it you want from me? Sister, bring us some chairs. Here, sit down. I assume you want to discuss your leaving.

LOUISE:
> Yes, Doctor.

THE DOCTOR:
> And why do you want to leave?

LOUISE:
> Because I'm cured. You have cured me.

THE DOCTOR:
> Yes, maybe. I think you look a lot better. Your eyes look healthier, don't they? *(He turns to the intern.)*

THE INTERN:
> Certainly the facial expression is more lively, more intelligent.

THE DOCTOR:
> You see! I diagnosed her from a depressive-manic profile according to Kraeplen. Whereas you …

THE INTERN:
> Me, I see her as more of a precocious insanity.

THE DOCTOR:
> If that's so, she wouldn't be in such a condition she is in today.

THE INTERN:
> Sometimes there are remissions.

THE DOCTOR:
> Not very likely.

(The left door opens. A woman's head appears and addresses the Sister in an aside.)

THE WOMAN:
> Sister, it's time for the coffin.

THE SISTER:
    Good. I'll be right there.

(The Sister exits left as the death bells sound in the distance.)

THE DOCTOR:
    (To Louise) So, you no longer suffer from your anxieties or hallucinations?
LOUISE:
    Me?
THE DOCTOR:
    You don't remember them anymore? Even better!
LOUISE:
    No, I'm feeling fine, Doctor. I feel—I am—how can I say it, I feel like I'm resurrected. I feel like returning to my home.
THE DOCTOR:
    I understand that. But one still has to be reasonable. *(To the intern)* Where is she from?
THE INTERN:
    From Fécamp, I believe.
LOUISE:
    Yes, my parents live over there.
THE DOCTOR:
    When it overpowered you, your crisis, you stayed with them?
LOUISE:
    Oh, no! I wasn't with them. I traveled. I've traveled since I was ten years old. I was adopt—
THE DOCTOR:
    So, your adopted family were the ones who discovered that you were mentally disturbed?
LOUISE:
    Yes.
THE DOCTOR:
    Do you think, after that, they would take you back?
LOUISE:
    I don't know.
THE DOCTOR:
    Everyone in the region will know that you have been at Saint-Léger. It's going to be quite difficult now to find another place to stay. You see, for patients released from the asylum, life can be unusually hard.
LOUISE:
    That's true. *(Suddenly secure)* But since I am cured, you can't keep me in the asylum for eternity! This is not a human existence.
THE DOCTOR:
    Of course, but wait a little bit.
LOUISE:
    Wait?
THE DOCTOR:
    Yes. Stay a little bit longer. It isn't fun, but it can only help you.
LOUISE:
    Oh, no!

THE DOCTOR:
> But yes, yes. And then, that will give us more time to observe you.

LOUISE:
> No. You see, I have to leave.

THE DOCTOR:
> Where are you going when you leave here? Do you have any idea?

LOUISE:
> I'll go to Paris.

THE DOCTOR:
> To Paris!

LOUISE:
> It's a big city. One always finds some work.

THE DOCTOR:
> Do you know anyone there?

LOUISE:
> No, but that doesn't matter. I will arrange it myself.

THE DOCTOR:
> You don't know a thing about Paris! Paris, my poor little one, pretty as you are, will swallow you up. And you'll experience so much misery, so much melancholy that your condition will return! But I will not permit that!

LOUISE:
> Doctor ...

THE DOCTOR:
> No, no, be reasonable.

LOUISE:
> You don't want me to leave?

THE DOCTOR:
> Of course, I do, but not immediately. First of all, you will receive my personal care. *(To the intern)* Remind me. *(To Louise)* And then, when I've found a nice place for you on the outside...

LOUISE:
> When?

THE DOCTOR:
> When? I don't know. Maybe in fifteen days, maybe in a week.

LOUISE:
> *(Energetically)* I don't want to wait!

THE DOCTOR:
> What?

LOUISE:
> One more week here! No, I can't!

THE DOCTOR:
> Calm down, calm down!

LOUISE:
> I don't want to stay here anymore! I want to leave! *(Lowering her voice)* I don't want to sleep in this room anymore.

THE DOCTOR:
> *(Shocked by her tone)* I see, there are other things... other things you haven't told me! *(He notices Louise looking away.)* Why are you looking over there?

LOUISE:
: I was checking whether the Sister is listening.

THE DOCTOR:
: You have problems with her? *(Louise lowers her head, not responding.)* That doesn't surprise me. But what has she done to you—made your life miserable? Because you didn't go to Mass?

LOUISE:
: Yes, maybe. But that's not it!

THE DOCTOR:
: So what is it? You can tell us. Is it something that happened under her care?

LOUISE:
: Yes, in this room.

THE DOCTOR:
: What happened?

LOUISE:
: That night, no one was here …

THE DOCTOR:
: No one? What about the other patients?

LOUISE:
: Yes, but the Sisters were gone. And then …

THE DOCTOR:
: Yes? Stop trembling. *(He takes her hand in a fatherly manner.)* Tell us.

LOUISE:
: I don't know how to say it. Just thinking about it turns my stomach!

THE DOCTOR:
: Please, calm down.

LOUISE:
: Fine. When the Sisters leave, when the lights are out, if you only knew how everything changes in the wing.

THE DOCTOR:
: What changes?

LOUISE:
: There are things going on that you don't understand. First, there is that door over there, you see! *(She points to the left door.)*

THE DOCTOR:
: Yes?

LOUISE:
: The Sister locks it when she departs. Last night, in the early morning, the door opened.

THE DOCTOR:
: You saw someone open that door?

LOUISE:
: It opened by itself. It was like a signal. The two old ones who sleep there, do you know them?

THE DOCTOR:
: Yes. Continue.

LOUISE:
: They got up.

THE DOCTOR:
> What? They got up?

LOUISE:
> Since there was no one there to stop them.

THE DOCTOR:
> Excuse me, but one of the women, the one from Normandy, wore a restraining jacket that I personally tied her in that night.

LOUISE:
> What does that do? The other one pulled her out of it.

THE DOCTOR:
> It requires a key.

LOUISE:
> She *has* a key. She has everything it takes to— *(She stops.)*

THE DOCTOR:
> To what?

LOUISE:
> I see how you stare at me! The both of you!

THE DOCTOR:
> *(To his intern)* I fear she still can't take any agitation.

THE INTERN:
> Obviously not.

LOUISE:
> My God! Do you think that I am lying or still mad?

THE DOCTOR:
> No, my child. So, from the beginning, what did they do?

LOUISE:
> Without a sound they crept close to my bed. They leaned over me, they watched me... with a fixed stare like they wanted to hurt me.

THE INTERN:
> To hurt her!

LOUISE:
> But they didn't dare. They looked towards the door and they shook their heads: "No, no ..." as if they were afraid. It seemed as if they spoke to someone else. And there *was* somebody else.

THE DOCTOR:
> Who was it?

LOUISE:
> One-Eye, who gestured to them.

THE DOCTOR:
> You think so?

LOUISE:
> Oh! I recognized her immediately with the black patch over her eye. She made signs.

THE DOCTOR:
> It's impossible.

LOUISE:
> Doctor, I saw her.

THE DOCTOR:
> I tell you, it is impossible! True, the other two women are not crippled. But the so-called One-Eye has been paralyzed in both legs for six years. She is bedridden. Therefore, she cannot rise or stand.

LOUISE:
> But I did see her, Doctor. She was there in front of the door, standing!

THE DOCTOR:
> I see, my child, that you are not yet cured!

LOUISE:
> I am cured. My mind is healed.

THE DOCTOR:
> No, since you claim things that are impossible—

LOUISE:
> I don't know how to convince you, but I did see her. I wasn't asleep. My eyes were wide open. I did see her. The signs she made to the others. They were in fear. I absolutely saw her!

THE INTERN:
> *(To the doctor)* She is having hallucinations again.

THE DOCTOR:
> That's what I think, too.

THE INTERN:
> It is quite possible, what she is telling us—

THE DOCTOR:
> *(Interrupting)*—are the warnings of a new crisis. Poor little one!

LOUISE:
> *(Frightened)* No, Doctor. *(To the intern)* But no, Monsieur, I tell you, I did see her.

THE DOCTOR:
> Of course, you saw it. You think you saw it. *(In an aside to the intern)* Now I've made up my mind.

THE INTERN:
> Me, too.

THE DOCTOR:
> The hallucinations have returned.

LOUISE:
> No, Doctor. No! I'm not mad anymore! Doctor, you can see that I'm in my right mind at this moment!

THE DOCTOR:
> Calm down!

LOUISE:
> I am excited but not crazy. I am not telling you stories. *(To the intern)* Isn't that true, Monsieur? I don't tell stories. Please believe me, I beg of you!

THE DOCTOR:
> *(To placate her)* Certainly, I believe you! I just need to make a few additional observations over the next couple of days.

LOUISE:
> For a few more days? And if it happens again at night?

THE DOCTOR:
You'll inform me.
LOUISE:
But you're not going to leave me here? If I can't leave immediately, at least put me in a different wing!
THE DOCTOR:
All the beds are taken at the moment.
LOUISE:
I beg of you!
THE DOCTOR:
Then tomorrow you will change wings. I promise you.
LOUISE:
Yes, but tonight... I'm so frightened! So frightened!
THE INTERN:
What a state she puts herself in!
THE DOCTOR:
Tonight the Sister is not going to leave you.
LOUISE:
She will leave!
THE DOCTOR:
I am going to give her an order.
LOUISE:
She will leave!
THE DOCTOR:
I'd like to see her try!
LOUISE:
She will go as soon you have left!
THE DOCTOR:
(Harshly) That's enough! If you continue to be so obstinate, that alone proves that you're not cured and I will be forced to keep you in the asylum... for a substantial period.
LOUISE:
My God!

(The Sister enters from left.)

THE DOCTOR:
(Calling her) Sister!
THE SISTER:
Doctor...
THE DOCTOR:
I came to scold this child because of her unreasonable nature. She is still very nervous. She is constantly afraid without reason. But, nevertheless, she suffers, and we must spare her of any unnecessary suffering. Tonight you will watch over her.
THE SISTER:
But, Doctor ...
THE DOCTOR:
Please! Your presence will prevent her nightmares.

THE SISTER:
> Nightmares are immaterial!

THE DOCTOR:
> They're important enough to be cared for.

THE SISTER:
> If she becomes too agitated, we could give her two spoonfuls of chloral.

THE DOCTOR:
> No, I prefer that you stay with her.

THE SISTER:
> That will be difficult for me, especially tonight.

THE DOCTOR:
> Why is that?

THE SISTER:
> We have a service.

THE DOCTOR:
> What service?

THE SISTER:
> For Sister Sulpice.

THE DOCTOR:
> Ah, yes!

THE SISTER:
> There will be a wake all night long to sing hymns, and all the Sisters are assisting.

THE DOCTOR:
> You will have to find someone to replace you.

THE SISTER:
> *(Bluntly)* That is impossible.

THE DOCTOR:
> That is *very* possible, if you want it.

THE SISTER:
> The Abbess will not tolerate anyone's absence for this service.

THE DOCTOR:
> I have to remind you that there are matters of humanity that are more important than the service in the chapel.

THE SISTER:
> I don't think so. It depends on one's point of view.

THE DOCTOR:
> I'm surprised that you hesitate, when I insist that your duty is to remain here.

THE SISTER:
> My duty is to obey the Mother Superior.

THE DOCTOR:
> Watching over the dead is good, but there are certain things of greater importance, which is to treat the living.

THE SISTER:
> *(Stubbornly)* My duty is to obey the Mother Superior.

THE DOCTOR:
> You must obey me first of all. The Mother Superior is not in charge of the halls of this asylum. It is me, the Medical Doctor! Do you understand that?

THE SISTER:
> (*Blankly*) Yes, Doctor.

THE DOCTOR:
> I insist that you stay the night, the *whole* night, in *this* room. Are you going to obey or not?

THE SISTER:
> I am nothing but a servant. My duty is to obey. (*She mumbles some words.*)

THE DOCTOR:
> What did you say?

THE SISTER:
> Nothing, Doctor. I said nothing. I am permitted to say nothing.

THE DOCTOR:
> (*Sternly*) That's good. (*To Louise affectionately*) I hope you're finally assured. (*Louise doesn't respond.*) Good evening, my child. Good night. (*To the intern*) Ah, the Sisters! The Sisters! (*As he departs*) They have great qualities. They don't make any noise. They are serious, devoted. But when it comes to ceremony they are stubborn!

(*The doctor and intern exit right, followed by the Sister.*)

LOUISE:
> (*Alone, she sits down on her bed.*) They didn't want to believe me. (*Lamenting*) My God! My God! (*The Normandy Woman and Hunchback reenter from the left. In the dark, they slowly advance toward Louise, who becomes frightened again and lets out a shriek.*) Ah!

NORMANDY WOMAN:
> You shouldn't be afraid like that, my little darling.

HUNCHBACK:
> We haven't even touched you yet and you scream.

NORMANDY WOMAN:
> Wait a little.

HUNCHBACK:
> A little bit.

NORMANDY WOMAN:
> The night is long!

HUNCHBACK:
> Yes, the night. It is good, the night.

LOUISE:
> Why do you look at me like that?

NORMANDY WOMAN:
> Can't we look at you?

HUNCHBACK:
> You are pretty.

NORMANDY WOMAN:
> Your eyes especially.

HUNCHBACK:
> They are not yours.

NORMANDY WOMAN:
> Certainly not.

HUNCHBACK:
> The old hag said it, "There's a cuckoo inside."

NORMANDY WOMAN:
> And, one day, she will fly away

HUNCHBACK:
> *(Making flapping movements)* Pffft! Pffft!

LOUISE:
> Go away. Don't come any closer. *(Calling)* Sister!

NORMANDY WOMAN:
> Don't be frightened, little one, the cuckoo will be released soon!

(They laugh as they move closer to Louise.)

(The Sister reappears through the right door while the two old crones silently climb in their beds.)

THE SISTER:
> What is it? Who called for me? You, again?

LOUISE:
> *(Emotionally)* Yes, Sister.

THE SISTER:
> It's always the complainers who waste our time. What is it now?

LOUISE:
> *(Pointing at the two women)* They're here.

THE SISTER:
> Of course, they are here, because they sleep in the same room as you do. So go to bed now, all three of you. *(She strikes a match and lights the bed lamp. The room brightens. She looks around. Voices and words from the next room can be heard.)* Hey, over there! *(She takes the bed lamp, opens the left door, and looks into the room.)* Silence! No more noise! It's time to sleep. Do you hear me?

(The noise slowly dissipates into a deep silence. She locks the door with her key. The two old women prepare to sleep. Louise sits on her bed quietly. The Sister puts the lamp on the shelf. Then she kneels down at the crucifix and says a prayer in a low voice.)

(Hunchback and the Normandy Woman murmur a prayer—a few words can be heard: "Saint Mary ... in the hour of our death ... so be it!")

THE SISTER:
> Amen. *(She rises. At this moment a bell rings in the distance. The Sister listens, hesitates, and walks slowly to Louise's bed, who still hasn't moved. In a soft voice)* Louise?

LOUISE:
> Sister?

THE SISTER:
> Are you going to bed, my child?

LOUISE:

(Hesitating) Of course, Sister.

THE SISTER:

You're not afraid anymore, I hope? You see, everything is calm. You are going to have a good night, aren't you?

LOUISE:

Yes, Sister. *(The ringing begins again.)*

THE SISTER:

Do you hear that bell calling me? It demands that I go and perform my duty to the dead.

LOUISE:

But Sister...

THE SISTER:

You do understand that I cannot stay here. You're not a selfish person. You have a great generosity of spirit. You know the dead need our prayers. The dead should come before the living.

LOUISE:

But the Doctor—

THE SISTER:

The Doctor is never going to know if you don't tell him. If you tell him, you'll cause me a lot of trouble. And then, my girl, think of all the scandal that you would cause! He makes a big thing out of everything. He'll complain to the administration and will demand an inquiry. The Abbess doesn't like that. Not at all. And we should not do anything to displease her. In fact, it's she who gives orders here. Do you understand me?

LOUISE:

(Resigned) Yes, Sister.

THE SISTER:

Good, my child. Be reasonable. We'll remain good friends, the two of us. It is in your interest, believe me. I can be helpful for your departure. So be reasonable. Good night!

(She moves to the right door while the curtain falls slowly and the bell continues to ring in the distance.)

ACT II

(The same set as the first act. Through the window moonlight shines with a greenish glow while the flame of the night lamp flickers in the glass on the wall shelf. Deep silence. A clock in the distance strikes ten. During the whole act one can hear—from time to time— the sound of an organ and the psalms of prayers from the chapel. Suddenly, on their beds, Hunchback and the Normandy Woman turn silently.)

NORMANDY WOMAN:

(In a deep voice, breaking the silence) Psst!

HUNCHBACK:
   (Replying in the same manner) What?
NORMANDY WOMAN:
   (Sitting up on her bed) Is she asleep?
HUNCHBACK:
   (Same manner) I think so.
NORMANDY WOMAN:
   Make sure!
HUNCHBACK:
   I'll check.
NORMANDY WOMAN:
   Wait! Somebody is walking, somebody is talking in the hallway.
HUNCHBACK:
   Maybe the Sister is returning?
NORMANDY WOMAN:
   Maybe. *(They return to bed. Silence again; the noise grows distant. They sit up.)* They didn't come in here!
HUNCHBACK:
   No, they went down the stairs.
NORMANDY WOMAN:
   That's right.

   (Pause)

HUNCHBACK:
   So, that's it for tonight.
NORMANDY WOMAN:
   That's what she wants.
HUNCHBACK:
   Must obey her. Absolutely!
NORMANDY WOMAN:
   Or she'll hurt us.
HUNCHBACK:
   Like the little one.
NORMANDY WOMAN:
   Remember what she demanded?
HUNCHBACK:
   What do you mean?
NORMANDY WOMAN:
   A towel.
HUNCHBACK:
   I don't have one.
NORMANDY WOMAN:
   Tear a piece out from your sheet, with your teeth!
HUNCHBACK:
   Good idea.

   (The sound of ripping cloth can be heard.)

LOUISE:
: (*After dozing, she sits up.*) What?
HUNCHBACK:
: She's waking up.
NORMANDY WOMAN:
: Quiet.

(*They remain still for some time.*)

LOUISE:
: I heard. Certainly, it's here. (*She looks around the room.*)

HUNCHBACK:
: (*Hides the piece of cloth under her pillow.*) That's it.
NORMANDY WOMAN:
: Wait for the signal.
HUNCHBACK:
: Wait.
  (*Silence*)
LOUISE:
: Who is talking over there? It's them. They aren't sleeping! (*She leans forward in order to hear better.*)
HUNCHBACK:
: There, she woke up!
NORMANDY WOMAN:
: She can hear us. (*They sit on their beds.*)
LOUISE:
: What are they doing, sitting so still? (*Loudly*) What is it? What do you want?
NORMANDY WOMAN:
: Don't be afraid, my little darling.
HUNCHBACK:
: Of course.
NORMANDY WOMAN:
: Was it the cry of the cuckoo which woke you?
HUNCHBACK:
: That's a sign of death. (*They laugh.*)
LOUISE:
: Be quiet! It's horrible to be here, with the mad—
NORMANDY WOMAN:
: Then you are even madder, you there!
HUNCHBACK:
: (*Laughing*) She thinks she isn't crazy anymore!
NORMANDY WOMAN:
: Because she will soon leave the madhouse!
HUNCHBACK:
: You will never leave.
NORMANDY WOMAN:
: If you leave, it's with your feet first! (*They laugh.*)

LOUISE:
> *(Frightened)* I can't stay here anymore! Alone...

NORMANDY WOMAN:
> You are not alone!

HUNCHBACK:
> Because you're with us!

(They climb off their beds.)

LOUISE:
> Leave me, or I'll call...

(A wheezing is heard from the room at the left. Louise, scared sick, stops. The two old crones, frightened, stay still.)

NORMANDY WOMAN:
> Be quiet! It's her!

HUNCHBACK:
> Shut up! She enters!

NORMANDY WOMAN:
> If she hears us, she'll be in a rage!

HUNCHBACK:
> And if she is in a rage, protect yourself!

NORMANDY WOMAN:
> Yes, must protect myself!

HUNCHBACK:
> *(Praying)* "Miserere..."

NORMANDY WOMAN:
> "Miserere nobis..."

HUNCHBACK:
> When you leave ...

NORMANDY WOMAN:
> ... with your feet first...

HUNCHBACK:
> *(Pointing to the left door)* She enters! There!

LOUISE:
> *(In front of the window)* The door is opening by itself! Help me! Help me!

(She attempts to run toward the right door, but the two crones block her and push her away. Panic-stricken, like an animal in a trap, Louise turns away. Suddenly, a dark figure surges up in front of her. One-Eye enters through the left door. She closes the door silently, rushes toward Louise, and knocks her down on a bed. A muffled scream is heard.)

(One-Eye holds Louise, who struggles on the bed as Hunchback brings the bed lamp closer.)

ONE-EYE:
> Light!

HUNCHBACK:
> Here!

ONE-EYE:

    More light! *(She puts a hand over Louise's mouth to silence her.)*

HUNCHBACK:

    (With the bed lamp) Voilà!

(Both Hunchback and the Normandy Woman lean over Louise.)

NORMANDY WOMAN:

    (To Hunchback) She holds her so firmly.

HUNCHBACK:

    She does!

NORMANDY WOMAN:

    What is she going to do?

HUNCHBACK:

    I don't know ... but *she* knows!

ONE-EYE:

    Normand, do you have the cloth?

NORMANDY WOMAN:

    Here it is.

    (She hands her the torn-up piece of sheet.)

ONE-EYE:

    (To Normandy Woman) Hold her hands! And give me a long needle!

HUNCHBACK:

    (Searching) A needle?

NORMANDY WOMAN:

    The Sister's knitting needle! On the shelf!

HUNCHBACK:

    (Turning) Ah, on the shelf.

NORMANDY WOMAN:

    In front of the Blessed Virgin.

HUNCHBACK:

    There it is!

(She gives the knitting needle to One-Eye.)

ONE-EYE:

    I can't see well enough to do my work!

(She jams the needle in the deep pocket of her asylum gown.)

NORMANDY WOMAN:

    I agree. It's too dark in here.

ONE-EYE:

    Bring the bed light closer!

HUNCHBACK:

    Here.

ONE-EYE:

    Closer!

(Hunchback obeys.)

NORMANDY WOMAN:
: (*Staring at Louise*) People say she's already dead. Yes, she is like a corpse.
ONE-EYE:
: No. When I am finished, the cuckoo will return to us!
LOUISE:
: (*Struggling against One-Eye's grip*) Ah!
ONE-EYE:
: (*Uncovering Louise's mouth*) Do you know who I am, child?
LOUISE:
: Where am I?
ONE-EYE:
: Stop moving!
LOUISE:
: (*Catching a glimpse of them*) What are you doing to me?
ONE-EYE:
: Don't scream. We don't want to do anything to you... only to those two eyes.
LOUISE:
: My eyes!
ONE-EYE:
: Those are not your eyes!
NORMANDY WOMAN:
: She thinks those are her eyes.
HUNCHBACK:
: Ha! Ha!
NORMANDY WOMAN:
: Ha! Ha!
ONE-EYE:
: (*With authority*) Quiet, you two! Do you understand, my little one, it's a service I want to render you. You were crazy once, weren't you? Don't you remember?
NORMANDY WOMAN:
: Of course she does!
HUNCHBACK:
: She doesn't remember!
ONE-EYE:
: While you were crazy, a beast got inside you, a cuckoo bird. She hid in your head. Behind your eyes!
LOUISE:
: (*Struggling*) Ah!
ONE-EYE:
: If you continue to scream, I am going to have to shut you up good. So listen to me! I'm going to rid you of the bird. Do you understand? She has stolen your eyes. That bird has removed your eyeballs and put hers in your sockets! Do you understand now? (*Screaming*) Those damned cuckoo's eyes are planning to rob me of my sight!
LOUISE:
: (*Filled with terror*) No, no! Have pity! Please!
ONE-EYE:
: (*Calmly*) Now you understand.

LOUISE:
> I beg of you!

ONE-EYE:
> It'll be good for you!

LOUISE:
> Please! I don't want to die!

ONE-EYE:
> You won't die!

LOUISE:
> *(Struggling)* Help! Help me!

ONE-EYE:
> *(Her hand over Louise's mouth)* Shut up! *(To the women)* Hurry, before the screams begin! *(One-Eye gags her with the piece of cloth, which also covers her entire face.)*

LOUISE:
> *(Resisting)* Ah!

ONE-EYE:
> Don't move, little one! It will be over soon. I only have to feel exactly ... where your eyes are. *(Pause)* But this cloth is too stiff! It's been starched!

NORMANDY WOMAN:
> What?

ONE-EYE:
> Too much starch in the cloth, idiot! Soak the damn thing in water and dry it on the stove! I must know precisely where her eyes are, Normand!

(One-Eye grabs the cloth from Louise's face and flings it at the Normandy Woman. One-Eye again silences Louise with her hand. Now in a panic, the Normandy Woman repeatedly dips the cloth in a water basin and throws it on the stove, which sends up plumes of steam.)

ONE-EYE:
> Why did you give me a starched cloth?

NORMANDY WOMAN:
> It's soft now! Look, it is completely soft!

(The Normandy Woman spreads the steaming cloth over Louise's face.)

LOUISE:
> *(Screaming)* Ah!

(One-Eye clinically touches Louise's covered face and smiles. With her other hand she pulls the knitting needle from her pocket and quickly rams it through the cloth into Louise's eye-socket.)

LOUISE:
> *(A new intense screaming)* NO!!!!

ONE-EYE:
> There! That's it! Blood is flowing on my hands. It's warm, it's good! It's just like the blood of an infant! A tiny, beautiful child! *(One-Eye stabs Louise's other eye.)*

LOUISE:
> Ah!

ONE-EYE:
: Like the old times!

(One-Eye laughs hysterically and makes flapping gestures as she dances around Louise's tortured body.)

(In a reflexive motion the blinded Louise pulls the knitting needle from her second destroyed eye and leaps up from the bed, as the bloody cloth falls to the ground. Vitreous fluid flows down Louise's mutilated face, which is frozen in a silent scream.)

NORMANDY WOMAN:
: *(Confused as she runs toward Louise)* The bird? Where's the bird?

ONE-EYE:
: Ha! Ha! Ha! Ha!

(Louise instinctively ignores the Normandy Woman, lunges toward the laughing One-Eye, and falls dead, holding the needle.)

NORMANDY WOMAN:
: *(Inspecting the corpse of Louise)* The cuckoo didn't fly out! Hunchback, did you see the bird?

(The crones stare at each other in disbelief as One-Eye continues her demented dance. Realizing that they had been tricked, Hunchback suddenly overpowers the ecstatic One-Eye and drags the uncomprehending ogress across the room to the stove. Hunchback forces the unseeing side of One-Eye's face down onto the red-hot plate. The face sizzles away in a burst of bloody steam as One-Eye screams wildly. Alarmed by the piercing shrieks, Hunchback lifts up the ogress' oozing head by her hair and smashes her one eye against the stove plate, killing her.)

(Long pause. Hunchback looks at the Normandy Woman.)

NORMANDY WOMAN:
: *(Coming out of her shock)* There never was a cuckoo!

(Noise from the right is heard.)

HUNCHBACK:
: Normand, listen! Footsteps!

(Hunchback blows out the bed lamp and climbs into her bed. The room is bathed in moonlight.)

NORMANDY WOMAN:
: *(Realizing their predicament)* They're coming! They're coming! *(She scrambles into bed and pulls a sheet over her head. A pause. Steps can be heard.)*

THE SISTER:
: *(Off-stage)* I assure you, Sister Agnes, I did hear noises. *(Enters, holding a lantern.)* What is it? Did someone cry out? *(She stops at the threshold. Silence)*

SECOND SISTER:
: *(Entering)* No. Just as I said.

A Crime in the Madhouse

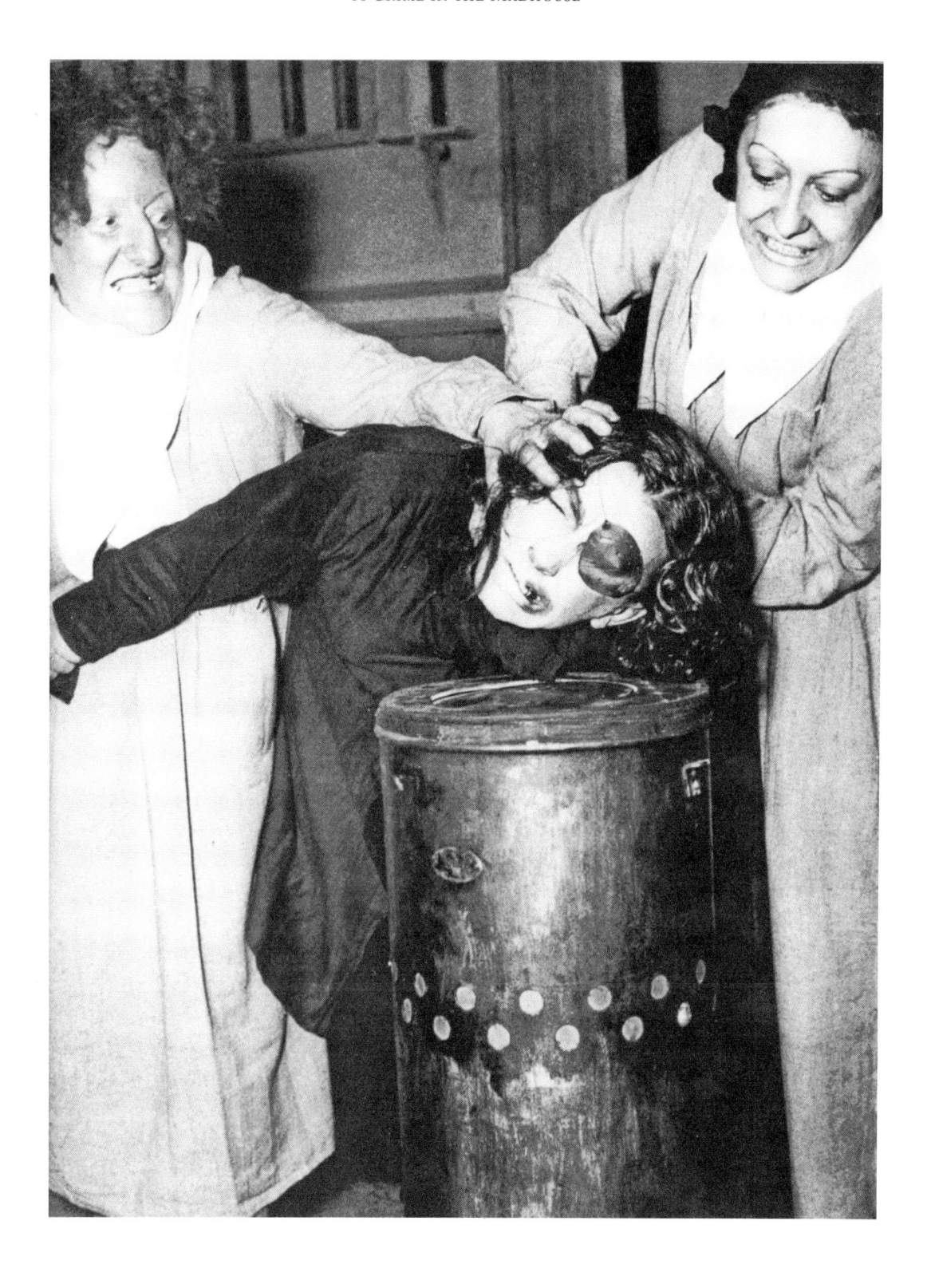

THE SISTER:

(*Illuminating only the sleeping forms of the Normandy Woman and Hunchback*) Asleep. Everything is quiet.

SECOND SISTER:

I told you! It's nothing at all. And you know Mother Superior doesn't like it when we leave before the end of the service.

(*A lyrical Vespers' chant of female voices can be heard in the distance.*)

THE SISTER:

(*While leaving*) Yes, I was mistaken. Let's return for Communion!

(*The Sisters exit with the lantern. After the door is shut, the curtain falls slowly on the Normandy Woman and Hunchback as they rise up in their beds and begin to cackle in the moonlight.*)

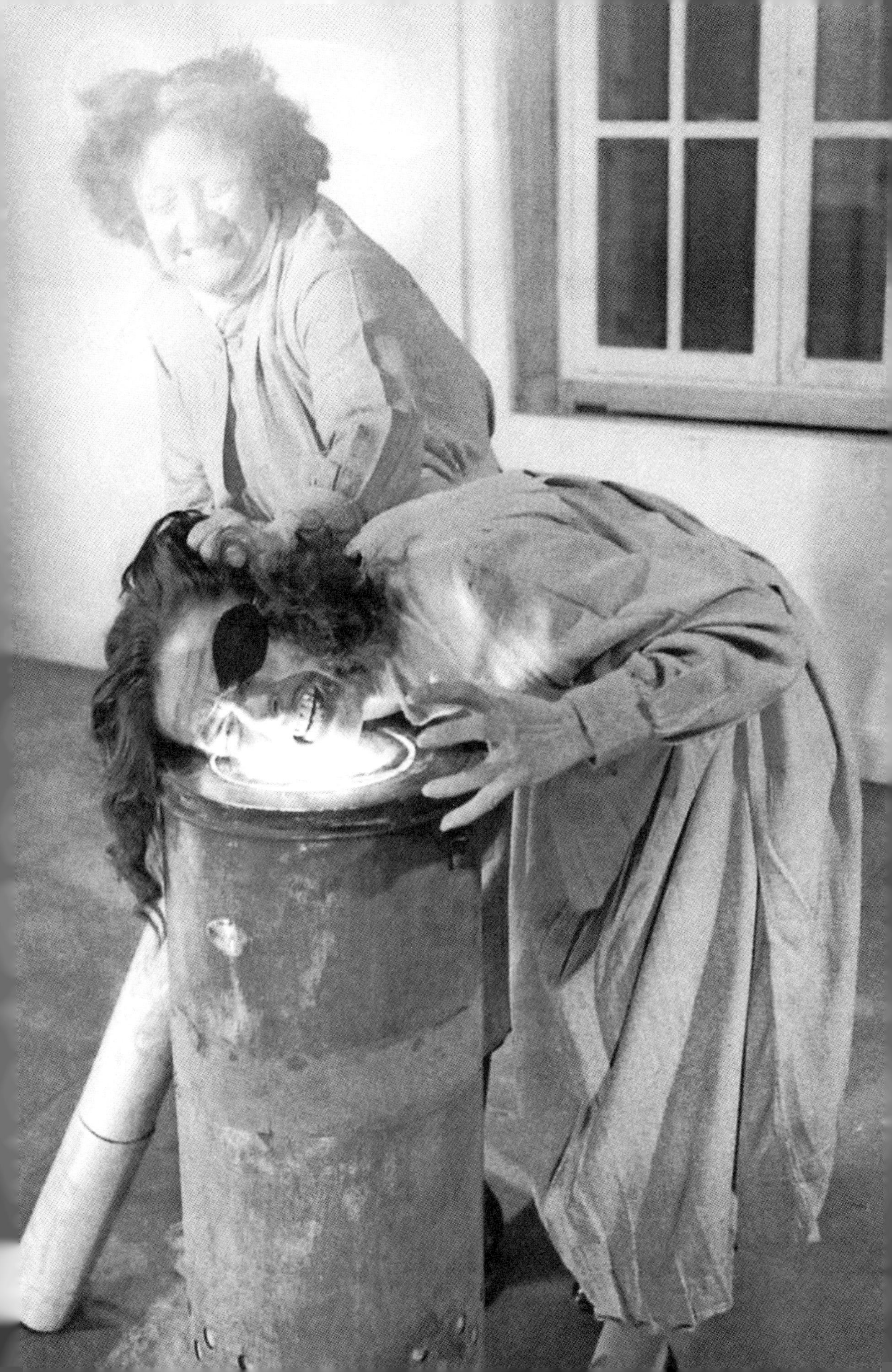

A WILD SAILOR, YVES, BRINGS TWO PROSTITUTES, ROSA AND NINI, INTO HIS BROTHER'S LIGHTHOUSE ON THE BRETON COAST. LOGONADEE, THE OLD, DRUNKEN KEEPER OF THE LIGHTHOUSE, WATCHES AS NINI PREPARES TO DANCE WITH YVES.

ORGY IN THE LIGHTHOUSE

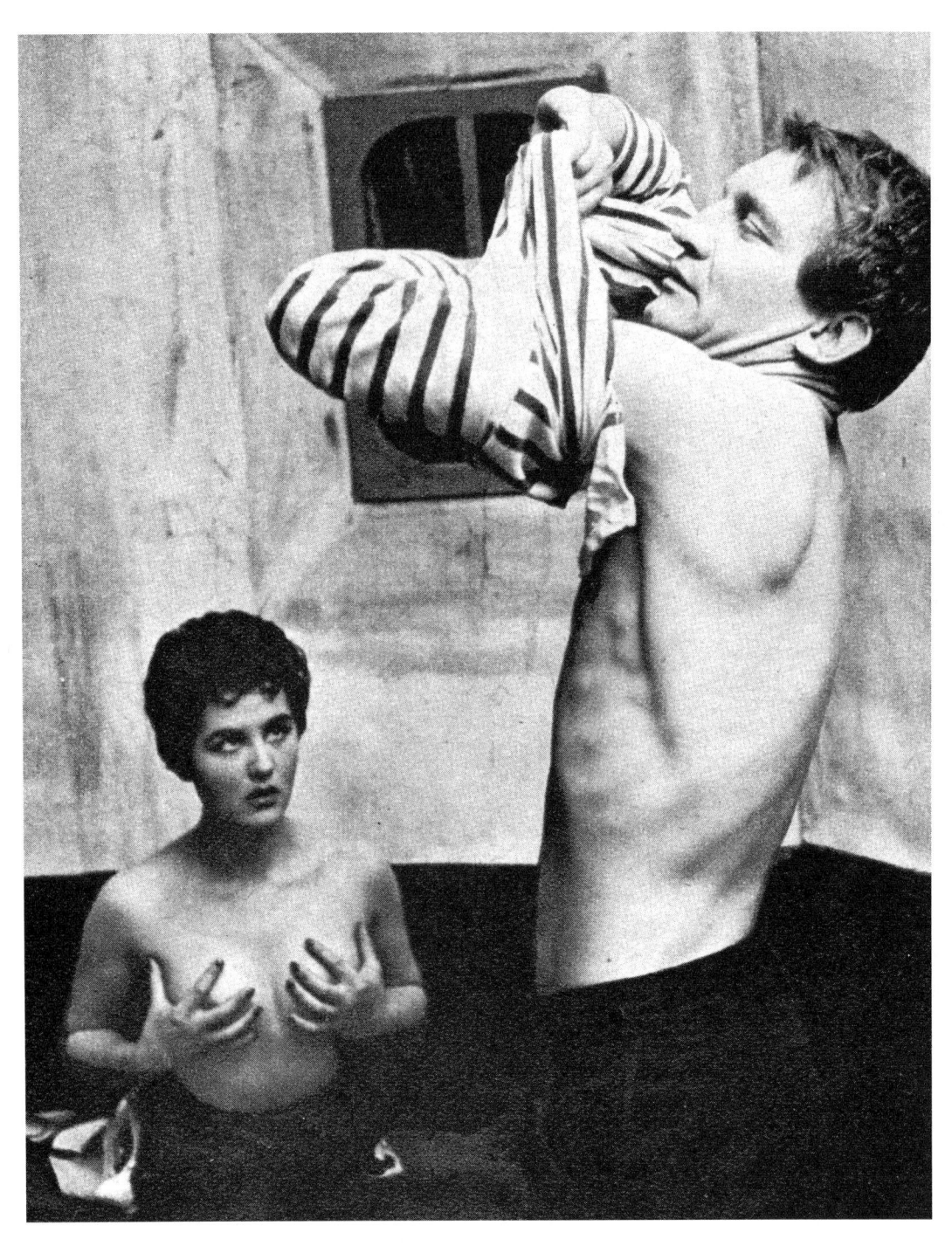

LATER THAT NIGHT, YVES AND NINI MAKE LOVE. DURING THEIR ORGY, THE BEACON OF THE LIGHTHOUSE GOES OUT AND A BOAT FOUNDERS ON THE ROCKS BELOW.

ORGY IN THE LIGHTHOUSE

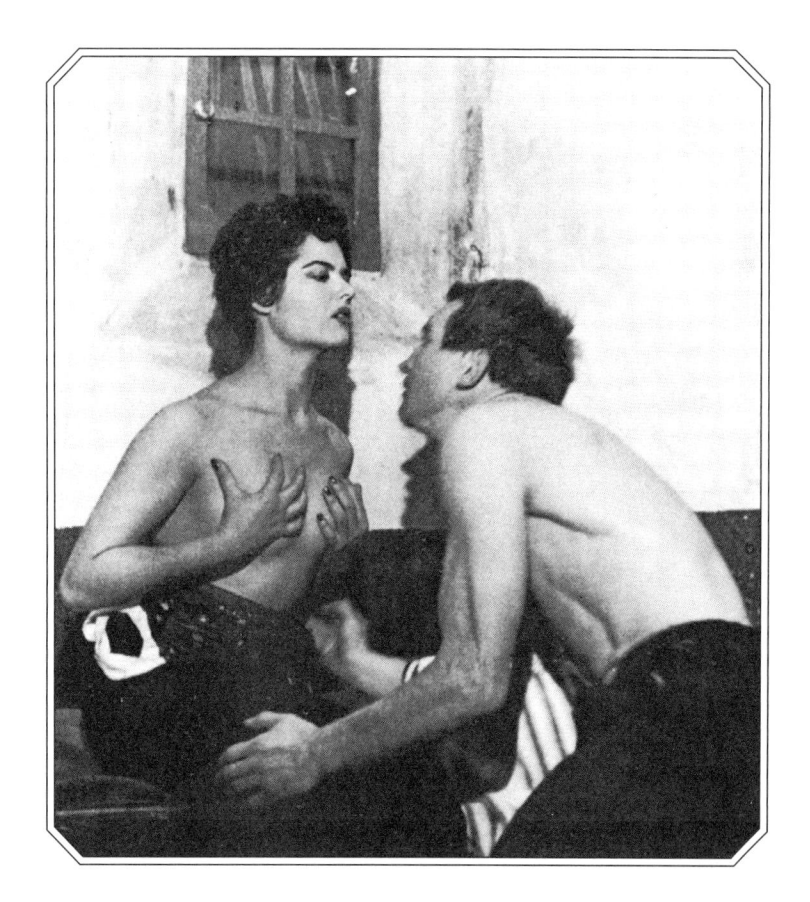

A Drama in One Act

BY ALFRED MACHARD (1956)
FROM THE COLLECTION OF BARRY RICHMOND,
WITH ADDITIONAL STAGE DIRECTIONS
FROM THE ORIGINAL PRODUCTION.

CHARACTERS:

Legonadee, an old, alcoholic lighthouse keeper
Yann, Legonadee's young assistant
Yves, Yann's older brother, a sailor
Rosa, a dark, cheaply-attractive prostitute. Flashily dressed
Nini, Rosa's shy cousin. A thin blonde girl, who has an occasional dry cough

(The top-floor of a lighthouse. Inside are two cots and a shelf with a carved figure of the Virgin. In the corner is a can of gasoline.)

(Legonadee peers into a telescope. Yann stands right beside him.)

LEGONADEE:
The streets are packed!

YANN:
They must be pouring in from every parish! The locals get crazy for the Feast of Guivic.

LEGONADEE:
What a day!

YANN:
Too bad we can't go ashore in the evening when they light the bonfires and the girls come out to dance.

LEGONADEE:
Sounds like you got hot pants, kid!

YANN:
You know I like to dance!

LEGONADEE:
Don't play the little saint with me. I was young once too. And I know what it's like to live without a woman's touch for weeks on end. But if I was at the feast tonight ... a drop or two of Calvados!

YANN:
That's your sin, Papa Legonadee.

LEGONADEE:
Since when is it a sin to appreciate something good?

YANN:
Easy. Let me have a look.

(Legonadee hands him the telescope.)

LEGONADEE:
Now what's happening?

YANN:
The procession has reached the quay. The priest is leading a long line of peasants.

LEGONADEE:
He's going to bless the boats now, right?

YANN:
Yes, everybody's kneeling.

(Distant bells are heard. Legonadee takes off his cap and kneels.)

The benediction!

(Yann puts down the telescope and kneels before the Virgin statue. Both men cross themselves.)

YANN AND LEGONADEE:
"Saint Mary of the Waves, protect the sailors ...."

(Yves' head appears through a trap door. Dressed in sailor attire, a drunken Yves holds a toy trumpet and blows loudly.)

LEGONADEE:
(startled) Jesus!
YANN:
What's that?
YVES:
Scared you?
YANN:
Yves! What're you doing here?
YVES:
Always ready to visit you, Yann. It isn't everybody's got a kid brother in a lighthouse.
LEGONADEE:
Next time don't bring the horn, idiot.
YANN:
You on leave?
YVES:
Forty-eight hours.
YANN:
But how'd you get out here?
YVES:
Sailed. Came through Plantiers Reef.
YANN:
The reefs! That's crazy dangerous with these currents!
YVES:
But a lot faster.
LEGONADEE:
He's a good sailor, this one. Did you tie up your boat tight?
YVES:
Don't worry. I know what I'm doing. Know all about the tides here.
YANN:
Where'd you get a boat?
YVES:
At Guivic. Le Pao loaned it to me.
YANN:
Did you see Mamma?
YVES:
She wasn't home.
YANN:
Not home?
YVES:
She went to the Isles ... this morning.
YANN:
She missed the feast?
YVES:
There are even bigger feasts there. She went over on Guermane's steamboat.
YANN:
Mamma on that little tub of Guermane's?

YVES:
    What's wrong with it?

LEGONADEE:
    That lousy tub is on its last legs. That's what wrong. Saw it just this morning, not more than a gunshot away. The wheezy old engine could hardly make headway against that damned current.

YANN:
    If I'd known Mamma was aboard I would have gone out on the catwalk and waved. She'd have seen me if they passed that close. She must have looked up here!

LEGONADEE:
    Sure she'd look up here. You're the apple of her eye, kiddo.

YANN:
    We've always been close.

YVES:
    Well, anyway, the boat isn't coming back till tonight, so I didn't want to stay in Guivic.

YANN:
    And you came out here to see me?

YVES:
    Right.

YANN:
    You went to church first? It's a feast day you know.

YVES:
    Sure, I know.

YANN:
    Why weren't you in the procession?

YVES:
    I didn't feel like it. I thought I'd come out here.

YANN:
    It's bad luck not to join the procession! Then sailing out here alone. You took a chance.

YVES:
    Who said I came alone?

YANN:
    What do you mean?

YVES:
    (lifts the trapdoor) Listen.

(Yves blows his toy trumpet and faintly, we hear a trumpet reply from below.)

LEGONADEE:
    What's that? Some guys from your ship?

YVES:
    Nah, what would I bring them for? Girls!

LEGONADEE:
    Girls! You know better than that! You know the rules! No visitors! And certainly no girls.

YVES:
    Take it easy. They're not coming up here. I made 'em promise to stay below.

YANN:
> You missed the procession to come out here with girls?

YVES:
> I wanted to catch the tide.

YANN:
> On a festival day?

YVES:
> You used to do pretty good with the girls on festival days at the bonfire.

YANN:
> But not till after the procession.

YVES:
> Well, it's after the procession now.

YANN:
> How many are there?

YVES:
> Two.

LEGONADEE:
> You know the rules. A lighthouse is government property.

YANN:
> They're waiting down there, huh?

YVES:
> They're inside, at the bottom of the steps.

(*A louder blast from the girls' horns and a laugh from below.*)

LEGONADEE:
> They're coming up?

YVES:
> Quit worrying. If I tell 'em not to come in here, they won't.

YANN:
> Two of 'em, huh.

YVES:
> Yeah, yeah, two of 'em.

YANN:
> Young?

YVES:
> What do you think?

YANN:
> Pretty?

YVES:
> And built! (*He indicates bosoms*) I tell you, these are the real items. And what's more ...

LEGONADEE:
> That's no reason to break the regulations.

YVES:
> What's more ... (*stops Legonadee from going into the trap*) ... they brought a few bottles.

LEGONADEE:
> Bottles?

YVES:
> (*winks at Yann as he speak to Legonadee*) Four bottles of Calvados.

LEGONADEE:
   Calvados? *(suspiciously)* Really?
YVES:
   Would I rap you, Pops?
LEGONADEE:
   I suppose not but it's still against the rules.
YVES:
   I bought 'em for you, Pops. At the store on the dock.
LEGONADEE:
   Nice thought.
YANN:
   After all, who'll know if they do come up here. There's just the three of us, and we're not going to tell anybody.
LEGONADEE:
   The regulations.
YANN:
   It's not like they're spies, you know.
LEGONADEE:
   How well do you know these girls?
YVES:
   I know them well enough, Pops! You think I'd waste my time.
YANN:
   And nobody's going to inspect us today.
LEGONADEE:
   Let them come up.
YVES:
   You won't regret it, Pops. *(He calls down)* Girls!

(The girls' horns sound, very near and they appear in the trap.)

LEGONADEE:
   Fast! Where'd you have 'em, right under the trap?

(The first to enter is Rosa. She is followed by Nini, who is less boldly aggressive than Rosa. Each carries two bottles.)

ROSA:
   Jesus! I'm sore from sitting on those iron steps. *(rubs her ass)* Which one's your brother?
YVES:
   (points to Yann) That one.
ROSA:
   (with a glance at Legonadee) Glad of that. *(looks over Yann from head to foot)* You did all right, Nini. He's cute. Hello, Yann. This is Nini, my cousin. She may not look it, but she's a smart girl. Very smart.
NINI:
   (shyly) How do you do?
YANN:
   Hi.

YVES:
> And that's Papa Legonadee. I told you about him.

ROSA:
> Hello, Pops.

NINI:
> How are you?

YVES:
> *(buttering up Legonadee)* I promised I'd show 'em a real lighthouse.

LEGONADEE:
> Mine, ladies. The most beautiful lighthouse on the whole coast. It stands 40 meters high ....

ROSA:
> *(cuts him short)* Don't tell me. I climbed the goddamn steps on my hands and knees! Where do you want the bottles?

LEGONADEE:
> I'll take them, ladies. Allow me.

(He takes the bottles from the girls and places them on the table. He draws the cork from one of them and sniffs the contents ecstatically.)

YANN:
> What's that on your cheek?

ROSA:
> Nothing. It's just a scratch.

YANN:
> It's still bleeding. How did you get that?

ROSA:
> *(snappish)* Ask your brother.

NINI:
> It was really awfully funny. This morning, when the procession was going by, Rosa looked at the priest and said ....

YVES:
> Shut up!

ROSA:
> *(signals Nini)* Yeah, change the record! It wasn't as funny as all that.

NINI:
> It's warm up here, isn't it?

ROSA:
> Warm? Hell, it's hot. *(looks around)* It gives you a crazy feeling, doesn't it. I mean being inside a lighthouse.

NINI:
> I didn't think it would be like this.

ROSA:
> What did you think it would be like?

NINI:
> I don't know—different. I thought there'd be a big light.

LEGONADEE:
> Oh, the big lamp. Yes, that is interesting.

NINI:
> I don't see any lamp.

Rosa:
> Where is it?

Yann:
> Upstairs.

Yves:
> Hey, Pop, show 'em the big lamp. You can explain how it works. When you come down, they'll give you a shot of Calvados.

Legonadee:
> Yes, yes, I'd like that. This way, ladies.

(Legonadee leads the way up to the ceiling trap door.)

Rosa:
> More steps! Jesus, you got to be a goddamn mountain goat to get around this place. Oh, well, a girl's got to be educated. You coming, Nini?

Nini:
> Where?

Rosa:
> Up on top.

Nini:
> No, I don't think so ... high places. It kinda takes my breath away being up on top.

Rosa:
> I thought it was being on the bottom took your breath away.

Nini:
> What?

Rosa:
> Never mind. Come on.

(Rosa drags Nini upstairs.)

Yves:
> Well, what do you think?

Yann:
> Fine. Like you said.

Yves:
> Which one you want?

Yann:
> They're both all right.

Yves:
> The dark one's my chickee.

Yann:
> The blonde's not bad.

Yves:
> She goes for you, kiddo. I can tell.

Yann:
> No, she's just ....

Yves:
> Sure, she goes for you big, big time.

Yann:
> You think so? You think she'd ....

YVES:
>A sure thing.

YANN:
>She's not married or anything, is she?

YVES:
>Married? These girls?

YANN:
>Sounds funny but I don't want to commit a sin.

YVES:
>Look, let me tell you the facts of life.

YANN:
>And especially on a feast day.

YVES:
>Kiddo! Who do you think these chicks are? They work at the Pompadour in Brest.

YANN:
>The Pompadour?

YVES:
>Sure, you know! It's a cathouse.

YANN:
>The Pompadour?

YVES:
>Yeah, I made a bet. I made a bet with a couple of friends of mine. Sancebe and Le Ruedee, the helmsmen on my boat.

YANN:
>What kind of a bet?

YVES:
>They said, "I dare you to take a couple of broads from the Pompadour home with you." What was I gonna do? "Take 'em to your home town for the feast day. I dare you." "You think I won't?" I said. "I'll bet you won't," they said.

YANN:
>You brought them with you?

YVES:
>What could I do? "Bet you a drink you won't." So I did. The boys even paid their busfare.

YANN:
>Yves, you didn't bring them to Mamma's house did you?

YVES:
>What do you think I am? I left them in a bar at the station when I went to Mamma's. I told the guys in the bar they were waiting to meet their husbands. Then when Mamma wasn't home, I brought 'em out here. Hell, kiddo, I thought I was doing you a favor!

YANN:
>Then I guess maybe Nini.

YVES:
>You don't have go knock yourself out to make it with her, kiddo. That's what she's here for.

(Legonadee and the girls reappear through the ceiling trap.)

ROSA:
: Key, knock off the low Mass. (*She blows her trumpet.*)
LEGONADEE:
: She thinks my big lamp is beautiful!
NINI:
: I got to see it lit!
LEGONADEE:
: You will, my dear, this evening.
NINI:
: (*to Yann*) He said that a lot of birds kill themselves up there.
YANN:
: Yeah, alot. The light blinds them.
NINI:
: I think it's cruel, that light.
YANN:
: It would be crueler to let the navigators pile up on the black rocks down there.
YVES:
: The coast is dangerous around here.
LEGONADEE:
: From up here they look like pebbles but they don't take long to split open a ship.
YVES:
: (*pulling Nini over*) Why are we talking about rocks? (*pushing Nini to Yann*) How do you like my kid brother?
NINI:
: (*Examining him professionally*) He's a good-looking boy.
ROSA:
: You want to kiss him?
NINI:
: Sure, if he wants it.
ROSA:
: You want to kiss her, kiddo?
YANN:
: You kidding? Sure.
ROSA:
: Well, go ahead. (*Nini goes to Yann. He kisses her, lightly.*)
ROSA:
: You call that a kiss? Show him, Nini.

(*Nini takes his face between her hands and kisses him, pressing her body against him. Yann laughs nervously.*)

ROSA:
: You sure aren't like your brother!
NINI:
: (*Yann's embarrassment has made her uneasy*) Gee, it's tight in here. Can't you open the door or something?
YANN:
: Done. (*Opens the door to the catwalk*) Look at that! We're going to have a storm.

YVES:
> *(goes to the barometer)* Falling!

YANN:
> Seven points since this morning. It's going to be a hellofa blow!

NINI:
> What does that mean?

ROSA:
> They told you a storm. *(to Yves)* Come look at the sea.

NINI:
> *(to Yann)* We gotta go. I'm scared of boats when the sea is bad.

YANN:
> You got lots a time.

NINI:
> No—no—I want to go. Rosa!

LEGONADEE:
> What're you waiting for, kiddo, you got that made.

YANN:
> But now she is going.

(Nini has gone out on the catwalk, where Rosa and Yves are looking at the horizon. But after one look downward she comes back into the room.)

NINI:
> I can't … I can't ….

YANN:
> What's the matter? You're white!

NINI:
> It's so high! So high! And the waves down there … the rocks. I got dizzy.

YANN:
> You're just not used to it.

NINI:
> If you fell …

YANN:
> It would make a lot of fish happy.

NINI:
> Don't joke about it!

(During the above, Legonadee has uncorked the bottles and inhaled the bouquet lovingly. Then he opens the cupboard.)

LEGONADEE:
> I'm sorry, we're not used to having company. We only have two glasses.

ROSA:
> *(entering arm and arm with Yves)* Don't worry, Pops. We'll work it out.

LEGONADEE:
> Of course, I'd be happy to drink out of the bottle and leave you the glasses. I'll just take a mouthful. I don't need anything fancy.

YANN:
> Look, Pops, just a short one. No more.

LEGONADEE:
> It's a feast day, kiddo. A little celebration.

YANN:
> I don't want to have to stand your watch. *(to Yves)* When he's loaded, you can't do a thing with him. He passes out cold like he was dead!

LEGONADEE:
> *(filling the glasses)* A drink for the ladies.

ROSA:
> *(taking a glass)* It's about time. Maybe it will liven things up. We came here for a laugh. Up to now I haven't seen anything very funny.

YVES:
> Let's laugh then. *(blows his trumpet)*

ROSA:
> Take a drink first. *(to Nini)* What's the matter, kid, can't you get him horny? You're slippin'.

NINI:
> *(Accepting this as a challenge)* He likes me. He just isn't ready yet. He's shy!

ROSA:
> Shouldn't you get him ready, for Christsake.

NINI:
> You take a drink too. Right here where I drank from.

(Yann takes the glass and does as she asks.)

ROSA:
> *(to Yves, pointing at Yann)* He's finally warming up. *(to Yann)* Why don't you give her a centime for her thoughts.

NINI:
> He already knows my thoughts, don't you, honey?

(Nini kisses Yann, and his hands begin to stroke her.)

ROSA:
> Look at that. Hold me tight, honey! Tighter ... squeeze me.

(Legonadee, taking advantage of the couples' preoccupation with each other, downs several long gulps from the bottle.)

ROSA:
> *(breaking away)* I don't know what's the matter with me. I'm beat.

Rosa throws herself on one of the beds.

NINI:
> *(breaking her kiss with Yann)* See! There's nothing to be afraid of.

Taking the initiative, Yann draws Nini back and kisses her.

ROSA:
> Come on, bite my neck. Make me feel it! *(Yves bites her.)* You pig!

(Rosa pulls away laughing.)

NINI:
(to Yann) You know, I like you. I really do.

YANN:
I like you too.

LEGONADEE:
Anybody want another?

YVES:
(embracing Rosa) In a little.

ROSA:
(pushes Yves away and moves toward Legonadee) No, give me it. I never turn down a drink.

(Rosa fills the glass and holds it out to Yves.)

ROSA:
Come on!

YVES:
Here's to you.

(Yves drinks from Rosa's glass, spilling a little, and passes it back to her. Meanwhile Yann slips the top of Nini's blouse from her shoulder.)

NINI:
I've got soft skin, huh.

YANN:
Yeah ... soft and smooth ...

NINI:
You like me don't ya?

ROSA:
(looking in the cupboard) What's all this stuff?

YVES:
Gasoline for the lamps.

ROSA:
Why do you need so much?

YVES:
For the big light upstairs.

ROSA:
Say, you got any records?

(Rosa takes one out of the cupboard.)

LEGONADEE:
Some organization in Paris sent it to us with some books. To keep us amused.

ROSA:
God, I wouldn't want to live here all the time.

LEGONADEE:
Especially in the winter.

ROSA:
Talk about a life! I'd be bored to death. Wouldn't you, Nini?

NINI:
: *(looking at Yann)* Oh, I dunno.
ROSA:
: And with no women around.
YANN:
: Yeah that's bad and when you do see one …
ROSA:
: Oh—so you do see women.
YANN:
: Sometimes.
LEGONADEE:
: Here's a souvenir from the last one.

(Legonadee takes a woman's shoe from the bookshelf.)

ROSA:
: A shoe? It's all stained.
LEGONADEE:
: Seawater.
ROSA:
: What do mean?
YANN:
: Poor girl. The tides brought her to us. Right at the foot of the lighthouse … on the rocks.
ROSA:
: Drowned?
YANN:
: Yes.
NINI:
: Aw, that's sad.
YANN:
: She seemed like a young girl. Nice figure … blonde hair ….
ROSA:
: Pretty?
YANN:
: You couldn't tell. The crabs had been at her face.
NINI & ROSA:
: Oh, my God! Don't.
YANN:
: There was a nest of them. The flesh eating kind … in her eye socket.
NINI:
: Oh.
LEGONADEE:
: Now, now! Don't get sick little lady. Easy, Yann.
YVES:
: Yeah, she's not used to talk like that.
ROSA:
: Who is?

YANN:
> I'm sorry.

YVES:
> *(aside to Yann)* You wanna spoil everything?

LEGONADEE:
> *(to Nini)* Here we have more funerals than weddings. It's the way the currents run. They bring in the bodies …. *(Nini turns away)* Come on, a good shot of Calvados will put you on your feet again.

ROSA:
> It's the heat that's making her sick. Come on, take off your dress. Let me help you.

(The girls take off their dresses, exposing their black stockings and garter belts.)

YVES:
> *(to Yann)* She likes you, kid. Go for it. Don't ever say I never got you anything.

YANN:
> You think she'd tell anybody?

YVES:
> Who'd she tell? Of course not.

YANN:
> Well, what're we waiting for?

(Now embarrassed, Yann laughs at his suggestion.)

LEGONADEE:
> *(hands a bottle to each of the girls)* Have a drink, you two.

(Legonadee looks at the half-dressed girls and chuckles.)

ROSA:
> What's the matter, Pops. You getting ideas at your age?

LEGONADEE:
> I'm not so old! You're a looker, you know.

ROSA:
> You married, Pop?

(Rosa puts an arm around Legonadee's neck.)

LEGONADEE:
> Well … yes, but ….

ROSA:
> Got any kids?

LEGONADEE:
> Eleven.

ROSA:
> *(pushing him away)* Christ! You're not a man, you're an epidemic!

(The girls laugh.)

LEGONADEE:
> It's all right. I've got what I want. *(cradles a bottle)* I'll just go upstairs and turn the wicks. *(chuckles)* Go to it, boys. It's all yours.

(Legonadee starts toward the stairs.)

YVES:
Yeah, come on. He's happy with the booze.

(Yves sits on a stool. Rosa drops on his lap, giving Nini a push toward Yann.)

ROSA:
Go on!

NINI:
(to Yann) I like you, and when I like somebody I can be awful nice to 'em. Give me a ventilator.

YANN:
A what?

NINI:
A ventilator. Don't you know what that is?

YANN:
No.

NINI:
Tell him. He doesn't know what a ventilator is!

ROSA:
Tell him! How can you tell anyone? Show him!

NINI:
Well. Open your mouth.

(Nini gives Yann an open-mouthed kiss.)

(Legonadee quietly slips down the stairs to get another bottle of calvados. He returns, admiring the label and shaking his head.)

LEGONADEE:
Calvados ... real Calvados! *(closing the trap door behind him)*

ROSA:
Hey, why don't we dance?

YVES:
You mean like at the Pompadour?

ROSA:
Sure.

NINI:
(embracing Yann) You wanna dance?

YANN:
I don't mind.

NINI:
You know how?

YANN:
Sure.

ROSA:
How'd ya learn, with the old man? Look, jitterbug! *(putting a record on the phonograph)* I could die dancing, especially the jitterbug.

Nini:
: Me, too.

(*Nini swings away from Yann, which brings her face to face with the statue of the Virgin.*)

Nini:
: Rosa, come look!

Rosa:
: What?

Nini:
: Look.
(*points to the statue and whispers to Rosa*) Don't she look just like the Madam at ....

Rosa:
: (*going into a gale of laughter*) She does! We ought to take it back and put it in the ....

Yann:
: What are you laughing at?

Rosa:
: What's it to you?

Yann:
: You mustn't laugh at her!

Yves:
: Yeah, don't start that business again like this morning!

Rosa:
: Calm down, baby. You want to know what she said?

Yves:
: (*menacingly*) Yeah, what'd she say?

Rosa:
: She said, "She looks like the Virgin at home we pray to everyday." Now what's wrong with that?

Yann:
: Is that all you said?

Nini:
: Honest, that's what I said.

Yves:
: Yeah.

Rosa:
: I swear it! (*Rosa pushes Yves away. Quite drunk now, he falls on one of the beds.*)

Nini:
: (*to Yann*) Come on ... You wanna dance or not?

Rosa:
: Come on, honey, dance.

Yves:
: No.

Rosa:
: Don't be so square. Come on! (*pulling Yves to his feet*) Hold me tight ... the way I like it. Tighter!

Nini:
: (*dancing with Yann*) You hold me tight, too. Don't be so shy. I won't bite ya.

(Yves suddenly pulls Rosa to him brutally. They stand swaying.)

ROSA:
Oh, God, I love it when you hurt me!

NINI:
(to Yann) Will you write me, honey? Will ya?

YVES:
Everything's spinning.

ROSA:
I like that feeling. Everything's spinning and your stomach gets all hollow!

(From outside harsh cries are suddenly heard approaching. They gain in intensity and then pass. Nini stops dancing.)

YANN:
What's the matter? Why did you stop?

NINI:
That screaming?

YANN:
It's just seagulls. They're coming back to the shore.

NINI:
What's that mean?

YANN:
Nothing. They always do that before a storm.

NINI:
I'm afraid.

YANN:
There's nothing to be afraid of!

ROSA:
Quit worrying, kid. *(to Yves as she turns off the phonograph)* Listen ... I know a song you'll like! *(singing)*
"There was a little hunchback who had a twisted dick
He was so all screwed up
The Madame said, 'Get out.'
She wouldn't let him in
In spite of all his gold.
She left him standing out
With his spout
Out in the cold."

Yves roars with laughter. Nini laughs, and Yann joins in, a little embarrassed.

(A sudden clap of thunder.)

NINI:
Listen! The storm!

ROSA:
I knew it was coming. I felt it in my bones. We're safe here, aren't we?

YVES:
(drunk) Sure, honey.

NINI:

Is it true what that old man said, the drowned people come back here?

YANN:

Yes, on the rocks down below. One morning we found five bodies!

NINI:

(sits on a bed) Five!

YANN:

(sits beside her) They were all swollen and black.

NINI:

Stop it. Be quiet.

(Nini buries her head against him and Yann begins to stroke her, at once protectively and lasciviously.)

ROSA:

Come on. Let's dance. *(puts on a record)* Hold me tight. I told you what it does to me! Oh, you bastard! Come here!

(Rosa throws herself on the other bed, then straightens up.)

ROSA:

Ouch!

(Rosa stands and rubs her buttocks, picking up the shoe she sat on. She looks at it a moment, then throws it across the room in disgust.)

ROSA:

Goddamn it! I sat on the dead girl's shoe!

(Rosa pulls at Yves' body, which topples over her. At that moment Yann and Nini fall prone onto the other bed.)

(Another flock of seagulls passes.)

(In the darkness, the phonograph ends and the sound of the storm increases until the wind is a continuous high-pitched shriek. Waves of lightning against the rocks below.)

(A faint glow from the portholes illuminates the room. Rosa is sleeping heavily on one of the cots. Yves lies on the floor beside her. Yann and Nini have fallen asleep in each others' arms, and lie entwined on the other bed.)

(There is a long pause, then Yves stirs, and groans.)

YVES:

Come on, fellas. Hit the deck! Hey, Sancebe, Le Huedee! I did it. I brought those dames home with me. That'll cost you the next round. *(a burst of thunder)* What do you know! Gunnery school! *(staggers to his feet)* Hit the deck. They're firing the 406's. *(a flash of lightning illuminates the portholes)* Where am I? How'd I get down in the hold? Fellas, fellas … *(staggers to a porthole)* Shitty weather! *(opens the port)* Ah, that wind feels good.

Yves bathes his face in the wind.

ROSA:

(*in the darkness, singing*) "There was a little hunchback who had a twisted spout."

YVES:

Who's that?

ROSA:

"He was so all screwed up
The Madame said, 'Get out.'"

YVES:

Rosa! Yeah, I remember! The lighthouse, that's it!

(*At this moment a siren is heard, its shriek mingles with the sounds of the storm.*)

YVES:

A lighthouse. Legonadee! Where are you?

(*Rosa sits on the bed, where she sways unsteadily.*)

ROSA:

Kiss me, honey. You know the way I like it.

(*The siren is heard again but louder.*)

YVES:

Listen! You hear that?

ROSA:

Yeah, come on, honey, hurt me ... like you did. You were wild. I love it when you hurt me.

YVES:

Shut up. (*slaps her*) Listen! (*again, the siren*) It's a siren!

ROSA:

It's a siren. So what does it mean?

YVES:

It's from a boat ... a boat in trouble. Out there somewhere. (*looks throught the porthole*) Damn, I can't see a thing. It's so dark. Where the hell is the light? The light! The light is out!!

ROSA:

What's the matter?

YVES:

Legonadee! (*rushes up the steps to the ceiling door*) Legonadee!! The light is out!! (*bangs on the door*) Legonadee!!! (*gives up and starts down*) Yann, Yann! Where the hell are you?

(*Siren becomes louder.*)

ROSA:

It's getting closer.

YVES:

(*by the porthole*) Closer to the rocks! (*lightning*) It's Guermane's boat! I saw her, Yann! It's Guermane's boat heading straight for the rocks. They'll all be killed, Legonadee!! Legonadee! (*beats on the door*) Wake up! Legonadee!!! (*shakes the door and pounds*)

NINI:

(*waking up*) Rosa ... Rosa, where are you?

ROSA:
: Here.

YVES:
: Legonadee!!!!

(*Loud sirens, then screams from the outside.*)

YVES:
: What's that?

ROSA:
: (*striking a match*) A ship.

YVES:
: Yann!! Wake up. Wake up!!

NINI:
: What's the matter?

YANN:
: Oh, my head!

YVES:
: Yann! Wake up. Wake up. For God's sakes, wake up!!!

YANN:
: What? What do you want?

(*A piercing siren.*)

NINI:
: (*whispering*) Yann!

YVES:
: Shut up! Yann, listen. The siren.

YANN:
: Siren? Yeah, siren.

YVES:
: It's Guermane's boat, calling for help! Guermane's boat! Yann, Mamma is on board!

YANN:
: Mamma?

YVES:
: (*shaking Yann*) Mamma! She went to the Isles on Guermane's boat! And the lamp is out!

YANN:
: Out?

YVES:
: Out! The lamp is out! Legonadee is drunk. Yann, can you hear me? Mamma is on that boat!! Listen to me!

YANN:
: Guermane's boat!

YVES:
: He can't find the passage in the dark! He'll hit the rocks!

YANN:
: (*rising from the bed*) Mamma …

NINI:
: What's wrong? Don't leave me. I'm scared.

YANN:
> Let go of me.

NINI:
> *(clutching him)* I'm afraid. What is it?

YANN:
> Get away from me!

(Yann strikes her.)

YVES:
> The hell with her! They need the light! We've got to wake Legonadee!

YANN:
> Where's Legonadee! Legonadee! Where is he?

YVES:
> I told you! He's up there dead drunk ... locked in! He can't even open the door!

YANN:
> He's got to wake up! *(throws Nini aside and dashes up the steps)* Legonadee! Legonadee!

(Yann pounds on the door.)

NINI:
> Rosa! I'm scared.

ROSA:
> Shut up, kid. So am I.

YANN:
> It won't give. The bastard's locked it! *(siren)* Oh, God, help them!

NINI:
> I wanna get out of here. I'm scared. Get me out of here!

ROSA:
> Take it easy, kid.

YANN:
> Shut up, you bitch. *(slaps Nini)* Shut up ....

ROSA:
> *(runs to Yves)* Can't we get out of here?

YVES:
> *(pushing Rosa away)* Get away from ... It's your fault.

ROSA:
> What the hell did I do?

YANN:
> The both of you. Coming here with your filthy talk. A couple of whores ... on a holy day. Dirty talk, dirty songs.

ROSA:
> Why us? What about you? You didn't mind when we got here.

NINI:
> You said you liked me.

YANN:
> I told you to shut up! You're worse than she is, laughing at the Virgin. You blasphemed on a holy day.

YVES:
> *(pointing at Rosa)* She's the worse one. At the procession today, she insulted the sacrament.

YANN:

    The Holy Sacrament!

YVES:

    Listen to me! Father André heard her. He turned to me. And you know what he said, "Get away from here with that woman. You have the Devil with you!" And he pointed right at Rosa!

YANN:

    The Devil? Father André said that?

ROSA:

    You're crazy!

YVES:

    Yann, the Virgin! The statue of the Virgin's gone! They stole the Virgin!

YANN:

    (to Rosa) You're gonna die!

ROSA:

    What is this? A joke?

YVES:

    You're gonna die.

ROSA:

    No, wait. Listen to me! I'll tell you the truth. Listen to me! It's her, Nini ... she's the one!

NINI:

    Rosa.

ROSA:

    She told me! It was her that said the Virgin looked like the Madame at the Pompadour. *(thunderclap)* And at the procession ... listen. She was the one. She told me to laugh when the sacrament passed.

NINI:

    Rosa, I didn't. Oh, God, I didn't.

YVES:

    (uncertain) Maybe it was you?

ROSA:

    Yes.

YANN:

    Wait a minute. She's lying. Father André said it was her, didn't he?

YVES:

    Yeah. That's right!

YANN:

    The Devil always lies.

YVES:

    Liar!! *(Yves seizes Rosa.)*

NINI:

    Oh don't!

    (Nina shrinks back into a corner.)

ROSA:

    Let me go! Oh God, please!

(Both Yves and Yann seize Rosa and drag her to the door.)

ROSA:
No ... I haven't done anything!

YANN:
Throw her into the sea.

YVES:
On the rocks!

ROSA:
No! Oh Christ, no! The crabs ... No!

YVES:
Open the door.

(Yann throws the door open. The sound of the waves becomes deafening. Rosa's screams are almost swallowed up in the roar.)

YANN:
Into the sea!

(Yann cuts her throat and they hurl her over the railing. Her scream recedes in the sound of the storm.)

NINI:
(cowering in a corner, whimpers) Oh, no ... Rosa ...

(Yves and Yann close the door and stumble into the room, falling on their knees.)

YVES:
(praying) Lord God, we have killed the Devil.

YANN:
Calm the storm and spare our mother!

YVES & YANN:
Hail Mary, full of grace! The Lord is with you. Blessed be Thy name, and ....

(The siren stops suddenly.)

YVES:
Listen!

YANN:
The siren has stopped.

YVES:
The boat missed the rocks!! They're safe!

YANN:
Thank you, Lord!

A sudden and terrifying crash, and then the cries and screams of many people, nearly drowned out by the sound of the wind.

YVES:
She hit the reefs ... the buoys. Come on!

(Yves starts toward the catwalk.)

YANN:
>Nini, so it was you! It is you! You stole the Virgin. I saw ... I saw the way you were looking at her!

YVES:
>*(on the catwalk)* It's too dark, I can't see.

NINI:
>You're crazy! Yann, please ...

YANN:
>It's you: you're the Devil. You laughed at the Virgin! You stole her!

NINI:
>I didn't! You gotta believe me! It was Rosa.

(Yann moves toward her menacingly.)

NINI:
>I'll show you. Look, here it is .... under the pillow!

YANN:
>Don't touch Her! Put down that statue, you filthy whore!

NINI:
>*(now angered)* Awright! Here's your goddamned Virgin!

(Nini throws the statue on the floor.)

YVES:
>If the light were lit, we could see where to throw the buoys!

YANN:
>Light! *(seizes Nini)* I'll give you light!

NINI:
>What are you doing? Yann, let me go!

YANN:
>Yves! The rope! Throw it!

YVES:
>What are you going to do?

YANN:
>We'll tie her to the hooks!

NINI:
>What are you going to do?

YANN:
>Burn the Devil. It's fire that purifies.

NINI:
>NO ... no! Oh God, no! Help me!

YVES:
>A light!

(Yves and Yann drag Nini to the catwalk and hang her from the hooks.)

NINI:
>Oh, God, no ... no ... no! Not like this!

YANN:
>The gasoline.

(Yves brings the can.)

NINI:
>Help!

YANN:
>Douse her!

(Yves throws gasoline on Nini.)

NINI:
>No ... please! I don't want to burn. I'm not the Devil. Are you crazy! I don't want to die. Not like this! Oh, Christ not like this! Have pity! Pity.

(Yann finds one of Rosa's matches and approaches Nini after striking it.)

YANN:
>*(to Yves)* Close the door!

(Yann throws the match toward Nini as the door is shut. A great light brightens outside the portholes.)

NINI:
>*(screaming)* Murderers ... I'm burning! Oh, Christ, I'm burning!

(Nini continues to scream.

(Yann and Yves tear the buoys and ropes from the walls. Yann throws open the door. Nini is still alive, still screaming, now charring horribly as she hangs on the hooks.)

YANN:
>Burn, Devil ... burn!

(Yann slams the door shut.)

YVES AND YANN:
>"Holy Mary of the Waves ... protect the shipwrecked!"

(The storm grows louder and Nini's screams grow weaker as the light from the portholes begins to fade.)

⚜

OPPOSITE: BLAMING THEIR PREDICAMENT ON ROSA'S THEFT OF A RELIGIOUS ICON, YVES CUTS HER THROAT.

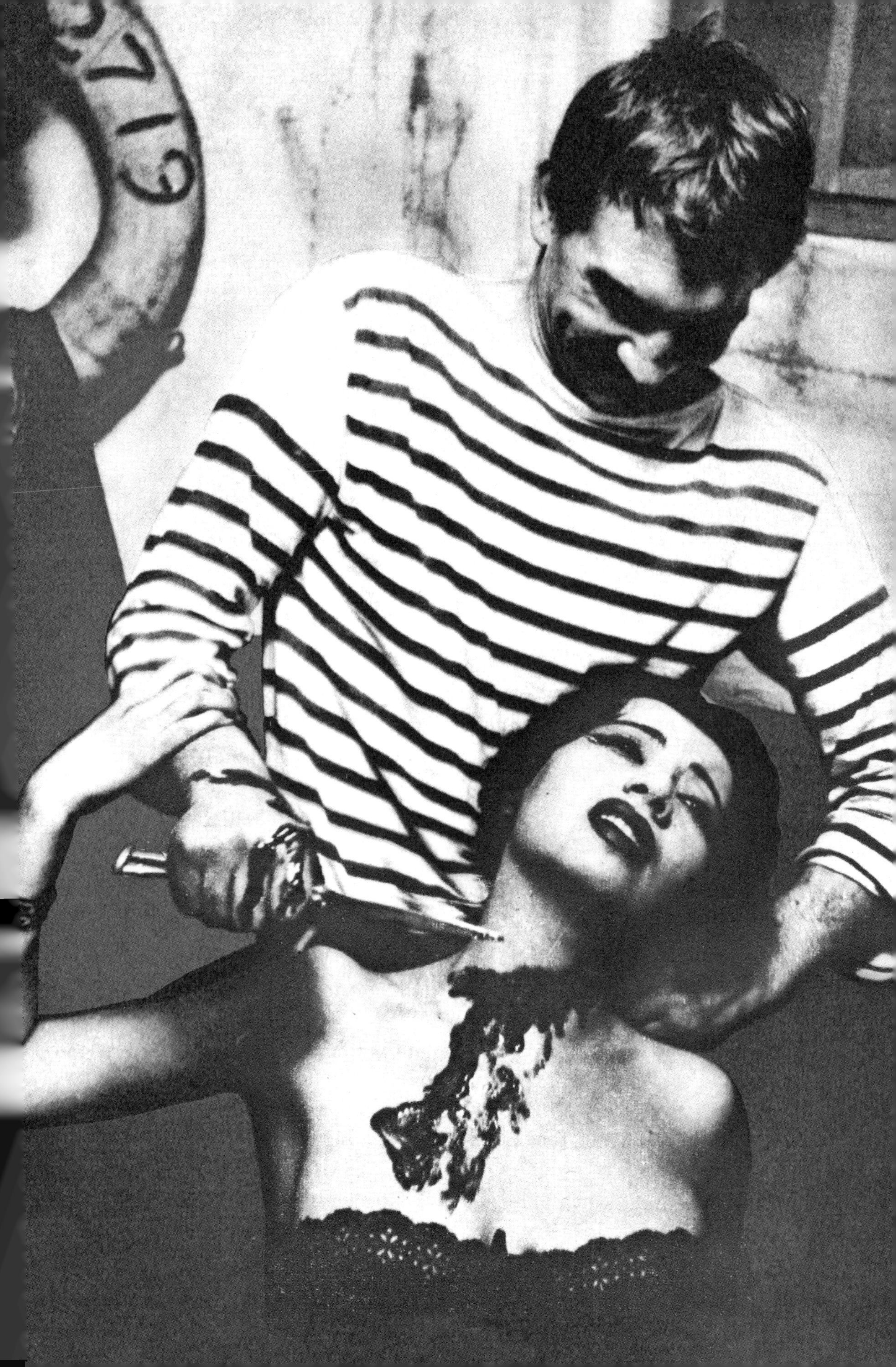

ABOVE AND OPPOSITE: WHEN THE BROTHERS DISCOVER THE DESTROYED BOAT CARRIED THEIR MOTHER, IN A FRENZY OF REPENTANCE THEY BURN николаи TO DEATH.

GG → Einfluß auf russ. Theaterszene?
evtl. Adaptionen / Übersetzungen ins Russ.?
Caligari → Expressionismus → Traum - Alptraum → Hovvas Traum